Intimate Conversations

∽ FOR COUPLES ∾

Intimate Conversations

～ FOR COUPLES ～

Turn Your Relationship into a
LIFELONG LOVE AFFAIR

Bill Syrios 2/11/14

BILL SYRIOS

Crossover Press

Intimate Conversations for Couples
© 2014 Bill Syrios

Printed in the United States of America

Cover Photo: Sándor Lau
Book Design and Layout: Luminare Press
Illustrations: Patti Sobel

Crossover Press
1247 Villard St
Eugene, OR 97403
IntimateConversations.com

ISBN: 978-0-9716683-1-7

LCCN: 2013955270

To Teresa,

from whom I have
learned so much—and for
whom an abundant appreciation,
admiration, and love has blossomed.

&

To Our Sons,

Luke, Andrew, Phillip, and Mark,
as well as their future women friends who
become wives. This book may contain more about
good old Dad than you wanted to know!
But when the appropriate time comes,
I trust that it will add a measure
of joy to your own passionate
lifelong love affairs.

Intimacy • Passion • Commitment

These three key ingredients of love have given playwrights, singers, novelists, actors, poets, and the rest of us commoners a lot to contemplate over the ages.

When merged, something wonderful, even magical happens—a lifelong love affair. And yet, bringing them together can pose such challenge and frustration.

To speak in generalities, we observe that men naturally desire passion but often find intimacy beyond their reach. Surely a man needs the relational value that intimacy brings into his life. But his lack of innate ability leaves him wondering if he can cultivate and sustain such a connection with the woman he loves. He secretly hopes she is willing to patiently help him grow in intimacy with her.

Women, on the other hand, treasure the connection of intimacy but often find passion more complex to sustain. A woman needs the vitality that passion brings into her life but is often disheartened as intimacy and passion become detached from each other with the man she loves. She secretly hopes he can learn to keep the two connected and open her up to greater depths of passion between them.

As partners commit themselves to love each other in the way that each feels loved, they realize the fulfillment of both loving and being loved.

It's certainly a subject worth talking about!

Conversations

Welcome

*Y*ou and the one you love are warmly invited into an intimate conversation.

It takes place between a couple over a weekend at their favorite vacation getaway. This encounter will surely change the course of their relationship, and yours as well.

So let's talk.

Con•ver•sa•tion

A spoken exchange of thoughts,
opionions, and feelings:
a talk

So Let's Talk

*I*ntimacy takes place as two people connect on a deep, emotional level, sharing their feelings and secrets. When that bond forms between members of the opposite sex, well, let's just say—other stuff also happens.

Well-known author John Gray describes what happens as a mixing of two distinct cultures, as if we're from totally different planets. An ancient author, the writer of Genesis, describes something similar: two unique reflections of God's image becoming one. However described, that synthesis provides a wonderfully confounding context for our attempts to achieve and sustain intimacy.

We can understand intimacy better by contrasting it to bonding. Bonding occurs when we share an important experience with another person. We study together to pass a class, we "rough it" camping for a week, we assist each other selling t-shirts in a school booster club, we complete an accounting task together with a fellow employee. Such experiences bring about bonding via "project sharing."

Men bond naturally. Since boyhood we've set goals and enlisted each other's help by joining together. In the process we connect and feel close. But that connection seldom includes the need to pour out our vulnerabilities and feelings. As a matter of fact, intimacy might actually get in our way, rather than help us complete our projects.

Intimacy comes more naturally to women. From the

time they are little girls, women learn the value of relating to each other in depth, and those relationships become the center of what's important and solid in a woman's world.

So the friction between men and women comes when a man thinks he is into intimacy but is actually into bonding, and when a woman, knowing the difference, finds herself frustrated and unfulfilled with that level of connectedness. Now, just for grins, add to the mix the fact that men often find their way to emotional intimacy through physical intimacy—something incomprehensible to many women—and what have we got? A real mess.

To try and sort this mess out I found a couple willing to talk about intimacy for an entire weekend. This couple represents the different perspectives that men and women often bring to such conversations. Beyond gender differences, we also find ourselves in various situations—happily married, unhappily married, just engaged, living together, girlfriend/boyfriend, single and glad of it, dating whomever comes along, separated and relieved, divorced and lonely, widowed and wondering "What now?"—to name a few. So any effort to create the all-inclusive couple would fail before the ink dried on page one.

Meet Matt and Sarah. This particular couple is married, happily at times and not so happily at other times. They certainly don't pretend to be the ideal couple. They're a typical couple struggling to figure out intimacy.

Some women reading these conversations will see themselves more accurately portrayed by Matt, and some men will see themselves more in Sarah. But most women, I'm going to guess 75 percent or more, will identify with Sarah, and the same percentage is likely true for men identifying with Matt. If you do find yourself part of the sizable minority, though, flip the dialogue, and if you find yourself alternately identifying with each of them, then flip-flop!

Either way, you'll quickly find their conversations dispensing with the superficial fluff and getting down to the genuine stuff of how we find our way into intimacy and passion. At times you'll consider yourself in familiar territory, and then you'll be in deep water. It will be fun, and it will be frightening. If you're looking for straightforward honesty, however, you won't be disappointed.

Interspersed within their freewheeling conversations are highlighted boxes and periodic interludes that summarize their thoughts and point out practical "how-to's"— a kind of right-brain/left-brain approach. Also along the way you will find places to add your thoughts. So, feel free to evaluate, disagree, have an "aha" moment, and focus on what's relevant to you. The important thing is to enter their conversation as a participant in the dialogue instead of an observer who stands on the outside looking in.

None of us naturally knows how intimacy and passion works for the opposite sex—we have to get into their gender world to see their perspective. Even then, when we think we've gotten it, something blows through our relationship that sets us back to square one, or close to it. Since we're all a mixture of feminine and masculine traits, relating to each other is both frustrating and fascinating!

Again, allow me to introduce you to Matt and Sarah. Actually, this couple is more special than first impressions might convey. They are, after all, willing to take a weekend out of their busy lives to explore what it takes to improve the intimacy and passion between them. By joining the dialogue, you've made a similar commitment. We're looking forward to seeing where it all leads.

Bonding vs. Intimacy

How would you describe the difference between bonding and intimacy? (See pp. 1-2.)

_____

_____

Does this difference between bonding and intimacy affect your relationship? How so?

_____

_____

In what ways would you like to see your relationship grow in intimacy?

_____

_____

Periodic questions such as those above are meant to help you get into the conversation as a participant. If writing isn't of interest, use them for personal reflection. If, on the other hand, you want more space to write, consider starting a journal to record your thoughts.

For Women who Identify with Matt and Vice Versa

Most women, I'm going to guess 75 percent or more, will readily identify with Sarah, and the same percentage is likely true for men identifying with Matt. If you do find yourself in the sizeable minority, though, flip the dialogue, and if you find yourself alternately identifying with each of them, then flip-flop!

A Couple's Quest

> The quality of our life has but one measure:
> the quality of our relationships.

O nce there was a man who enjoyed sex. Actually, that is an understatement. He yearned for the sense of admiration a man feels from a woman who obviously likes him and who joyfully anticipates bringing his body inside her own. Since the English language so broadly employs the word love, one could say this man loved making love.

The man's name was Matt, and Matt loved sex so much that he would do nearly anything to experience it—climb the highest hills, swim the widest seas. No obstacle could keep him from finding a woman interested in him.

So he set out on his quest to follow such passion.

Likewise, there once was a woman who thrived on relationships. She yearned for a special connection with a man full of understanding and affection. Someone who felt affirmed by her nurturing spirit and could, in turn, nurture her as well. She loved being cherished.

The woman's name was Sarah, and Sarah loved being cherished so much, she would do nearly anything to experience it—gladly baring body and soul. For Sarah, just as for Matt, no difficulty could stand in the way.

So she set out on her quest to attain such intimacy.

Incidentally, Sarah liked making love and Matt liked his relationships. As we know, however, a difference exists between liking something and loving something. The man was as clear about his priority as the woman was about hers: He loved sex. She loved being cherished. They both sensed, however, there was more to it all.

While on their quest, Matt and Sarah crossed paths and found themselves drawn to each other. Thinking they had discovered kindred spirits, the couple eventually made a vow to look after one another, come good times or bad.

The first years went by quickly—like something out of a favorite fairy tale, but it wasn't long before Matt and Sarah's relationship grew more complicated. The fairy tale turned unsettling now and then as they experienced hazardous twists and turns in the road. They saw their friends struggle too. Some had even called it quits.

Maybe, the couple reasoned, very few fully comprehended how challenging their "for better or worse" pledge could become. They weren't naive. The infatuation subsided early on. They were prepared for that, but they wondered about the passion? Did it have to be a casualty in their relationship as well? How can a person who loves making love and a person who loves feeling loved both have their desires fulfilled—of being loved? It was a question that hung over their life together like a cloud.

The passing years did nothing to eliminate the difference in orientation. Quite the contrary. Between them persisted loyalty and affection, but also plenty of tension and disappointment. Differences can either give a complementary edge to a relationship or a contentious one. At the moment, the latter was winning out.

Sarah suggested they try something unusual to get back on track: a "conversation weekend" at a cabin they had occasionally vacationed in as a family. Such a peaceful setting might provide just the place to get down to the real issues and reaffirm their commitment to each other. Matt's enthusiastic response encouraged her.

Of course, given their differing orientations, he'd likely want to talk about issues related to physical intimacy. She, on the other hand, would seek to focus on matters of the heart—emotional intimacy. No matter. Whatever the topics of conversation, they looked forward to spending time with each other. So they rented the cabin, asked his folks to watch the kids, and packed up. Plans unfolded into reality and, with that, anticipation. What would happen next?

> We all know the destination—love.
> But on the way there, sex makes the trip
> thoroughly entertaining!

Let's Begin with Some Basic Questions and See Where the Conversation Takes Us

How do you (my partner) most deeply experience intimacy and passion?

Familiarity kills infatuation, but does it have to destroy passion as well? Why or why not?

How can a person who loves making love and a person who loves feeling loved both get their desires fulfilled—of being loved?

What does it take to turn an ordinary relationship into a lifelong love affair?

Any others: _____

_____

_____

Do you find it difficult to think up key questions for facilitating in-depth conversation between you and your partner? If so, you're not alone! Consider getting the e-book of intimate questions entitled *So Let's Talk* from our website: IntimateConversations.com

The bottom line: Matt was as clear about his priority as Sarah was about hers: He loved sex. She loved being cherished. He was into passion, she was into intimacy. But they both sensed there was more to it all.

On a scale of 1 (little), to 10 (lots), how do you relate to this couple's priorities stated above? _____

_____

_____

Friday Journey

Recognizing Self-Protective Ways

After saying their good-byes, the couple started their journey. "It's nice of your folks to watch the kids," Sarah said, making a last wave to their send-off party.

"You know they love doing it, and the kids love it too. So, have we officially started our 'talking weekend'?" Matt asked.

"This has to be every woman's dream come true: A weekend to talk and an eager man to talk with. Did something get into the water that I don't know about?"

"Hey, I'm a talking machine," he grinned at her sarcasm. "Just wind me up and get ready to di-a-logue."

"Actually, would you mind if I take a few moments to just sit and do some thinking?" Sarah asked, stretching back into the seat. "I wanted to write out some thoughts before we left but I didn't find the time to do it."

"No problem," Matt replied, with a glance at the rear view mirror. "A few days ago when you suggested we do some journaling before we left, I liked the way you put it. You said, 'We should write down everything we've ever wanted to talk about if the right moment came along because this is that moment.'

"As you know, I'm not much for introspection, but I did jot down a few things, and that got my mind in gear.

So, I'd also like some time to collect my thoughts, if you don't mind taking over the driving after a while."

"Sure. I'd be happy to," she said.

With that, they drove for several hours, alternating between driving and writing down their thoughts, periodically making comments that served to build even greater anticipation for the weekend together. They stopped for lunch at a favorite cafe and then began the most scenic stretch of highway, taking time to savor the view.

Sarah was the first to break through the small talk and asked, "So, tell me, what did you write down?"

"You first. What would you like to talk about?"

"Well, in general terms," she began, "I'd like to see how you and I can stay better connected. It seems that just about the time we get there, we lose it."

"Hey, you told me we were going to talk about sex," Matt replied with a grin. "Isn't that what you said?"

"Did I say that?" she said, looking his way. "I'm sorry, that talk is scheduled for next weekend."

The good-natured humor helped them relax. After a brief moment she continued, "One thing I've been thinking about is our first few years of marriage. It may be a long time ago now, but some of the mistakes we made then still plague us today."

He nodded and said, "I'd second that. The first couple of years were great; then, all of a sudden, the honeymoon came to an end. At the time we talked about the changes we were going through with new jobs, moving, and the like, but I don't think we realized how seriously those changes were affecting our relationship."

"Do you recall the stress test you found back then?" she asked. "It was a test someone devised to add up stress points for the life transitions a person is going through.

"The death of a spouse, for example, is the most stressful event at 100 points. Then it goes down from there to other things like moving, changing jobs, starting a family, etc. Even if they're positive things, any change adds to the stress and when you rack up a certain number of points, you're more likely to get sick—physically and emotionally.

"After we made our third—and fourth—moves, we went through a lot of other changes and my world began to close in on me. The sense of safety I initially felt so strongly with you started to fray, and that led to even more anxiety. Then, when we started a family, a big wave of depression washed over me. You seemed to cope with stress better than I did except when the changes happened to me. You just couldn't handle watching your wife go into a tailspin, and you started trying to fix it."

He looked her way and sighed. "We've talked about this before. It was the first time I'd seen you become so despairing, and I didn't know what to do. At the time your reactions seemed extreme. It felt as if you were pulling away from me and becoming more demanding at the same time. Your depression turned to anger, even hostility, and I began backing out of our relationship emotionally."

She paused and then replied, "I certainly had no intention of alienating you. It's just that I began to feel like you didn't really care what was going on with me because you kept invalidating my feelings. You'd tell me that things would get better or not to worry so much or that I was overreacting. All I really wanted was for you to listen to me. With all our moves my support network of family and friends became paper-thin. Depression was my way of grieving the losses in my life, but without someone to affirm the validity of my grief, it made getting over it that much harder.

"At some point I concluded that you really didn't care, or at least you didn't know how to express your concern. That squelched my desire to reach out to you for support, but trying to cope with it on my own didn't work any better, and a 'cold war' broke out between us."

"Especially in the bedroom," he stated.

"That was all part of the same issue. We were creating self-protective walls where open spaces used to be. I know I started to close down sexually and became more and more critical, which just drove you farther away.

"You insulated yourself from the negativity by spending more time at work and being defensive about your priorities, which made me feel even more unloved. Neither one of us was mature enough to step out of our self-protective shells long enough to see things from the other's point of view and break the cycle."

"I remember talking about it—a lot," he said. "Our talks so often turned into arguments, and then we'd argue about the way we were arguing. Periodically we'd have a breakthrough conversation, but sooner or later we'd fall back into our old habits again and even that became disconcerting. Who were we really, a happily married couple or an unhappily married one?

"How sad that marriage is supposed to be a commitment to love and protect each other, but within just a few years we were both developing self-protective strategies that were anything but loving. I suppose we thought protecting ourselves from hurt would insulate us from pain, but it only served to bring on more pain."

She thought for a moment and said, "Well, we were naive. As a young couple we thought we had it together.

We were sure we'd do things better than our parents. Little did we know that we were headed for the same traps we had watched them fall into—plus a few of our own!"

"You know, this 'relationship thing' is a lot more challenging than I ever thought it would be," he said. "I remember thinking early on that marriage was going to be fun and easy and full of incredible sex."

"Well," she said, pausing, "it's been fun and we've had some incredible sex, but I don't know about easy."

"Our opposite personality types made sure easy would never happen," he replied with a grin.

"That and a huge lack of maturity," she added. "Relationships will always produce some hurt—and at times, a lot of hurt. That's unavoidable. We're just never going to be perfect partners for each other. But the question is, what do we do with that hurt? Do we take the risk of honoring our commitment to keep loving each other or do we insulate ourselves with defensive behavior?

"One way to define love is to say it is the opposite of self-protection—opening ourselves up to each other, rather than closing ourselves off. From what I've seen, insulating ourselves from hurt comes naturally to us all. So I'd say the greatest challenge is to live without self-protective strategies, continuing to risk loving each other even though we know we'll be hurt again." She reached out to squeeze his knee and said, "Those early years were difficult. I'm so glad we survived and decided to make a better ending to our story."

"Aren't we about ready to write another chapter during the next few days?" Matt asked.

"No, silly, we're talking this weekend," Sarah said.

He sighed. "Now, I'm really confused."

Self-Protection:
The #1 Enemy of Intimacy and Love

We all have a tendency to relate in ways that maintain our comfort and avoid interactions that could prove threatening. Such self-protective strategies undermine intimacy in our relationships and with it our hope for maturing as individuals and as lifelong loving partners.

Check Off Your Self-Protective Strategies

Consider a difficult relational situation in your life. Are you taking a risk or are you playing it safe by:

___ Withdrawing in hurt, not reaching out for support?

___ Looking to shift the blame, not taking responsibility?

___ Being defensive and prideful, not open to change?

___ Being critical, not being respectful and complimentary?

___ Capitulating, not developing appropriate boundaries?

___ Being swayed by what others think, not quietly confident?

___ Counting success in terms of externals, not internals?

___ Taking the easiest path, not doing what's right?

___ Being quick to give advice, not listening with empathy?

___ Withholding feelings, not taking the risk to share them?

___ Avoiding commitment, not deepening commitment?

___ Building up resentments, not seeking to deal with issues?

___ Developing a demanding attitude, not a thankful spirit?

If growing in intimacy and love is our goal, we must take a hard look at our self-protective strategies. The call to intimacy and love is, at the same time, the call to abandon self-protection.

The Hostess and the Guest

*B*y the time the couple finished unpacking, evening was fading into night. After setting up their home away from home, they bundled up and headed for a favorite outcropping. The moon's light danced on the lake below them. Looking for a way to resume their discussion, Sarah asked, "So, where do we go from here?"

"I think you called this meeting," Matt answered.

"Now, I know you want to talk about our sex life, and you know I want to talk about our love life—our relationship in general."

"That's a little bit simplistic," he replied.

"Oh, so you don't want to talk about sex?"

"Well," he said, caught up short, "I don't want to talk just about sex. There are definitely other things I'd like to discuss—although, at the moment, I can't remember what they are!"

She laughed. "We came here at my request—and I really appreciate your willingness—so we'll start with you first. What's on your agenda? Fire away."

"You know, it's funny, women are forever deferring. It's one thing that makes you attractive to men but it gets you into trouble at the same time."

"What do you mean?" she asked.

"Anytime there's a burnt piece of toast around our kitchen, it ends up on your plate—never mine or the kids'. I don't even know if you're conscious of it, but you always put our needs ahead of yours. It's a great quality of femininity, until you get to the breaking point of feeling taken for granted. That's when it can get… "

"Volatile," she said, completing his thought.

"Well, most women are givers by nature, which leads us to over-give. So, enjoy our generous spirit and be sensitive when you see us hitting our limits! We don't start getting bent out of shape until we begin feeling unappreciated or used.

"Whatever it takes, my goal is to be more than just a giver to you. I want to be your advocate. When we see the issues from each other's point of view and champion the other's position, we build enormous trust. Then, even in the midst of disagreement, we each feel that I'm on your side, you're on mine. We're advocates for each other."

"Great point, and very challenging! Being each other's advocate means humbly acknowledging that another person's perspective is just as valid as our own. Given this as a goal, I'll propose a pledge between us."

She looked at him and replied, "A pledge?"

"Yes, a pact while we're here to look to the future."

"Is this different than our relationship outside of this weekend?" she asked, puzzled.

"Not really. We don't usually dwell on the past. But

we've never before set an entire weekend aside for the purpose of talking. When you suggested this weekend, I began thinking about the ideal situation that would help us handle so much intensity. I envisioned an opportunity in the next few days to forget our past and start fresh. It's like what we've just done in coming here—we've left most of our stuff at home and brought with us just the smallest bit of 'baggage' from our real lives."

"It's hard to leave your memories behind," she said.

"True, but let's pledge to give up the disappointing ones, and any hurt, and begin from a place of newlywed bliss—even if that's naive. In this new place we have only ourselves and a wide-open future to work with."

"I'm for whatever helps us lower our defenses," she said. "If we can't talk freely, there's not much reason to talk."

"Agreed. I just know that sometimes too much honesty has been more hurtful than helpful, and I don't want that to happen again."

"What about this," she proposed, "If our dialogue gets too uncomfortable, then we should signal the other by waving a hand—or whatever—to indicate it's time to move on. But up until that signal we are free to describe, in complete honesty, all our thoughts and feelings. We're agreeing to suspend judgment and hear each other out. When we disagree with each other, we do so agreeably."

"I like that," he said, squeezing her shoulder. "No thought or feeling or desire poses a threat. This beautiful place acts as a sanctuary where we can talk and listen with no hidden agendas or unstated expectations, working hard to understand each other. After the weekend, we'll go home and determine what to do with what we've experienced."

"I should warn you, there may be a lot of handwaving

on my part," she said smiling. "So, like I always do, I'll defer to you. Where do you want to begin?"

"I don't know. What do you think? Oh well, let's start with sex. Hey, you can't wave your hand already!"

"I need to be careful about over-giving," she said, broadening her grin. "Go ahead, I'll save it for later."

"Thank you," he replied. "I guess I'd like to start out by defining the act itself. Are you ready?"

"Ready as I'll ever be."

"I've been thinking about a simple observation that leads to an insight. Here's the observation: When a woman has sex, she opens herself up. When a man has sex he comes inside. Of course, sex has to happen some way, but no matter how creative a couple is, it always happens in the same way: There is an opening up and a coming in."

"Are you trying to say that these two actions represent something? That they carry a deeper meaning?"

"Exactly," he continued. "The act of making love itself serves as a reminder on the deepest level. By opening herself up, a woman invites an 'outsider' into the sanctuary of her home. By accepting her invitation, the man loses his 'outsiderness.' They become one person, joined together in the sacred place where life begins. This completes the most intimate, even holy, union that two human beings can have with each other."

"So, what's the reminder here?" she asked.

"The intimacy of lovemaking involves two distinct roles: The woman is the hostess and the man is the guest. She extends hospitality, and he enjoys that hospitality. Lovemaking then becomes the sensuous embrace of best friends, coming together to celebrate everything they hold dear in their relationship.

"It's like building a campfire on a cold night and sitting next to its glow. Within the context of a committed relationship, sex offers us the intense fire of passion, while an intimate friendship offers the ongoing warmth of coals."

"That campfire has had us sizzling on many a night," she said, leaning back into his arms, "and left its glow between us for days afterward."

"That's what it's about," he said, gently squeezing her waist. "Then, as a man finds his greatest pleasure in giving pleasure to a woman, lovemaking reflects the giving and receiving roles of a relationship as a whole. It's the act of love that melds together our physical, emotional, and spiritual selves. Now, with this weekend's conversation, we'll add a little to the intellectual side!"

"So this weekend, we're just talking," she replied playfully. "Gosh, I'm so disappointed."

"I suppose, but I might consider some kind of invitation from the hostess, as her most humble guest, of course," he said, tightening his arms around her.

"Well, if I'm going to play hostess for this affair," she replied, "I might just invite my guest to a little campfire for two. And it's getting chilly, so let's head in."

Back at the cabin, Matt and Sarah spent the rest of the evening warming up together next to their fireplace. As they prepared for bed that night they felt invigorated from their ongoing conversation. It didn't take long for the embers of warmth to turn into flames of passion.

In the act of sex there is an opening up and a coming in. The act reminds us of the two primary roles played out in sex: that of hostess and guest.

Guidelines for Intimate Conversations

Collect Your Thoughts

- If possible, prepare for the talk(s) with some personal reflection and journaling.
- Write down things you've always wanted to talk about if the right moment came along.
- Distill your thoughts into a few key areas.
- Aim to go deeper rather than broader.

Abide by Conversation Ground Rules

When Listening:	When Talking:
Seek to understand	Be straightforward
Suspend judgment	Express it sensitively
Avoid defensiveness	Proceed to your point

Focus on Mutual Goals

- Share your own feelings and views.
- Listen to your partner's feelings and views.
- Identify better ways of thinking and acting.
- Develop realistic, concrete steps for change.
- Build trust by being each other's advocate.
- Reaffirm your love and commitment.

And Don't Forget

Two monologues have never equaled a dialogue.

Interlude on Intimacy

In•ti•mate

Marked by a close acquaintance,
association, or familiarity.
Relating to or indicative of one's deepest nature.
Essential or innermost.
Marked by informality and warmth.
Very personal, private.

Conversation typically exchanges information.
Intimate conversation discloses
affections and passions—our personhoods.

While the couple enjoys a first night's sleep at their weekend getaway, let's also take a break to consider just what intimacy is.

Intimacy melds people together. It undergirds our friendships by deepening our respect for, commitment to, and trust in each other. Pursuing intimacy requires a sustained effort, and this effort rewards us with a deep and lasting union with the important people in our lives.

The Heart of Intimacy

Intimacy takes place as we disclose who we are—
in-to-me, see. It's about being known.

Intimacy is *not* about being validated or accepted. If we
seek acceptance more than intimacy we end up "shaping
our sharing" to avoid potential rejection. Our partner may
warmly reciprocate when we share ourself, and we certainly
appreciate it when he or she does, but if we need his or
her validation, that need becomes more important than dis-
closing who we are.

Intimacy requires a willingness to disclose ourselves with
no assurance of another's acceptance.

Intimacy begins with Me

It takes root as I grow in self-awareness and courage: Self-
awareness of who I really am inside—not an idealized view
or a deflated view of myself. And courage to honestly talk
about myself—my anxieties, my dreams, my secret desires,
my disappointments, my growing pains, my joys.

Intimacy becomes a shared experience as both partners disclose their "inner worlds" and find acceptance.

Intimacy then creates an Us

It forms a unique partnership marked by qualities of
respect, empathy, and affirmation. Such mutuality grows
into a radical connection of trust and the deepest form of
togetherness between us—the feeling of being understood,
valued and loved by another human being.

Intimacy Busters

Intimacy's great potential has limitations in the face of three intimacy-destroying behaviors. The Triple-A Intimacy Busters are abuse, addiction, and adultery. (There are also personality disorders that make achieving intimacy impossible.) If you are a victim of any of the intimacy busters, seek counseling to consider confrontation, separation, or divorce.

Abuse: Intimacy cannot coexist with abuse. If you or your children are threatened with or are experiencing physical or sexual abuse, leave the relationship as quickly as possible. Emotional and verbal abuse seriously jeopardize trust as well. Look for help from professionals, as well as family and friends.

Addiction: A spouse consumed by drugs, porn, alcohol, or gambling will serve the addiction before the happiness of a mate or the well being of a family. Addictions can be hard to identify and treat. An addict must be willing to face his or her addiction and follow the difficult road to recovery.

Adultery: You deserve your spouse's sexual faithfulness. Certainly there is a difference between a chronically unfaithful spouse and one who, after an affair, determines to make different choices and is willing to rebuild the marriage.

As the offended spouse, you are not responsible for your mate's actions. Such situations necessitate that you draw up appropriate boundaries regarding his or her behavior. Those boundaries act as a critical safeguard to your self-respect. Counseling should be sought to give clarity and help you determine your best course of action.

Tough love is love—applied in a tough situation!

Twelve Don'ts When Relating to Him

1. Don't nag, pout or whine at him.
2. Don't be impossible to please or fail to be happy.
3. Don't embarrass him in public or ridicule him ever.
4. Don't think he doesn't love words of praise or your affirmations.
5. Don't think unkind words won't wound him.
6. Don't stop cheering him on or telling your friends what a great guy he is.
7. Don't think he doesn't need decompression time after work or some "guy time" with his buddies.
8. Don't assume his work aspirations are not your business, too.
9. Don't think your appearance makes no difference to him.
10. Don't fall in love with your kids more than with him.
11. Don't think he doesn't appreciate your touch.
12. Don't underestimate how important sex is to him.

Circle which numbers you need to take more seriously.

Saturday Morning

WHERE HE'S COMING FROM

*M*att got up early the next day with plans to serve Sarah breakfast in bed.

"Well, this is quite the role reversal," Sarah exclaimed, as he asked for her breakfast order.

"What do you mean?" Matt inquired.

"I thought I was the hostess in this relationship!"

He smiled at her and sat down on the edge of the bed. "As I've told you before, sex gives me lots of energy to focus on you and keeps me coming back."

"Yeah, back to bed for more," she teased.

"True, but that's not the only thing that's true. Great sex, or even run-of-the-mill sex, keeps me coming back to you. I'm sure it's difficult for you, as a woman, to comprehend just what sex does for a man. If a woman's identity centers around relationships and feelings, the basic identity for a man comes from work and sex.

"I'd say that men just don't spend a lot of time thinking about how we feel, or how others are feeling, for that matter. So for me, having sex is like getting zapped with electroshock paddles. That jolt brings my emotional center alive. Then I can start seeing beyond my task-centered orientation and enter into your relational world.

"I'm sure this is no big surprise, but I can go all day

> Differences between the sexes—where do we start? Women connect to belong, men compete to win. Women form circles, men climb ladders. Women are like radars, aware of the needs, feelings, and concerns of people around them. Men are like lasers who, once they become aware of a need, are able to focus in on meeting that need.

without ever tapping into my feelings. I do this and do that; push, push, push; make things happen; and I never think about how I feel or what's happening around me.

"So, sex helps me to feel. It turns on my emotions. Beyond that, making love pumps all kinds of gratitude and appreciation into my soul. Those feelings give me hope and strength to face the world out there, and the desire to listen and spend time with the world in here—you and the kids. Sex has the power to help a guy evolve from being a taker to being a giver, maybe even a nurturer. There's not much that sex won't do for a man!"

"But will it get breakfast made and get the dishes washed?" she asked, trying to suppress her grin.

"Let's try it and see how it goes," he said, pretending to dive on top of her. As he stretched out, he hesitated and then sat up beside her again. "There's one more thing, if you would be so kind as to indulge me a little longer. In all of this, I don't think I've adequately described what making love does for me."

"Sounds like an infomercial," she paused as her words sunk in. "'But wait—there's more!'"

"I'd like to go right-brained to describe the experience," he proposed, touching her knee with his hand.

"Go ahead," she said, settling back on the pillow.

"Imagine yourself preparing for a warm, soothing bubble bath," he began. "As you step into the water, you immediately feel its comforting invitation. As your body slowly slips below the water line you are surrounded by a sensation of warmth and peace.

"The center of your inner self pulsates from a sense of caring that quickens all the nerves and muscles in your body. The day's irritations and frustrations vanish, leaving you with only a heightened sense of anticipation that comes from feeling very much alive. Picture yourself lying in this warm channel, enveloped by understanding, acceptance, and affirmation. You are naked, but your body is blanketed by the security of a loving environment.

"I hate to wake you out of this state, but for me that feeling of being enveloped comes from being inside you. Even though only a small part of me is in you, it feels like my whole body is surrounded by your caring presence. I feel so secure and wonderful, as if you had spread your loving embrace all around me from head to toe.

"Now it's your turn; what does sex do for you?"

"It's wonderful," she said, with a pause, "but more complicated. I don't need sex to switch on my feelings, because a woman's feelings are already switched on—nearly all the time. So I'm not looking for something to jump-start my emotions or surround me as you've described—unless it's with hugs or cuddles. Making love can bring me a great sensation of fulfillment. Often, though, this comes as a net energy drain rather than an energy boost. Sometimes sex represents the safety of infancy for me, as it does for you. At other times, though, it feels like the vulnerability of my teenage years."

"A net energy drain," he repeated. "I'm not sure I really understand that. What specifically do you mean?"

"Let me put it this way: I'm the one who opens up and lets you in. That's a vulnerable place to be, especially if I'm feeling out of sorts already. If sex is the culmination of our connectedness during the day, I'm fully engaged and energized. But if sex brings with it a sense of intrusion, instead of feelings of warmth and love, I disengage.

"As we talked about last night, I assume the role of a hostess, which takes a lot of internal energy to fulfill, much like any caregiver. You said that sex energizes you and helps you put your world in order, but I need to have my world in order to be energized for sex. Then sex connects me with my femininity and deepens my love of life.

"Remember, when I get going, I want sex as much, or more, than you do. I was the one all over you last night, after all. And as you know, in the moment of passion I can start 'carrying on' with delight—at least, if no one else is in earshot. I'm a pretty expressive person, but that can be a little over the top, even for me."

"I love your 'carrying on,'" he said. "You know men live for those sounds of appreciation, right? You can't say enough ohhhs, ahhhhs, and oh-yeses. Here's a little secret: It's a thrill when I first come inside you and you act a bit physically overwhelmed. After all these years I love that shiver that lets me know I can still take your breath away."

"Well, there's nothing staged about it. We talked one time about faking orgasms, and I said I wouldn't because I didn't want you to think you were getting me somewhere you weren't. Sex is confusing enough without reinforcing your desire to please me in a way that you're not."

"I want you to be as specific as you can be about the

kind of touching you like and don't like. Hearing you say 'that feels good' feels good to me too. And moaning communicates delight and abandon, like you've dug into your favorite chocolate dessert. It's cute on you, very cute."

"I like you talking like that: 'It's cute on you'," she said. "That's girl-talk. It may seem like a foreign language, but it's worth learning. I find it much less threatening than guy-talk, especially when talking about sex."

"And how, exactly, would you describe 'guy-talk'?"

"I know it when I hear it. All of us girls do. You know I'm no prude. Nevertheless, I rarely even name body parts—especially using any of the crass options. Talking in such specifics can taint the real thing for me. Technical descriptions replace the sweetness of sex with graphic detail. Instead of treating its delicate mystery under a soft candlelight, you're using a glaring spotlight.

"It's like expressing what chocolate tastes like, and instead of saying 'it melts in your mouth,' you could say 'the saliva starts the digestion process by dissolving, etc.' You've used three technically correct words—saliva, digestion, and dissolving—but it makes something that's really good sound rather yucky."

"So do you want us to be more vague?" he asked.

"No, I want to be specific. For this weekend I'll try to set aside my normal discomfort because I'd like to fully understand. Believe me, though, it will not be easy to listen to vivid descriptions of sex. Things will get scary if the act of sex becomes detached from our relationship— if you see me more as a task-fulfiller than as a lover.

"No woman wants to make sex into a performance-oriented athletic event. If it becomes that, we begin feeling pressure to perform, which can lead to a sense of fear and inadequacy. That mentality adds to our self-consciousness about our bodies, so much so that some of us make love only in the dark to avoid being seen. But the beauty of sex in a committed relationship is the very lack of judgment. We don't go 'sizing up' each other as another sex partner."

"You did say something about 'carrying on'!"

"That's about as athletic as I'm likely to get!" she replied. "Maybe I should amend my description from 'carrying on' to 'expressing pleasure in a verbal way'!"

He matched her grin with his own. "Okay, but when you 'express pleasure in a verbal way,' I feel like I've won the lottery. I don't know whether to describe it with girl-or guy-talk. All I know is that I love it."

"Like childbirth, orgasms have a way of extracting all my inhibitions. And while sex can be over for you so fast, I have multi-orgasmic possibilities! So, I'd say, in the final analysis women have a deeper sexual capacity than men. I've also heard a little 'carrying on' from you as well!"

"Oh, so that's what I do—I carry on?" he challenged.

She mused. "I must say, I do wonder about something. Given how pleasurable it can be, you'd think great sex would carry over in increasing my desire for it. It's as if I have little memory from one time to the next of the physical gratification of making love—like an electrical cord getting detached from the outlet and then needing to be reattached before it can carry current again. If there's any reminder of the pleasure of sex, it's the relational side effects that keep me coming back for more.

"For you, the desire for making love helps to overcome the hassles and hurdles of getting into it. For me, life's practicalities can easily overwhelm my desire. When passion and pleasure come knocking, I'm often too caught up in everyday life to open the door.

"I'm glad you keep knocking, otherwise, my sexuality might get buried by the mundane. I'd say the one with the stronger hormonal drive should keep pursuing, and the one with the weaker hormonal drive should remain open to that pursuit. I hope you can stay positive even if things aren't happening. Whatever might be going on with me, it won't end your horizontal pleasures forever. If you keep seeking to connect with me, sooner or later—and likely sooner—I'll want to connect with you too.

"For now I'd better get up and take a shower. I will take you up on that breakfast offer, though. How about a bowl of oatmeal and some fruit?"

Where He's Coming From

Ladies, sex helps a man feel. It turns on his emotions. It takes him back to infancy. It pumps all kinds of appreciation and gratitude into his soul.

It provides him with hope and strength to face the world. Sex gives a man the jolt he needs to get out of his task-centered environment. There's just not much sex won't do for a man!

[Sex] is the most Godly and lofty of all human pursuits. The powerful pull of sexual craving, rather than being seen as a sinful desire to indulge the flesh, is rather seen as an irresistible urge pulling us outside of ourselves, thereby guaranteeing that we do not remain selfish and self-absorbed.

—Shmuley Boteach

Twelve Don'ts When Relating to Her

1. Don't invalidate her feelings or patronize her.
2. Don't intimidate her with your anger, ever.
3. Don't stop listening even if she has a lot to say.
4. Don't forget to pamper her or to touch her often in non-sexual ways.
5. Don't neglect to tell her what you are feeling.
6. Don't avoid saying, "I'm sorry, please forgive me."
7. Don't assume she knows you love her unless you tell her so.
8. Don't tell her how to "fix it" as if her feelings don't count.
9. Don't neglect taking pride in how she makes everything look, especially herself.
10. Don't come home from work thinking your job is done.
11. Don't ignore your role as father in the family.
12. Don't assume sex works for her or means the same to her as it does to you.

Circle which numbers you need to take more seriously.

Where She's Coming From

O n his way to the kitchen, Matt walked by the open bathroom door and caught a glimpse of Sarah. Her presence acted like a magnet, drawing him into the room. Sometimes she put on her makeup before putting on her clothes. He had never discouraged the practice at home, and he wasn't about to start now!

"You look great," he said, as he slid up behind her.

She touched his hand on her shoulder and met his eyes in the mirror appreciatively. "Thanks Matt. And to think it only takes one hour and one pound of cosmetics."

"Hey," he replied, grinning, "I'll bet it won't take an ounce over a half pound to get you to magnificent!"

"Men," she sighed, "make the rite-of-bathroom-passage so easy. You need all of three items in here: a hairbrush, a toothbrush, and a shaver—and I need 300."

"Hey, you don't have to use 300. Why do yourself up so much when it's just us? It's fine with me if you want to go natural. I like you made up too, but we're a little far into this marriage thing for you to try to impress me."

"Actually, vanity doesn't motivate women to use makeup as much as the need to improve does. We want to improve everything important to us. The more important something is, the more we want to see it improve.

"That's why we're always working on our key relationships and why it doesn't make sense to just talk about sex. For us, sex is all about our relationship. So I don't mind talking about sex, as long as I'm assured that you see it in the context of our overall connection as a couple. I can't work on improving sex without your willingness to improve our relationship as a whole. One leads to the other, and then one thing leads to another!

"Sure there's a place for better sexual techniques, but a woman's urge to improve focuses on every aspect of life. Did you notice what I did when we arrived?"

"What you always do; you arranged our move-in."

"When we got here I could immediately envision us living in this place, and I went to work, setting things out neatly, efficiently, and beautifully. Many women love organizing all kinds of stuff, whether it's a special moment to bring someone joy, or a fun experience to share, or making something beautiful to look at. We love to realize a concept, to create something out of nothing like a party, a dessert, a quilt, or a nicely arranged living room.

"As 'environmental beauticians' we have an eye for decorating a home or styling our hair. That's why men get in trouble when they express dismay or displeasure over the time and energy that goes into these efforts. It's just our nature and you should be happy that someone in this world wants to add a touch of beauty."

"So how does all this apply to makeup?" he asked.

"If nothing else, every day I get a chance to improve myself and create a work of art right here," she replied, pointing to her face. "I'm not the Mona Lisa, and I'm no Leonardo da Vinci, but it's the best I've got."

"Oh, you're a work of art all right," he said, wrapping his arms around her. "Now, we've got just one more thing to do before you put your clothes on."

"We just did that last night, or have you forgotten?"

"Indeed, memory is my problem," he replied. "I can't get this body out of my mind."

She sighed. "That's not your only problem."

"Oh yeah?"

"Well," she began, "when it comes to sex, you should not tell me what I'm going to do. That kind of come-on feels demanding and will not get you the results you want. It's more of a turn-off than a turn-on. Even asking for sex is not the best approach."

"I don't want to manipulate you by being indirect about my intentions," he protested.

"Do you want a little education here or not?"

"Yes," he said, putting the toilet lid down for a seat.

"There's just not a lot of testosterone flowing in these veins," she said, holding out her arms. "So turn down the pushiness and turn up the subtlety. Women long to be nurtured; maybe you could say we have an affection drive. Since we don't have anything close to a guy's level of testosterone, most of us don't have such a strong sex drive. I could go on last night's lovemaking for a week. So, the direct approach is not going to work with me, particularly if we've recently had sex. Sometimes, it just does not compute in my brain that you are ready to go for it again less than eight hours from the last time."

"I know, you've said that before. It's so depressing."

"Being depressed is also a turn-off," she replied, "because it makes your advances so tentative. When you want to make love but don't think it's going to happen, you can come across like a car salesman who says, 'You probably wouldn't want to buy this car, would you?' Not exactly the best salesmanship. A woman loves to baby her man if, and only if, he doesn't act like a baby!"

"So, you're saying," he replied, placing his finger to his head as if it were a gun, "I'm damned if I do, when I approach you in a too-straightforward manner, and I'm damned if I don't, when I approach you hesitantly."

As the words settled into the air thick with moisture, she took his finger and guided it over the haze of the fogged-over mirror, drawing a line. On the left side she put an S, in the center she made another S, and to the right she wrote a third S. Letting his finger go, she stated, "The left S stands for 'too slow,' the one in the middle stands for 'subtle,' and the right one, 'too straightforward.'" Then she checked the middle S. "This is where you need to be."

Too	√	Too
Slow	Subtle	Straightforward

"Sounds like the story of the three bears: The advance can't be too cold or too hot, it needs to be just right."

"Exactly," she agreed, as she redrew over the check on the mirror's clouded surface, "but it's even a bit more challenging than that, because 'just right' changes. Sometimes I want your advances to be on the slow side of subtle, and sometimes on the straightforward side of subtle, and a lot of the time just plain subtle. It all depends on the state I'm in when the process begins."

"Okay, so how 'bout if we just create three signs: 'Very subtle,' 'Subtle,' and 'Not too subtle,'" he joked as he made two additional checks on the mirror.

√	√	√
Very subtle	Subtle	Not too subtle

"Hey, you can learn this or not. I'm not a water faucet that will respond any old way you turn it on. Do you want more sex? If so, I'm telling you how to get it."

"Honey, you certainly know how to get your man's attention! I know we've been through this before, but I obviously need a refresher course. Tell me again, in no uncertain terms, how I can get more sex."

"First, I should tell you how you can guarantee yourself less sex. Your approach to me just a minute ago was sweet, but too blunt. Don't tell me we're going to have sex. Unless I'm obviously 'hot to trot,' don't come on to me directly at all. You can think it, you can envision asking me directly, whatever. Just don't let the words come out of your mouth!"

"My lips are sealed," he said, tightening his lips.

"When you ask, 'Can we have sex?' it puts all the burden on yours truly," she replied, pointing to herself. "Then I'm saddled with the decision of whether to go ahead and please you, or not. That's a no-win situation for me because all the responsibility for making it feel right falls on me. It's

> *There's sometimes when I want to be gentle and treated like a lady, and other times when I want to be treated like a biker mama.*
>
> –Vicki, interviewed by Laurence Roy Stains & Stefan Bechtel

no-win for you because you end up with a frustrated wife at best and an angry one at worst."

"So you're saying there's just not quite enough subtlety in the statement, 'Can we have sex?'"

Sarah balled up her fist, as if to punch Matt's response right out of the room, and then continued. "If I resist your advances, don't go into a self-pity, woe-is-me act, either. Consider it a challenge—woo me. Did you catch that? Instead of 'woe is me, woo me.' I love the attention."

"Very good," he said, smiling. "Woo, yes. Woe, no."

"Employ that subtle charm of yours. Maybe it's buried, but it's there. Think of a house. Before you get me to the play room, you need to spend time with me in the sitting room where we can talk and connect emotionally. Since I'm turned on by my emotional attachment to you, engage me on an emotional level, not an analytical one.

"Come into my world by asking questions that take me out of practicalities and motherhood: Something useful like, 'How can I help?' or even something fun like 'If you could be anywhere on vacation right now, where would you be?' or 'What has been your most fulfilling experience this last month?' I love the nurturing.

"Those questions challenge my current 'to do' list and elicit an emotional response. They're just a start, but they fan the flame and open me up to deeper longings. Maybe it would help you if I got a little crude here: You've got to get into my heart before you get into my pants."

"Whoa, this sounds like a primer on seduction," he replied, looking over to her.

"Call it what you will. You know there are many ways into a woman's heart—choose one! If it doesn't go very far, take another. Create a bridge into my world by helping me visualize and imagine. Use humor, make it fun, quote poetry, rent a romantic comedy, read me sweet music lyrics or sensual words from the Song of Solomon. Look at photo albums and talk about the kids. Ask me about my hopes and dreams. Spend time partnering on a project. Give me a half-hour foot massage. Take me on a bike trip to the nearest park or on an imaginary trip to a wonderful place or to the store for some bargain hunting!

"Here's an analogy: think of a candle. My passion is like its flame—it can flicker and die in the wind of a harsh word, a strange noise, a sick child, PMS, or stress. Your goal is not to romance me, as to make an emotional connection. If I feel the oneness of us coming together—even in a struggle—my desires will turn sexual and the flame will burn bright.

"Whatever you do, though, don't beg: 'Please, pretty please, can we have sex?' Begging is for the canine species. I'm just not going to be aroused if I look into your big droopy eyes and all I see is a hound dog. However dramatic or sincere it may be, thirty minutes of begging does not constitute foreplay!

"Begging also has a couple of cousins—whining and pouting: 'We never have sex.' Instead of coming off as vulnerable, which is a real turn-on for me, begging, whining, and pouting communicate self-centered neediness, which is definitely a turn-off. The candle flame dies out."

"I know there's a big difference between meeting needs and meeting neediness," he stated. "I don't want the demands of a needy wife any more than you want them from a needy husband, n-e-e-dless to say. And I don't want you acquiescing to my desires as a long-suffering wife any more than you want a self-pitying husband."

"Again, it's about attitude," she said, looking at him

in the mirror. "Meeting needs gives me a wide latitude and allows me the freedom to say, 'No, not now.' Meeting neediness pushes me into a corner where I feel like I have to endure sex or suffer the consequences: self-pity or anger or the silent treatment. Instead of being free to choose, I'm being forced to oblige. Imposing that kind of obligation on me will lead to passive resistance at best and fullblown anger at worst. It's the opposite of nurturing me."

"I hear what you're saying," he replied, "but there can be a fine line between having needs and being needy. Everyone has needs. The issue is how those needs are expressed. Do we demand attention or do we communicate in ways that respect our mate's right to say 'no' to us? At times I'm not quite sure which side of that line I'm on."

"Well, I can tell—usually. Unless I'm out of it, I enjoy meeting your needs. That's what nurturers do, and the more vulnerable, humble, and sweet you are, the better. I'm reminded of when you lost your job a few years ago and you began to retreat emotionally. I started feeling anxious myself as you went into a funk. I remember fighting my own fears and trying to affirm you at the same time. I'd say, 'You're really good at what you do, I'm sure you'll be able to find another job.' But nothing I said made any difference.

"Then it dawned on me that what you really needed was reassurance on a deeper, non-verbal level—a sexual level. By the time I realized it though, making love was the last thing I was interested in because you were pulling away from me and hiding in your cave. By sheer force of will I decided I was going to go into high gear sexually, which became even more difficult after you rebuffed my first couple of attempts. I knew you wouldn't hold out long, so I kept at it until you finally melted.

"I realized sex was working when you started opening up to me about your fears with hope, rather than anxiety, in your eyes. After you found a new and better job, I overheard you telling your parents that it had been tough, but you really appreciated my support during the whole ordeal. I don't even know if you recognized it, but the support you received came in the form of three months of high-octane lovemaking."

"Oh, I recognized it! At first I thought it was about sex, but it didn't take me too long to figure out what you were doing. What can I say though—it was great!" he said.

"Well, it was partly about sex. I realized, maybe for the first time, how powerful sex could be as a source of comfort and healing for both of us. Sex made us a team— literally—strengthening our mutual resolve. Your anxiety and depression lifted. It nearly wore me out, but my hope returned, and I felt very needed in the best of ways.

"You know, in normal times too, I enjoy satisfying your sex drive—whether it's comfort sex or morning quickies—as long as I know it's ultimately about us and not just about your needs. For sex to be fulfilling to me, the relationship between us must be fulfilling on an emotional level. Otherwise, the well is going to run dry quickly and you're going to be a very thirsty man."

"So, tell me how you really feel," he said, raising an eyebrow. "You know, instead of beating around the bush!"

"Actually, I want to beat you over the head when you approach me in a demanding way because it sets off a kind of knee-jerk resistance in me. I'm not saying you can never come on strong or even ask for what you want, but be assured, I know what you want. When you are so direct, I often can't help hearing it as a demand."

"I back off when you indicate you're not into it."

"You generally do, but that hasn't always been the case. Since suggesting this weekend, I've been thinking about why I react so strongly to what I view as demands."

"And what have you come up with?" he asked.

"How about I finish dressing, and we'll discuss it over breakfast," Sarah said, looking at him in the mirror.

"Sure," he replied. "I'll see you then." He squeezed her shoulders gently and turned to walk out of the room.

Where She's Coming From

Gentlemen, turn down the pushiness and guy-talk. Turn up the seduction of tenderness and subtlety. Don't ask, "Can we have sex?" Don't go into self-pity. Remember, thirty minutes of begging does not constitute foreplay! Women are natural need meeters, not neediness meeters.

A woman has an "affection drive." Unlike a man, her sexuality is not so much based on hormonal urges but on a deeper, heart-felt desire for emotional connectedness. For her the "Big O" is not orgasm; it's oneness.

At any given time a woman's passion resembles a candle flame which can very easily flicker and die out. She needs to feel an emotional union before a physical union feels right.

Women have a far more mature approach to sex than men...Unlike men, women have always treated sex as an act of love, a consummation of the road of intimacy. This is why her sex drive is so much stronger than a man, because the well from which it courses runs so deep.

—Shmuley Boteach

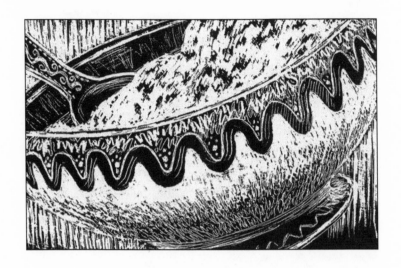

We're in This Together

S arah found Matt in the dining room with an old favorite, oatmeal. "Thanks," she said, spying the raisins he had added just for her. "So where were we?"

"Talking about you feeling pressured," he replied.

"Yes. There are a couple of reasons. First, while navigating my way around the dating scene, I felt like I was a leaky dam holding back a sea of testosterone. I feared I could crumble at any time and be swept away."

"Meaning?" he asked, encouraging her to continue.

"Well, during high school and college I was constantly feeling pressured by guys I dated to 'give it up'—to go further than I wanted to go physically, even on a first or second date. My waist-to-bustline ratio was rather good back then and that just made me more of a target.

"Some guys were gentlemen who took 'Let's slow down' or 'No' for an answer, but others took my affection for them as a green light for their hands to go anywhere. Their version of dating was to win my heart as fast as possible so they could have my body. In retrospect, I can't remember a sexual encounter that I didn't feel pressured into to some degree. I was constantly confused as to whether this whole dating and sex thing was for me.

"I've told you this before, but in a couple of situations my 'No' was not taken seriously. I wasn't physically restrained, but I was emotionally intimidated. Giving into such pressure cuts at the heart of a woman's self-respect."

"I hate hearing about this. It still makes me angry."

"The hostess–guest analogy helps explain it," she continued. "As a woman, I'm a hostess who seeks to give myself—heart, soul, and body—to the one I love. Like any woman, I'll go to great lengths to serve my primary love relationship."

"But the intimidation you experienced violates that trust, because your body was being taken, not given."

"Right. So my response early on was to constantly be putting on the brakes. Maybe guys felt I was giving out mixed messages because I loved the affection, but I wasn't ready for an intense physical relationship. I was actually seeking a special man to build a future with—not to have sex with. It just became apparent in my circle of friends that sex was expected as part of the dating scene.

"I've heard that now the average adult has ten sexual partners before they get married. If I had it to do over, I would have waited for my maturity level to catch up with all those hormones. Besides opening myself up to health risks, I fell victim to plenty of emotional risks.

"I found that sleeping together speeds up relationships artificially. You feel closer than you are and, as a result, make unwise choices. Then came that awkwardness with your ex-partners. Even the act itself lost pizzazz. Instead of being something special to share with your life partner, it became an ordinary date experience.

"Some of the women I knew became angry. They began feeling used, realizing that for men it was only about sex. Other friends of mine didn't seem to mind knowing these fleeting relationships wouldn't end up in permanent commitment. One of them even called a guy she regularly slept with her f'in buddy. But for me, without the security of a commitment, I never felt free to give away my heart along with my body and settled for an advance–resist mentality instead of a letting-go mentality.

"I would typically hold out sexually until my need for acceptance or security from a particular guy became greater than my discomfort with how far we were involved physically. The pattern got set, at least in my mind. A guy would come on to me sooner or later, and I would look for any way possible to nicely hold him back. Then I would give in. As far as guys in my life went, you were more of a gentleman than most—that was one reason I was so attracted to you. I knew I had met Mr. Right because you took—and still take—my feelings about such things seriously. I felt safe and valued by you."

"Thanks for making my shyness a virtue. You can bet I wanted to go all the way with you, but from the start I saw our future as long-term and felt we should go slow," Matt replied

"Such shyness is a virtue. You did make up for lost time, though, after we got married! For whatever reason, the link between sexual advance and resistance continued for me. When I felt a demand, I found myself putting on the brakes. Even now I sometimes catch myself avoiding sex when, in fact, what I actually want is to open the flood-

> *Blushing is the color of virtue.*
>
> —Diogenes

gates and allow those sexual feelings to flow.

"Did you notice I wore my locket this weekend?" she asked, touching the oval pendant at her neck. "You gave me this on our honeymoon. The little picture of us inside reminds me that everywhere I go I take our intimate experiences along. They're here, hidden in this little locket.

"The locket reminds me of the emotional, even spiritual, strength our sex life gives to me. It enables me to go out into my world and not feel alone. It helps alleviate my nagging doubts about whether I matter to you or not. In it are a multitude of joyful, very personal experiences no one but you and I know about. They're ours alone."

"What a wonderful, secret-filled locket!" he replied.

Sarah smiled. "Well, you share all the delights of this locket with me. I hope they reassure you of my love and, as you mentioned, energize you to take on all the opportunities and challenges of your world. If our wedding rings represent our public commitment, this locket represents our special, private love affair. It holds our secret pleasures."

"What a great illustration. I must say that men seldom, if ever, think that way; we're too simple and direct. If I put it in our language, I'd say a man wants a woman to love one thing above all else—sex—and to love it because she finds great joy in communicating her admiration through it. That woman makes her man feel like a man.

"Men admire women for everything they strive to be, men appreciate women for everything they seek to do, but men love women who love sex—or who are willing to learn to love sex," he explained.

"But love is an action, not a feeling!" she exclaimed.

"Well, you are the English major, but can't the word 'love' be used as both an action and a feeling? As an action, love changes what we do. This is the most important kind of love because it requires serving another person. But as a feeling, love can also describe our appreciation of that other person. So, men feel love for women who love sex."

He paused and continued, "Some men have given up thrones for women who made them feel masculine. If you polled husbands of beautiful women who dislike sex, versus husbands of plain women who like sex, I'll bet the men with the plain wives would rate as happiest in their marriages. It's much more about disposition than it is about looks. As a matter of fact, if a plain-looking woman took to lovemaking like some hot seductress in a sex video, she would begin to appear to her husband as a gorgeous model regardless of her looks."

"So now it's my responsibility to make sex good?"

"No, I don't mean to say that," he said. "We both share that responsibility. Here's a little secret that some women may not know, however: For a man to really enjoy sex, his partner must also enjoy it. Otherwise, she's just accommodating him—and he can tell. Such passive accommodation eventually leads to a sense of failure in men. I can handle failure in almost any area and not feel like a failure, but sex is different. The more I strike out in the bedroom, the more my insecurities increase, and my manhood shrinks!

"Even if I was a huge success in everything else, all that would amount to a hollow mockery without sexual success. When a man is sexually satisfied, life is good and he can take on the world. When he's sexually frustrated,

> A woman willing to set aside other priorities and other distractions for the sake of sex tells her mate that she admires him in his most fundamental essence. With joy she surrenders her body to his embrace. That's true admiration. What more could a man want his woman to desire than himself? If she wants his body, he won't be able to keep his mind off her!

the world takes him on—and puts him in his place, and living with a beat up, insecure man is not a pretty picture.

"We physically neuter dogs and cats. Women psychologically emasculate men bit by bit if they belittle them—their dreams, their abilities, their attributes. A man is most vulnerable at this most fundamental level: Does his wife find him attractive and worthwhile enough to have sex with? Every time a wife rejects her husband and is insensitive to his sexual needs, he suffers. Eventually such a man either shuts down or leaves, frustrated in knowing how to love himself or his spouse."

"I understand your point," she said, "but you seem to be contradicting yourself. What about the hostess–guest analogy? If sex is not seen by men as a right, but a privilege, then women always have the right to say 'No.'"

"Of course they do, but if that refusal is communicated harshly or continually, sooner or later it no longer registers as a 'No' to sex but a 'No' to the relationship. I don't think this is a contradiction; I very much respect your right to say 'No.' As a matter of fact I've got something to say, and maybe this is the best time to say it. I'd like to apologize."

"For what?" she asked, looking over to him.

"About a year ago, you mentioned an incident regarding my pushiness that has really haunted me."

After a moment's quiet, she exclaimed, "Oh yeah?"

"You described a particular situation earlier in our marriage: We were in bed, and I was pressuring you for sex. You made it clear that you didn't feel like it, but I ignored your feelings and pushed harder until you gave in. Since then I've realized how totally inappropriate such bullying is. Like you mentioned before, I didn't restrain you, but I used intimidation to get what I wanted.

"At that time, and I know there were others, I was operating as if sex were an entitlement that was mine for the taking. That was clearly wrong. I was being selfish, and I'm really sorry for my attitude and my actions."

Sarah reached over, gently placing her hand on his, and said, "I appreciate your apology, very much. You know that when I say 'No' it's not about you, it's about me: I just can't handle it at that time."

"That's helpful to hear you say—again and again—because so often I take your 'No' as a personal rejection, even though up here," he said, pointing to his head. "I realize that isn't the case."

"Well, once in a while it is about you," she said, breaking into a grin, "but, you're right, a 'No' to lovemaking is not a rejection of you. At that moment I may very well want all the affection I can get, including making love, but I just can't seem to get into it."

"The difficult thing for me is that when I feel aroused and start to initiate sex, I'm in a vulnerable state myself. I know this may be hard to understand, but sex unleashes my strongest feelings for you. So, it's hard to cope with your lack of interest in me at that moment.

"It's like when you have some stored-up feelings you need to off-load. If I turn a deaf ear and act like I'm not interested, how do you feel? Your refusal when I want to make love can be just as painful. Sometimes I feel upset, sometimes hurt, and other times I'm embarrassed—maybe I'm being out of place with my strong desires."

"I don't want you to feel that your yearning for me is ever out of place. I love that you find me sexually desirable. I know, though, at times that isn't communicated."

Matt nodded and said, "If I get turned down a few times in succession, I can begin to lose my confidence and start second-guessing whether I'm even an adequate sexual partner, or worse, whether you really like me or love me. Depression tends to trigger anger, which grows and simmers under the surface.

"If this scenario gets repeated more than a few times, the dynamic gets really confusing. I feel like I'm doing what you said you dislike so much—begging for sex— which, I'll tell you, I like even less than you do. It's a threat to my manhood. Sex then begins to feel like a power struggle, with you exercising all the control.

"I've noticed that when we've gone a long time without making love, I begin to shut down. The thought of having sex is more tiring than the thrill of making it happen. Instead of firing me up more, at some point abstinence cools me down. By that time I've put large amounts of energy into suppressing my sexual appetite and lost my determination to overcome the obstacles. I can still get aroused, but I get stressed out just thinking about how to deal with what I anticipate will be more rejection."

"What happens in my world can be even more complicated," she said. "You've got to understand your own analogy of who's opening up and who's coming in. When I'm up for it, sex amounts to a loving give-and-take experience for me. When I'm not, it feels like take-and-give, with you doing the taking and me the giving.

"Since a man comes inside a woman's body, he must make sure that he comes not as an intruder, but as an invited guest. I've endured enough pushy experiences in my life that my protective walls go up quickly. I'm probably overly sensitive about it."

"I imagine we're both over-sensitive because even though I realize a 'No' is not a rejection, that doesn't change how I feel about it. When I initiate sex, it's like your big, tough man has just become tender and sensitive, with feelings that can easily get hurt. I realize it's easy to treat me as the man you see, who may be pressuring you or begging you or whatever, but it's that sensitive guy who requires a 'tender rejection.'"

"How can I do a better job at that?" she questioned.

He paused and said, "By thinking more like a mom than a wife at that moment. Instead of seeing me as your adult husband, realize that I'm struggling with adolescent feelings. Then you'd feel lots of motherly concern and give me some kind of verbal or nonverbal reassurance."

"I'm not sure I can promise anything, but what kind of reassurance are you referring to?" she asked.

"First, it helps me deal with being turned away when you still make the effort to touch and cuddle with me rather than pulling back. Sometimes you say affirming things like, 'I'd love to be able to get into it with you, but I'm struggling with...' or 'Would you mind taking a rain check tonight, but certainly later...' And I absolutely love it when you say 'Not tonight, but tomorrow morning for sure.' That puts me to bed with a smile.

"Of course, the very best way to affirm me and soften

the sting of rejection is to stroke me down south. I don't think it's possible for a man to feel such caring and feel rejection simultaneously. It's reassuring, even when it's clear that's all there's going to be."

"I don't want to have to give you a reason every time, but I will try to use those reassuring statements, or at least an explanation, even some stroking, more often."

"Thanks. Those efforts communicate that you really care for me. I also appreciate subtle signs of openness, like body language changes. Here's one thing you do that's a quiet thrill: I'll be rubbing your thighs or your bottom and you slightly spread your legs. It's like you're opening your whole self to me and saying, 'I like what you're doing to me, and I trust you to go a little further.'"

"I do like it, as long as you're careful about stimulating me directly. That can close down the openness fast."

Sarah's disarming tone set Matt at ease. He reached out for her hand. "You mentioned there were a couple of matters that make you feel pressured. What's another?"

"That's easy. My whole life can feel like one big demand. The kids, my work, our house, the meals, and then you—and your sex drive. It's not that I don't see sex as a good thing, it's just that I so often feel overwhelmed. If I can't find a way to relax, then having sex becomes another item in my overflowing 'inbox.'"

"You know, I'd do anything to help you relax and deal with the demands that bring on unhappiness," he offered.

She sat back and paused. "Anything?"

"Well, a man also loves a woman who is happy. A happy woman feels good about herself, and her man feels that success as well. Failing to make your wife happy, on the other hand, is like failing in the bedroom: it's death.

A common reason why a man leaves his wife—first emotionally, and then in divorce—is because he concludes that, no matter what he does, he cannot make her happy."

"Men have a lot to do with that!" she interjected.

"Sure. But remember, men are simple. We interpret complaining and nagging and attempts at changing us as profound unhappiness. Men hate playing that game: 'If you really loved me, you could guess what's on my mind.' We need simple, clear, and repeated explanations of what we can do to help ensure our wives' happiness. Sure, some men are unwilling to do what it takes, but most are just clueless when it comes to the complexities of intimate relationships. We need guidance and lots of it!"

"You've told me this before," she said, "and I have consciously tried to remind myself that my happiness is very important to you, and a blessing to both of us. If my happiness is your goal, I'd say I can support that goal— wholeheartedly—and be quite happy doing it!

Equal Satisfaction

If ever win/win applies, it does so within marriage. It is utter foolishness to believe that one spouse can win while the other loses. Over time, and not very much time, the partners' level of marriage satisfaction will even out.

If you are dissatisfied in your marriage, recognize that your spouse is likely just as dissatisfied. You both are in a lose/lose situation. There is only one alternative: To seek your partner's satisfaction so that he or she wins—with your respect and love. This is the only way you will win with theirs.

The Heart of Passion:
Generalized Differences in Sexuality

	Men	Women
Orientation	Physical	Relational
	Compartmentalized	Wholistic
	Physical oneness	Emotional Oneness
	Variety	Security
	Very high priority	One of many priorities
Stimulation	Sight	Touch/Attitudes
	Smell	Action/Words
	Body-centered	Person-centered
Needs	Respect/admiration	Understanding/Love
	Physically needed	Emotionally needed
	Not to be put down	Time
Sexual Response	Acyclical	Cyclical
	Quick excitement	Slow excitement
	Initiates (usually)	Responds (usually)
	Difficult to distract	Easily distracted
Orgasm	Propagation of species	Propogation of oneness
	Shorter, more intense	Longer, more in-depth
	Physically-oriented	Emotionally-oriented
	Orgasm usually needed for satisifaction	Satisfaction possible without orgasm

Adapted from *Lonely Husbands, Lonely Wives*
—Dennis Rainey

Notwithstanding the challenges, sex allows two lovers to share life's supreme bonding experience and carry it with them as a "locket of love." When they are physically apart, they are still emotionally close—two halves of the same soul.

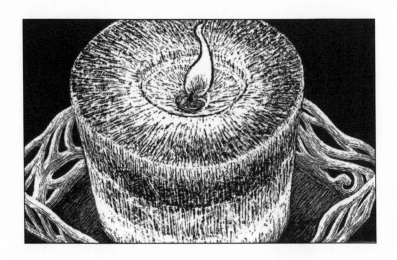

Lessons from a Candle Flame

Pas•sion

Intense emotion; strong feeling of enthusiasm,
deep sexual desire; powerful craving;
yearning, ardent love.

*A*fter breakfast, Sarah asked, "Would you get me a match? I've got an idea." When Matt returned from the kitchen, a short pillar candle stood in the middle of the dining room table. "Do you remember what I said about a woman's passion?" she asked, as she lit the candle.

He looked at her and said, "That it's fragile like that flame. It doesn't take much for it to flicker and die out."

"Fragile, yes, but if you doubt whether that flame is hot, go ahead and touch it! Just because you get aroused more easily, don't assume that you enjoy sex more than I do. A man's desire stems from a superficial hormonal drive, but a woman's desire flows from the deepest level of her heart and soul. Your climax lasts for just a few seconds, while mine can go on and on, giving me a much longer and deeper experience. A man's sexual interest peaks at around 17 or 18, and a woman's, maybe 20 years later. Guess who's closer to their sexual peak?

"Let's keep this candle here all day. It will act as a reminder that a woman's sexual passion, though deeper than a man's, is also more fragile. You've heard it before—a man heats up like a microwave and a woman, like a slow cooker. I get just as hot or hotter, only more slowly."

"Well, I have heard that sex begins in the kitchen!" he exclaimed.

"What that means for a woman is this: Sex starts with *partnering*. The more I feel like you want to be with me, even if it's just doing dishes together, the more my sexual desires emerge. Then I get the urge to merge."

"Oh, I'd hate to start manipulating you for sex!" he joked.

"Go right ahead and manipulate me like that!"

"Like what?" he asked, looking at the candle.

"Like working together, playing together, talking together. Say the word with me slowly: 'To—get—her.'"

"Very tricky, dear. I get—you," he said with a grin.

"For me," she said, "the starting point of togetherness is talking. Let me ask you something: Do you think it would help if I talked less and you talked more? Talking is the way I connect, but I also know I can make you crazy by 'over-detailing it.' You get bored and check out.

"I don't want to turn you off by talking things into the ground. I've got girlfriends who can handle that level of talk. What I want for us is a sense of sharing. When we share back and forth, it assures me of your interest. How can we get you to talk more and me to talk less?"

"I've heard it said that men like action and women like talking. It all started with our ancient ancestors. Men were the hunters, right? For thousands of years my forefathers spent lots of solitary time quietly watching and waiting, in search of game. Their lives revolved around the singular focus of hunting to provide food. They conserved energy and talked only enough to make a point. And feelings, well, feelings only made them vulnerable to fears, something a hunter must control to survive."

"Sounds quite modern, actually!" she said.

"Granted, and women were the gatherers. Your foremothers tended to a broad range of activities with children, family, and friends. You connected with each other for affirmation and support to get all the chores done. Whereas men learned to focus, women multitasked with each other and talked for hours on end.

"Times have changed. I don't bring home the bacon. I don't even bring home a paycheck; it's deposited electronically. In many households, the woman brings home half the income—or more. But even though our survival needs are met, we still have different orientations because I'm a male and you're a female. So what's the surprise if I'm comfortable with silence and you have a greater need to talk?

"You've said that you talk to process. I talk to exchange information. When I talk or listen, I like simple, direct, and concise speech—just the facts, ma'am. You can tell me all the little details if you want. Just realize that it's a strain for me not to go into 'half-listening mode.'"

"Understand my perspective," she said. "Words join my private world to yours. I talk to process what's going on in me and to connect with you. So please try to listen.

"In the primitive world I imagine my ancient counterpart fought side by side with her man for survival. Likely she was overjoyed just to see him come home from the dangers of the latest hunt. And if he saved their child from a bear attack, I'm sure her sexual desires would turn white-hot. Now I just take it for granted that you and the kids will come home in one piece, so when you return after a hard day of 'making money,' that just doesn't fan the flames of passion for me.

"Call me hard to satisfy, but I've got to have more than a survival-mentality relationship to get me sexually aroused. I need a soul connection with you. That's why talking and listening are so important. Please, don't act disinterested or cut me off or stonewall me with silence. Instead bring me into the inner world of your feelings and thoughts. I know this can be a struggle for you."

"It helps when you draw me out with questions."

"You tend to get upset with my questions," she said, "and act like I'm a busybody, or I'm being intrusive."

"I'm sorry about that," he replied. "Keep expressing curiosity and be patient with short answers. I don't have an innate need to talk—not with your level of detail anyway—but with the right, gentle prompting, I'll do better."

"Realize that you go a long way by just changing your speech to 'us language.' My heart skips when I hear, 'We're partners in this' or 'It's just the two of us' or 'We're in it together.' I love 'us language.' In my feminine world, 'together talk' communicates commitment and connection. 'Together time' confirms it. It's a feeling of partnership that takes any taint of manipulation out of your pursuit of sex."

"I understand what you're saying," he said. "The more I'm there for you emotionally, the more you're able to con-

For a Woman:
Intimacy Awakens Passion

For her, sex "starts in the kitchen" with partnering. The man's attention and affirmation is the key to unlocking her sexuality. While a turned-on man can come across as demanding, a turned-on woman turns on a man. Sex works best when a man holds back his passion slightly behind a woman's, and focuses not just on technique but on creating a loving experience.

For a Man:
Passion Awakens Intimacy

Sex brings him into the kitchen, creating a desire for partnering. A woman's openness to her own pleasure is key to unlocking his desire for intimacy. While her sexuality comes from her heart and soul, his sexuality leads him to find his heart and soul. Sex works best when a woman cultivates her own pleasure and lets her body lead them to mutual joy.

Intimacy + Passion + Commitment
=
a Lifelong Love Affair

Generally a woman brings the gift of intimacy to a relationship and the man brings the gift of passion. Of course there are exceptions, but when these two ingredients are cultivated, they work their magic of magnetism, drawing a couple together. When commitment from both is added as a third ingredient, magnetism turns resolute. Such security provides a powerful safe haven for the couple, as well as children, family and friends, even society as a whole.

nect sexually. The reverse is also true: the more you connect with me sexually, the more I'm pulled in emotionally. Then I end up tapping into my emotions, and you, into your sexuality. It's one of those paradoxical things: If we live unselfishly, we enjoy the benefits of selfishness."

"Sounds profound, but you wouldn't want to talk it into the ground," Sarah said, smiling.

"So, now I'm the one talking too much!" Matt laughed.

"Oh believe me, I can handle it."

The conversation took a breather as the couple sat quietly, caught up in their own thoughts.

"Okay," he spoke up, breaking the silence. "Can we go over this hostess–guest analogy again?"

"Sure," Sarah said. "I really like that analogy. But the odd thing about it is that each person is asked to take on what is traditionally the least natural role for them."

He paused briefly and asked, "How so?"

"Since a man typically has more hormonal drive, he is usually the more assertive one. To get the kind of sexual relationship he wants, however, he must play the role of the less assertive one—the guest."

"When I hear you say 'play a role' it almost sounds like 'pretending,'" he replied, looking at the candle again.

"I'm not using the word 'play' in a pretending sense, but in the sense of the roles we take on. The strongest actor can assume the role of the weakest character. Likewise, the one most driven to get something can channel that energy into being a very good recipient.

"It's a matter of attitude. If a man wants sex, he needs to pursue it passionately, but from a more submissive, humble position—as an appreciative guest. A hostess who feels appreciated can then draw on that as a source of strength. If she senses she's being taken advantage of or taken for granted, her ability to give dries up, but if she is honored for her gift, she is energized to give even more."

"Maybe this is obvious, but how do you best honor a hostess within the sexual experience?" Matt asked.

"You honor a hostess when you treasure the gift of entering her body as a celebration of your relationship as a whole. When she feels that the timing is right, that you've entered into an emotional oneness together, then she will relax and invite you to become one with her physically."

"It sounds like being thanked is not good enough!"

"Not even close," Sarah responded. Even worshipping the ground I walk on isn't good enough! It has to get intimate. A woman needs to know her man is 'in it' with her on a heart level, before he comes into her on a physical level. This is true, even if the 'it' is a fight.

"About a month ago we got into an argument about how much money we need to save. You weren't antagonistic, just firm in your viewpoint, but you asked me questions about what I thought and genuinely listened. You made your points, I made mine. It ended up being a great shared experience in figuring out our future.

"I don't think you realized it, but that encounter became sexual for me. When that much emotion gets stirred up, the make-up sex can be intense. Even in a fight, I still feel emotionally connected if you bring me inside your world and seek to come inside mine. Staying 'in it' with me constitutes the highest form of romance from a man—relating to his woman with intimacy and respect.

"It's just a sad reality that women are often treated disrespectfully, especially when it comes to sex. Just look at how we're viewed as objects in the male fantasy world."

"Do you feel dishonored by me?" he asked.

"No," she said, "but I am suspicious about your level of satisfaction with our sex life. When you bring up the subject, I sometimes feel you are doing it to subtly communicate your disapproval. Sensing your unhappiness about it shuts me down fast; it confirms my fears that I can never do enough to please you. Sex is never intense enough, never creative enough, never frequent enough. I then feel defeated. The candle flame flickers and dies."

"Are you saying I shouldn't be honest about what I say? I don't know how else to tell you what I want and what pleases me. How can I communicate that I want more or different sex without communicating some degree of disappointment with where we're at now?"

She paused and replied, "Think of your goal. You don't want to discourage me. You want to build trust by communicating acceptance, and by being my advocate. That will be set back by criticism. It will help you stay positive to think like a guest who wants yet another favor from the hostess. New requests are presented thoughtfully and with gratitude for what you've already received."

"If there is a problem in that analogy, it's here," he said. "You mentioned that a hostess gives—that doing so is just part of your nature—but there are many giving and taking roles in our marriage. In some, you're the primary giver and I'm the taker; in others, the roles reverse. It didn't take long for us to realize that I should balance the checkbook, whereas you're better at shopping for the kids. I mow the lawn, you keep the social calendar, and so on.

"If making love provides a critical bond to our marriage, then planning and pursuing sex becomes a responsibility, like doing laundry—only more important. Fitting lovemaking into our busy lives often requires more than a spontaneous urge. Creating good experiences takes work. It's enjoyable work, to be sure, but work all the same.

"With this in mind, the one who takes the primary initiative becomes the sexual giver, in a sense, and the one who receives that initiative is the sexual taker. This is a way of seeing it that's different from the hostess–guest model."

"I agree with you, at least to an extent," she replied. "Unlike mowing the lawn, the role of sexual giver is important enough to warrant shared responsibility. Neither one of us should have to do all the 'sex work' because, like you said, sex can be both work and play. So, whoever makes the effort to keep sex happening with regularity, with creativity, and with fun, serves our relationship.

"But the hostess–guest analogy still applies because a woman gives to the sexual relationship in a unique way: Biology dictates that the man comes into her space, her body. So we play in my home. When we have sex, even at your request or pursuit, I must take the same initiative a hostess takes in opening up her home. My body has to prepare for a visit and my mind has to say, 'Let's get into this.'

"Because you have more hormonal drive, you start the process more often. Once I'm engaged, though, we both have the opportunity to give to each other. Sometimes one of us gives more to the work of lovemaking and the other will coast. The next time the roles reverse. Over time, the sex workload tends to even out.

"But remember—every time I say 'Yes' as a willing hostess, I serve our relationship—even if you've taken the initiative up till then. Of course, if I grudgingly comply with your advances, I'm not being a giver. Dutiful giving is a contradiction in terms. A gift must be joyfully given."

"How can I encourage that sense of freedom?" he asked.

She looked over and said, "It helps if you verbalize your appreciation in physical terms. When you think I look good, tell me! As far as appearance goes, guys aren't the only ones looking. If you haven't noticed, women are very body-conscious. We look at each other as much, or more, than men look at us. I don't think I'm unusual here. Imperfections in my shape certainly don't need to be hinted at, much less mentioned outright."

"I love your looks," he said. "Honey, you can be so hard on yourself, especially when you get near the scales."

"Well, all the more reason to keep up the positive strokes. A woman's physical self-image is fragile; any hint of negativity or attempt to fix it is very discouraging. I know society's ideal and I know my reality. Each year that youthful figure I used to see in the mirror slips farther away. Pregnancies, hormonal changes, and insecurities take their toll.

"If you want to help me keep a positive self-image, communicate unconditional acceptance of my features and my figure—whatever the pointer on the scale may say. Beauty is in the eye of the beholder, right? So, look for what you can praise. Complimenting a woman on her looks helps her feel good about herself and her sexuality. As I get older it's important—for both of us—that I hold onto a healthy body image. So, I'm focusing on accepting my body as it is rather than always trying to change it."

"You wouldn't say acceptance turns a blind eye to a partner's desire to see some changes, would you?" he asked.

"It depends. If the area of change has to do with the body, sensitivity is in order. I think it's legitimate to talk about staying active and fit. This is something largely under our control. Sooner or later, though, we will likely gain weight, lose hair, grow saggy, contract a disease, or undergo any number of changes that affect our bodies in ways we have little or no control over. As this happens, negative feedback will only serve to bring on relational hurt and make any attempt to change more difficult.

"Relational behavior, though, is different. It's always within our control. A good partnership not only recognizes appropriate boundaries but helps the people involved to mature. So, we do have the right to hold our partner accountable for the way he or she treats us, our kids, and our friends, as well as how he or she conducts our mutual affairs. Of course, a little tact never hurts!"

Matt nodded and said, "This may lack any degree of tact whatsoever, but would you be willing to take a run at another sensitive subject, oral sex?"

"Yeah, so much for the diplomacy," she replied, "but why not? Just be careful that you express your point without criticism. Could you handle it if I were to criticize your sexual performance and demand something better?"

"Well, I'd like to think I'd be open to hearing you out, but when it comes to communicating, I don't know how to let you know what I like, except to let you know what I like! Is there any other way?" he asked.

Sarah thought for a moment and said, "I'll make you a deal here. I won't wave off this subject if we can also discuss our different approaches to spending money."

"And what does money have to do with this?"

"That will come later. For now, it's your turn."

"Okay then," he continued, "so I guess we'll go back to oral sex. In bringing up this issue, you may think I'm dissatisfied about its frequency, but in talking about it I'm expressing a desire, not a demand. Can you see that?"

"It's not so simple for a woman; at least, not for this woman," she stated. "Your role in the analogy you've proposed is that of a guest. Right? There is a certain etiquette that goes along with being a guest. Since a guest is on the receiving end—the one being served—he has to be careful not to communicate criticism. So, before we go any further, I'd like to recommend a test for determining whether a man really views himself as a guest or not."

"And what's that?" he asked, looking at her.

"The test," she replied, "is whether the man is willing to stay positive and not criticize the woman's sexual responsiveness. A hostess will be open to feedback on how she is doing over time, but anything which hints of disappointment or criticism must be avoided."

"Sounds like unconditional acceptance again."

"Right," she replied. "Acceptance gives us breathing room. We need that space so we can relax and let down our guard. Then we can listen, learn, and grow in the only way possible—on our own timetable.

"When we accept each other as individuals, we end up accepting ourselves as a couple. Remember when I altered that old cheerleader outfit and football uniform that I found at a yard sale? I thought it would be fun to dress up, do a few cheers, and seduce the star of my football team—you, but we were too self-conscious to get into it."

"You mean I was too self-conscious," he replied.

"Well, that's my point," she said. "Theater and drama were a big part of my life. The role you're most comfortable with is simply being yourself. So, sexual role-playing may not work for us as a couple, and that's fine."

Matt paused and said, "You'd think I'd be into role playing, especially since you took the initiative. But I so quickly reverted out of character, which killed the whole idea. You do know I like to experiment, though."

"Oh, I know you," Sarah continued, "but I think we forget that experiments, by their very nature, are meant to be tried more than once. Being creatures of habit, it's easy to fall back on the tried and true. We know how to push each other's buttons, so it's good to find new buttons to push. When we do try something new—a position, a location, an approach—we should do it a few times to feel comfortable before we decide whether it's something we want to add to our repertoire or not."

He looked up with a grin and said, "Sarah, do you recall trying to put a condom on me with your mouth?"

"That was a long, long time ago!" she laughed.

"I found it a thrill but you felt clumsy—and, like you're saying, the first time became the last time. Sex should be playful. It's easy to take ourselves too seriously. So what if we fumble around? It's just the two of us. They don't call it 'fooling around' for nothing. We can laugh about it—if not then, than later. Sex and fun go together."

"I agree and would consider any fantasy encounter if it helps make our relationship more special," she said.

"That's good to hear you say because at times when I suggest some spice for our sex life, I do so with trepidation. If you were to shut me down, I might even act like I was kidding out of embarrassment. I don't want you thinking I'm some kind of perverted sex maniac!"

"I should tell you, then, that our one-time condom experiment had more to do with my reluctance to give myself over to oral sex than a reluctance to experiment."

"So, you're okay with talking about oral sex?"

"That depends. How were you going to talk about it?"

Kosher Sex

How did the Creator expect men and women to enjoy sex together when they have such different sexual metabolisms? Men must exert considerable control to slow themselves down if they are to achieve the same pace as the woman they are with. In fact, the lack of sexual passion in marriage, [and the] leading contemporary cause of divorce, is directly attributable to men who don't take the time to romance the women they are with. This seems like a colossal biological imperfection in humans. The only answer to this question is that God intended us to practice sex where the focus is not on pleasure, but on the achievement of unity and symmetry between man and woman.

Any truly successful marriage must...distill the contradictory ingredients of passion and intimacy. We do indeed want our spouse to be both our lover and our best friend. And this is what kosher sex is all about. For kosher sex is passionate lovemaking that leads to intimacy.

Sex for pleasure is an end in itself. But kosher sex is a journey whose destination is a couple who feel joined not only by the same roof or children, but especially through the enjoyment and pleasure they constantly give each other.

Great sex makes you feel amazing and has you howling and swinging from the rafters together with your lover. But kosher sex is not measured during the lovemaking itself, but the morning after, when you can't get your partner off your mind.

Excerpts from *Kosher Sex*
—Shmuley Boteach

"Like a guest requesting an additional favor from the hostess," he replied. "It's no secret that I enjoy it. That's just honest. What could I do to help make it better for you?"

"Good start," she said. "You to me or me to you?"

"Well, both, but let's start with me to you."

"I don't know," she mused. "I'm not sure I'm ready for more. Can you tell me exactly why you like it so much?"

"This may surprise you, but oral sex amounts to the most intimate experience I have with you."

She paused and asked, "More so than intercourse?"

"Yes and no. I would say that intercourse lays bare both my body and soul; I find this is more and more true as I get older. So, normally I want to climax in the safest, most intimate place available—inside you. That's why I love it when you kiss and stroke my face while I'm climaxing. I like it, too, when you grab my bottom and pull me deeper into you, as if you are trying to absorb my body. It feels like you really want me deep inside you.

"But oral sex communicates a special vulnerability. Sometimes intercourse can be more passive, but oral sex requires one or both of us to take extra initiative. Whatever the case, connecting our body openings brings such a warm, soothing sensation of pleasure and intimacy.

"When you redirect my attempts, I feel a pang of rejection. It's not that bad, because you're usually not stopping the lovemaking; it's more like exclusion. This is your most vulnerable part. I'm being held up short and closed off.

"When you let me perform oral sex on you I feel so fulfilled by your openness to me—literally and figuratively. It's funny, but sometimes I still catch myself thinking, 'Is this okay? Is this right?' because it feels a little decadent, in a wonderful sort of way! Mostly though, I feel deeply trusted and appreciated as you open up before me and communicate your enjoyment of the experience. It seems like I'm connecting to the center of your being."

"That's the center of my being?!" she exclaimed.

"Hey, this is embarrassing enough."

"Tell me about it! I know some women who are completely turned off by oral sex. They're hung up on thinking that place 'down there' is gross and disgusting. And I also know a couple of women for whom oral sex is non-negotiable—they must have it nearly every time!

"I'm somewhere in the middle. Receiving oral sex definitely heightens the pleasure I experience as you focus on one part of my body, then another. I can't say I'm completely comfortable with it, though, especially if I haven't showered recently. I need to be clean in order to relax and give myself over to the sensation. I don't mind you raising my awareness of why you like doing it. But I'm less comfortable talking about it in specific detail, and more comfortable just letting it happen naturally when it does."

He reached out to touch her hand and said, "I don't know why that area of your anatomy is such a magnet to me, but it is. Maybe I'm drawn to the place where human life comes from. Or maybe it's your womanly scent, which is all part of the turn-on for me.

"I've heard that a man is drawn to the softness of a woman. From a purely physical point of view, that translates to your breasts and genitals. Whatever it is, I very much enjoy the opportunity to bring you pleasure there. Is it possible for you to see this as one of the most intimate expressions of my love for you?"

"I suppose," she said, after a moment. "I love the passion, but I can't handle the intensity of oral sex as often as you want to give it. I like both but if I had to choose one over the other, I'd pick intercourse. It's the face-to-face contact—another one of those 'togetherness' things."

"I love the togetherness of intercourse, too," he said, "but what I really enjoy is when I sense you getting into the pleasure of it. There is nothing that turns me on as much as seeing you turned on, and if you are willing to let me perform oral sex on you, I know you're definitely into it! I can't think of a more fulfilling experience for a man than seeing his woman driven wild with pleasure."

"Believe me, getting driven wild with pleasure is not something I'm against. I do like you bringing me to climax that way. It's just too intense for me to want it all the time. When life itself begins to feel overwhelming, more intensity of any kind is not something I crave."

He paused in thought and then began, "I'd assume we all have an 'internal intensity meter.' It would help me to better understand just how that meter works for you."

"Let me ask you this: Can you see yourself craving intercourse three minutes after you've come to a climax?"

"No, not likely," Matt exclaimed, looking at her. "I can see where you're going with this."

"I experience a similar kind of sensory overload. When we begin foreplay, I may already be feeling an emotional overload from my life in general. So, I find myself unable to deal with the extra feelings brought to the surface by our lovemaking. It's similar to how you feel after a climax, only my overload is emotional and not physical. This is a hump which is hard for me to get over."

"That's a helpful explanation," he replied. "I want to be as sensitive as possible to relieve that overload and keep the candle flame burning bright. How can I do that?"

"Sometimes you just can't. It's not your fault; my feelings are already topped out, and I just can't take any more. Sometimes you can, but my openness is so fragile that it takes a lot of patience and tenderness on your part. Often I want sex for closeness, not passion. I don't always need or even want an orgasm. One thing is for sure—your best chance to get me over the hump from resistance to openness is to start up north by helping me relax. And, stay north for quite a while before moving down south."

"You mean that I should begin with a kiss," he said.

"Yes, and not heavy kissing at first. A direct assault may be necessary for an invasion. But you are not invading a hostile populace, you're winning the allegiance of an initially reluctant populace. So go slow, but keep going—with passion. If we slow down too much, my arousal will plummet and plummeting arousal is not what you want!

"The first territory to win over is my lips. If you can change my mouth from reluctance to willingness, the rest of my body won't be far behind. There is a fine art to good kissing, you know. Making love starts with making out. A good kiss is often the first act of good lovemaking."

"And how would you describe good kissing?"

"Good kissing starts with good breath," she stated. "I'd rather kiss a rusty pipe than connect with bad breath. Yuck! The best kissing avoids anything slobbery—just a little moistness. Beyond technique, however, a truly memorable kiss requires absolute, total concentration. The universe stops. Nothing else matters except our embrace.

"To use a sports term, there's a basic 'play book.' Of course sometimes it's best to throw out the playbook and trust your intuition. But usually, let my openness dictate how far the kiss is going to go. Don't force my lips open or push your tongue into my mouth. Stay passionate but avoid pressure. Keep your kisses light until I can handle more. I like the way you comb your fingers through my hair, too. Focus some attention on my neck, then move back to the lips. Work on slowly coaxing my mouth open."

He raised his hand and asked, "How slow is slow?"

"Let's put it this way: no woman on her deathbed is going to tell her husband, 'I wish we'd spent less time in foreplay.' You'd be wise to stay above neck level and away from the 'hot zones' for a good 10 to 15 minutes. Remember the microwave and the slow cooker? If your arousal takes two minutes, mine takes 20; if yours takes three, mine takes 30. You're good with numbers."

"That means you're ten times slower," he mused.

"Then do the math with me," she said. "Way back, when we were first dating, we made the decision not to go 'all the way,' but that didn't stop you from being quite creative and spending very long periods of time warming me up. You didn't even know it, at least I don't think you knew it, but a few times I had a fully clothed orgasm. I've forgotten about this till right now, but it happened."

"I didn't know that was possible. So you faked not having an orgasm! Whoa!" he exclaimed with a smile.

"Unfortunately, after we got married your foreplay sped up a lot. So, in our first few years I rarely had an orgasm. Maybe I forgot that having an orgasm was very much my responsibility, not just yours. Maybe I got embarrassed, like it was too self-focused. I probably was not specific enough to help you get me there. But now you know the direction to travel—north to south—and you've got a flickering, but hot, candle flame to light your way!"

The Kiss

A kiss can be a comma, a question mark
or an exclamation point.

—Mistinguett

"Mike doesn't have technique…but when Mike kisses you
he isn't doing anything else. You're his whole universe…
and the moment is eternal because he doesn't have any plans
and isn't going anywhere. Just kissing you." She shivered.
"It's overwhelming."

—Anne, *Strangers from a Strange Land*

Give me a kiss, and to that kiss a score;
Then to that twenty, add a hundred more:
A thousand to that hundred: so kiss on
To make that thousand up a million.
Treble that million, and when that is done,
Let's kiss afresh, as when we first begun.

To Anthea: Ah, My Anthea
—Robert Herrick, 1591–1674

What's an occasion when you savored a great kiss?

Kissing bridges the gap between intimacy and passion. It keeps the pilot light of intimacy lit so that passion's fire can ignite at a moment's notice. Feed the flame by locking lips regularly and often!

Saturday Walk

STARTING AT THE NORTH POLE

*R*eady to take their walk, Matt and Sarah met on the porch. "What a beautiful day," she proclaimed, looking at the hills forming a backdrop over the quiet lake.

"Yes, and what a beautiful lady," Matt replied, as he slid his hand from the small of her back to her bottom.

Sarah smiled. "You've been handsy all morning."

"Yeah, but I have learned something," he said, patting her gently, "starting south isn't going to get me very far. North is the feminine starting location of choice."

She clasped his hand and descended the steps, "Better yet, think of it as starting at the North Pole."

"Sounds chilly," he mused, squeezing her hand.

"Right! Often I need time to thaw out before I start to warm up. Think about entering me in stages: First you enter my presence, then my mind, then my heart, then my mouth, and so on. Like traveling from the North Pole to the equator, it's a process."

"But not a formula," he added.

"Men like the tried and true. I've made my point about this before, however, so you know better, right? Just because something worked well once doesn't mean a repeat is in order. Anytime you turn sex into a predictable, step-by-step process, you're going to turn me off."

"So, what's the best unpredictable way?" he asked.

"It's best to help me relax physically before you be-gin arousing me sexually. You could turn on some music, draw a warm bath, give a massage, pour a glass of wine. Be tender. Hold my hand and give me your full attention.

"Start with my head—both inside and out! What I mean is: Talk to me. Look in my eyes. Stroke my hair and ears, my neck and lips before even thinking of moving your hands or mouth farther down. Take your time. Talk to me. Be fun and conversational. Be humble, vulnerable, and appreciative. Tell me about your day. Share a struggle or a joy. Ask me about my day, and listen attentively.

"When I begin to relax, quiet whispers or silence can work effectively. Sometimes shared silences communi-cate that a great bond of unity exists between us. Usually, though, I like some talking—before, during, and after.

"Keep your kisses gentle. Lightly touch and stroke my body in circles rather than straight lines. As you work your way around, start at the edges and move in. From what I know about biology, foreplay drives blood from the extremities toward the pelvic region, getting it ready and willing for you to end up there.

"But arousing a woman is more art than science. Do you remember a few months ago you slowly undressed me and at each step you told me how much you liked my body, either with words or kisses? You may not have real-ized it, but you started on the edges, touching, stroking, and nibbling my shoulders, back, arms, and legs. Then you slowly moved in to my waist, thighs, and chest. By the time you got it all off and focused on the sweet spots I was so turned on, I couldn't wait. I wanted it bad."

"You liked that, huh?" he said, slowing their pace.

"I did—and I loved your sensitivity. You employed 'the tease': moving me forward, then backing off a little. You treated my body with care and appreciation. There are occasions when I'm ready to go like a rabbit. Usually, though, slow and steady like the tortoise will win this race. Think of me as being testosterone challenged. You, on the other hand, are testosterone charged."

"That's the reason why," he replied, "the males of most mammals are more sexually assertive than the females. On a purely physical level, our reproductive systems are continually producing millions of sperm looking for release. I'm sure that's why men masturbate more often than women. And that's why frequency is such a big issue for us, prompting the humiliation of begging our women to put an end to our misery with 'mercy sex!'"

"That's why it's your place, as the more hormonally charged, to set a mood that gets my hormones to kick in. It's my responsibility to be open to your attempts.

"That happens best when you exercise restraint by taking time to cuddle, caress, and relax me, which slowly arouses me. I know your body is pressing toward climax— all those millions of new sperm cells want nothing more than to find my little old egg! I love it, though, when you take time to talk, to lock and unlock your fingers through mine, and stroke my hair. I need the 'slow burn.'

"I've heard that a woman's skin is more sensitive than a man's. Every square inch of my body can bring me pleasure if you touch it or kiss it. Also eye contact—from across the room or a few inches away—adds lots of fuel to the fire. So, treat my skin and eyes like important erogenous zones.

"Ultimately, though, the area of my body that is the most sensitive is right here," she said, placing his hand on her chest. "It's my heart. So, if you work on making love to that organ first, all the other body parts will come along for the ride. Just one word of warning about this area: Don't fondle my nipples too quickly or directly."

"You mean the east and west axis," he stated.

"Want to know a secret about a woman's breasts?"

"Oh, you bet," he replied without hesitation.

"The road south leads over them," she said. "If you can take the hills, it won't be difficult to occupy the valley."

"That analogy alone gets my motor running."

"Well," she continued, "then put some creative energy into building my interest by teasing me there."

"Boy, I sure could use a tutorial," he stated, smiling.

Sarah led Matt by the hand to a large rock, where they sat down. She faced him, grasped his hand, and placed it on her shirt, cupping her breast. "This is really quite simple."

Matt realized they were alone but took a nervous glance around anyway. "So what happens now?"

"You're going to massage my breast."

"You can order me around like that all day long."

"You said this weekend was a sanctuary of learning, right? Well, here we are, in a lovely sanctuary, and you're about to learn something. Now, my point: You crave release, but I love the buildup. With that in mind, how would you massage my breast?"

"Slowly," he said hesitantly.

"Yes, but always remember the word 'tease.' Sometimes for all your effort you will not be able to win over my mouth, but if you take the time to win over my breasts, you can still gain the entry you desire. You realize that I'm giving you the keys to the castle gate here, right?"

"I am your humble servant, my lady!"

Grasping his wrist, she moved his hand and said, "Gently run your fingers back and forth under the edge of my bra, and then go back to my neck and ears. Dip down into the cups but don't linger there." She then turned her back to him and lifted her shirt far enough for him to unhook the clasp. "When you unfasten my bra, take some time to rub and lightly scratch my back along the strap line, because it's almost always sore there."

"That feels great," she said after a few minutes. She then drew his hands around her chest and up inside her loosened bra. Reaching back with her hands, she cupped his neck and pulled his head in behind hers.

After a pause, she began again. "When my bra is off, you can squeeze gently, just don't grope. Stroke my breasts lightly on the sides and the bottom. Rub lightly in a swirling motion up and around, even use the back of your hand. Circle the area between them. Graze the nipples, as if by accident. If I'm getting into it, instead of plunging ahead, back off briefly—it's all part of the tease.

"That's good," she continued, as she brought her arms back down and motioned for him to fasten her bra.

"Hey, I'm just getting the hang of it!" he protested.

"The idea here is to build up my interest slowly and then ease off, but not completely. Stroking is superior to squeezing, just like you've been doing. My body will begin heating up and you'll have me yearning for more."

"Sounds like that Pointer Sisters song: You want 'a man with a slow hand and an easy touch. Someone who will spend some time, not come and go in a heated rush.'"

"For sure. When it comes to love I want a slow hand. Those lyrics express the desire of every woman's heart."

"And the challenge for every man's hands!"

"You know, if you're so anxious to use your hands and want to go south," she continued, lifting her legs up to his lap, "you should first go all the way—to my feet!

"You know how ticklish my feet are. The good news is that all those nerve endings are connected with corresponding nerves elsewhere in my body. So when you massage my feet you are in touch with all those other nerve endings and, in effect, massaging my whole body. It's great."

"As long as I don't expect something more," he said.

"That's right. Just think of a foot massage or a face massage or a back and bottom massage like any other thoughtful thing you do for me: It's part of an effort to get me over 'the hump' of life's stresses, which holds me back from wanting more. Sometimes it will work, sometimes it won't."

"I'm often aware of your transition points," he replied. "Sometimes your body visibly relaxes and I know you can move ahead. Another 'you can go further' signal is your willingness to move from lip kissing to French kissing. Making out usually reveals just how open your body is to making love. And if you let me go from stroking your breasts to kissing them, I definitely know you're over the hump."

"The hump I experience is usually emotional," she said, "but it can also be physical. One way you could help with that is to always be conscious of your personal hygiene, particularly any time you think we'll get intimate."

"You mean how I smell," he stated.

> *I admire the fact that a man can have a beer belly, a bald head, yellow teeth, bad breath, athlete's foot, and no job and still think he's the best catch in the sea.*
>
> —Tarita, interviewed by Laurence Roy Stains & Stefan Bechtel

"I can have a lot of sensory issues and I don't have the extra hormonal umph you have to help me overcome them. So don't let anything you can control—bad breath, rough hands, prickly face, sharp fingernails, or an unbathed body—distract me from the experience.

"I love Mr. Clean not Mr. Natural. Brushed teeth, a shaved face and clipped fingernails improve your odds dramatically! You're coming to a feast, and I'm the main course. So come appropriately attired. Dirty clothes or body odor turn me off, while a sweet-smelling, clean-shaven man starts me thinking, 'Let's get physical.'"

"I like clean too! I also like those fruity fragrances you wear sometimes, and freshly shampooed hair is nice."

"I like some fragrances on you too," she said, "like the after-shave you occasionally use or the smell of baby powder when you put some on your neck and chest. And that musk in your medicine cabinet—enough said!"

"How about this: As a wonderful way to end the weekend, we can shower together tomorrow and then apply a little fragrance to each other to celebrate our time together. But there are no expectations and there are," Matt caught Sarah's eyes as they spoke together, "no formulas."

The mutual chorus brought a wave of relief from the conversation's intensity. As they stood up, the couple hugged each other silently. "Let's head down and explore the lake," he suggested. "The shoreline here is so pretty."

> *A woman responds to accumulated touches in many parts of her body until she reaches the desire to be "filled up" while a man quickly responds to direct touch of his genitals and feels a need to "empty out."*
>
> —Linda Dillow & Lorraine Pintus

How Passion Works for Her

Start and stay north—above the neckline—for a long while before heading south. Think of being at the 'north pole,' working to relax her before pursuing arousal. Slowly win over a woman's mouth. Work on taking the hills before seeking to occupy the valley. Avoid the grope, employ the caress. Tease her by building up her interest, then backing off—but not completely!

To the men: What would it be like for you to make love and not reach a climax? Our partner's orgasm is ultimately a shared responsibility. The reality is that many men don't know how to help a woman reach orgasm and many women don't know how, or feel reluctant to help. But the above question should encourage you to do everything possible to figure out how to help her reach absolute pleasure.

If It's Not Working for Her

By its very nature, sex is about letting go of control. Some women from alcoholic family backgrounds or who have experienced abuse find losing control a very scary proposition. These women often find themselves avoiding sex or having to struggle through huge emotional hurdles until their bodies become sufficiently aroused. One way to deal with this is to channel the need for control into being the one who takes the initiative.

Because such deep hurt doesn't just heal itself, counseling may prove quite helpful. Also, fear cannot exist within someone who is thoroughly relaxed. So practice relaxation techniques that put body and mind at ease.

CHERISH IS THE WORD

*A*s the couple reached the water's edge, Sarah said, "I've been thinking about what you mentioned, that men feel love for women who love sex, and I wonder—do I really fit into that group? Sometimes I really love sex, but other times, I don't. I know you love me, but given that criteria, can you say you feel love for me that strongly?"

"Of course I do," Matt said, furrowing his brow. "It would probably be better to say that a man feels love for a woman who is open to his desires. Sex is just the most basic of those desires. When we first got married I felt that you were open to everything I wanted to do, from scouting out a new location for lovemaking to rafting the rapids with me. Slowly but surely, life between us got complicated, the trust level dropped, and that openness shut down.

"During the first few years of motherhood our sex life dried up almost completely. I know there were lots of issues affecting you, like hormone changes, energy drain, even weight gain, but it seemed to me that you and I got lost in the shuffle. Increasingly I began feeling way down on your list of priorities. I know I pulled away from you, too, and our feelings of love for each other went cold. The kids kept us together during that time—them and a lot of prodding by family and friends to get some counseling."

"In my mind it was the counseling that acted as a turning point, helping us to start reconnecting. We really needed the intervention of a third party to help us understand where the other person was coming from," Sarah reflected.

"I remember," he replied, "thinking at one point that what I had in our relationship added up to more than what I lacked. I began seeing the positives rather than just the negatives. So, for the past few years I'd say my feelings of love for you have been on a big rebound."

"Because I love sex again?" she asked.

"You're really pinning me down on that point."

"Well, I want to understand where you're coming from because I'd like to make a similar point," she said.

"It's more because of your attitude," he replied. "Some women get into sex because they're starved for attention. That's not you—at least, it's not you anymore. Some woman get into sex because they have a higher testosterone level than normal. That's not you either. If I were to guess, I'd say you're average for a woman. You have a deep capacity to enjoy sex but you're not as captivated by it as I am."

"Until I get going," she replied.

"It's before you get going that I'm referring to," he stated. "Like you said, without something to ignite a spark, you have little or no natural sex drive. But I have seen you become positive about sex again. At first I think it was more an act of will. You were going to enjoy sex even if it killed you, because you knew that's what I wanted, but that sense of obligation seems to have gone away."

She turned toward him and said, "It made all the difference that you were willing to refocus your attention on being my life partner, not just my sexual partner. I guess we got into a non-vicious cycle!"

He thought for a moment and replied, "I should tell you that I see that same kind of effort and attitude change in other aspects of our life as well. You've taken a lot more interest in some of my other passions, even following football and basketball. Your strategy seems clear: You've obviously tried to grow enthusiasm in these things for the sake of our relationship and I love you for it!"

"Okay, one more time," she stated, "to make sure I have this right. The reason you'd say it's important for me to work on loving sex—and your other passions—is because I'm loving your essence—your masculinity. I'm making your greatest interests my greatest interests—starting with sex, right?"

"Yes! Again, I'd be happy to describe it: Sex from a desirous woman nurtures a man's soul. Men love sex because we feel so tangibly loved through sex. And we love women who love sex—or are willing to learn to love it—because, like you said, it makes us feel like men.

"All of a sudden I think of myself as someone special—as God's gift to women, if you will. It's all because one woman thinks my body is God's gift to her, and her body is God's gift to us both. It might only be one woman out of three and a half billion on the planet, but her opinion of me, at this most basic level, is the only one that matters.

"I think, 'Wow, this human being really cares for me! She loves me so much, she wants me and this body of mine.' It takes the hostess and guest analogy a huge step further. A hostess can give out of obligation or she can give out of joy. If she's doing it freely, out of joy, the guest will feel more than just served, he'll feel admired."

"So, to put your statement in broader terms, you'd say a man feels love toward a woman when she finds her greatest joy in him. A man loves a woman who admires him. Sex is just the most basic evidence of her admiration."

"Yes, that's it," he replied. "I'd agree with that."

"You know, you're describing what a man who is passionate about a woman's interests does for her as well. A woman loves a man—again using love as a feeling—who seeks to make her needs his most important concern. Women know men have all kinds of goals, ambitions, and pursuits in life that are important to them. When I see you set aside time and energy you'd give to those things and instead focus on my concerns—I love you for it!"

"Then you know I'm taking you seriously," he said.

"Oh, it goes deeper than that! It's difficult to decide on the best word for this feeling—treasured or cherished. But I think I'll go with cherished. A woman loves a man who cherishes her. I suppose being cherished is very similar to being admired, only with a more feminine twist."

He paused briefly and asked, "So if sex is the ultimate act of admiration for me, a kind of 'manly applause,' what is at the heart of feeling cherished for you?"

"Cherished," Sarah repeated aloud as she slowed the pace. "Let me ask you. How do you act toward something you cherish?"

Matt paused and said, "I take special care of it."

> To cherish is not to lose ourself but to extend ourself by surrounding another person with our affection.

"Exactly," she agreed. "When you cherish something, you do everything in your power to keep it safe and protected. If sex is fundamental to your sense of well-being, then feeling safe is fundamental to mine.

"From my reading of history I know that my ancient foremothers and their children were totally dependent on a man's protection and provision. As much as women's status in society has grown, it is obvious, and sometimes painfully so, that we still live in a man's world.

"Men control most of the financial resources and hold most of the positions of power and influence. Men are just plain stronger. So we women can end up feeling vulnerable: physically, emotionally, and sexually.

"This is how my special man—you—becomes part of the solution for me, rather than part of the problem."

"You've lost me," he said. "Exactly how do I become part of the solution? By helping you feel safe?"

"Yes, which counteracts the fear and worry that I often have," she said. "To feel cherished is to know that another human being places my needs and desires above all others, even his own when needed. That's reassuring!"

"Is that kind of reassurance another word for unconditional love, tenderness and affection?" he asked.

A man willing to focus his affection on his mate above those things that so naturally draw his time and energy— his career, his ambitions, his pursuits—lets her know that he cherishes her. Within such an environment a woman's tendency to feel insecure finds relief and her natural inclination to nurture and love blossoms. That love finds all kinds of avenues of expression—especially back to the man who made her such a priority to begin with.

"Unconditional is the key word," she agreed. "This is where love changes from a feeling back into an action, bringing with it an endeavor to cherish, especially during my weakest moments—when I'm the most difficult to love and the hardest to live with. At those times I may be feeling unsafe, unsupported, devalued, taken for granted, lonely, or just out of sorts. That's the time to set aside your own feelings and make the choice to love me."

"Well, isn't that the test of love for all of us? It's pretty easy to love someone when they're at their strongest—looking good, feeling positive, and fun to be around. It's when we're at our weakest—angry, depressed, fearful, anxious, jealous, inconsistent, critical, withdrawn, or just plain nasty—that we're so hard to love."

"That's quite the laundry list of unpleasantness."

"You like that, huh?" he said, squeezing her hand.

"What I don't like is when I become some of those things and you back out emotionally," she stated. "I don't really blame you, but I don't feel cherished by you either.

"Some women get naggy, possessive, clingy, or needy when they feel insecure. Others, like me, withdraw into our own little despairing world of loneliness, close all the doors and windows, and shut others out. We can get nasty, but in a more passive sort of way. We stop relating."

He looked at her and said, "The problem with that, as we've talked about before, is that sometimes I don't know how you're feeling unless you tell me. You said that a woman is born to nurture. Well, there's a masculine parallel: A man is born to rescue. Particularly when you're vulnerable—when you express a need in a hurting way instead of an angry way—I want to ride into your world to save you. If you break down and cry, nothing can stop me:

> A woman is born to nurture and a man to rescue.
> When you see the depths of love a mother has for
> her child, you get an idea of the lengths a man will
> go to rescue his damsel in distress. When you need a
> man, you motivate and empower him.

I've got a damsel in distress who needs me.

"But when you just stew all day in depression or make
me a target of your anger, all the time dropping vague hints
about what's wrong, I get no sense of vulnerability to turn
on that innate rescue-mentality. You seem like you can deal
with it alone or, worse yet, I end up confronting the wrath
of the dragon from the damsel! So I run and hide. I know
that's not a mature reaction, but I must admit I fail the test
of love regularly."

"When you shut me out I have nowhere to go but into
a deeper funk of feeling insecure and sorry for myself.
Then I start to get really unpleasant to be around."

"How can I halt that downward spiral?" he asked.

"First of all, don't criticize me for being needy. You
don't come out and say 'Don't be so needy,' but I feel
judged when you act like I should cope better or that what
I'm facing is not a big deal. It is a big deal to me.

"Financial stress brings you down the fastest and hardest—and maybe that's a point of empathy for you. Your
feelings when you're stressing about money or your job
are similar to the ones I'm talking about. I just have different points of vulnerability. Please be my advocate.

"Another big way you can take care of me and show
your love is to let me into your life more deeply. It seems
that it has to reach crisis proportions before you're ready to

talk deeply about something."

"I know you often hear me say 'I'm fine,'" he said, "but remember, men process their problems internally."

"I know," she said, looking at him, "but as much as possible I want to be involved so I feel a part of what's going on in your life and in our life together.

"Also, being included in decisions is proof of your respect for me. I want to know that my opinion is valued and that I am an active partner in our decision-making. If you exclude me and leave me on the sidelines, I begin to feel insecure, like I'm not that important to you."

"You know you're very important to me," he said.

"The more deeply we connect, the more I feel that. My need to connect is at least as strong as your sex drive. This is the point that so often gets us into trouble. Not getting enough sex should act like a warning light—the oil's low and I may not be getting enough partnering."

"You can also call that light an idiot light!" he mused.

"You bond with your buddies watching a football game or cooking burgers at a picnic or fishing, and you feel close. Shared experiences are great, but you can do lots of things together and never share confidences. I'm looking for something deeper out of our relationship. I want to share on a feeling level—heart-to-heart. Bonding is a good first step but bonding is not intimacy.

"When it comes to intimacy, I want us to be friends who get naked with our deepest secrets and feelings. Really getting naked with you then becomes the icing on the cake. I'd love for us to share with each other as explicitly on an emotional level as we do on a physical level.

"Emotional intimacy with you brings security to my life. It assures me that you like talking and listening to me and being with me: 'This guy really wants to share our lives together. He loves me in my most basic essence, my femininity.' A woman loves a man who cherishes her."

"I really do want to step into your world more often and to open up my world to you," he replied, "but yours is truly a different world from mine. Remember that pact we made to respect our emotional differences?"

"That I wouldn't ask you how you feel," she stated.

"Yes, and I wouldn't ask you to apologize," Matt replied.

"So how do you feel about that now?" she asked.

"Like you should apologize for asking! Kidding aside, though, don't you think we had good reasoning behind that pact? The reason you don't want to be pressured into an apology is not because you never do anything wrong. Rather, you've said relationships are everything in a woman's world, and consequently you are always trying hard to be sensitive and caring. To throw a failure in your face by forcing the issue and saying you should apologize is quite hurtful, particularly coming from a man, who is likely a lot less sensitive than you would be in the first place.

"The same is true when you pressure me to share how I feel. I was born and bred in a man's culture. In my world we don't talk about our secrets, our embarrassments, our failures, or our frustrations unless we have a very good reason to do so. So it's best not to expect it."

"I respect your male culture and I'm not asking you to talk about your feelings like I would. I'm just asking you to go 'cross-cultural' for intimacy's sake. Talk as deeply about things as you can. I'll encourage you, and I'll keep sharing my feelings. Just be sure to keep listening to me.

"I'm not expecting to have the same kind of connection

that I might have with a woman, but I don't want to settle for the intimacy level you and your buddies seem content with either. We have a truly special relationship that calls for a unique closeness and togetherness."

Matt stopped and found a flat stone to skip across the lake. "It's a tall order to respect each other's differences and to keep crossing the gender divide into each other's territory. Surely that's the mark of a mature marriage."

They stood in silence and watched as the ripples from the stone spread over the water's surface.

Going "Cross-Cultural"

Men generally connect as they participate together in projects and tasks—bonding. Women go further—sharing their feelings. Intimacy takes place as those feelings are met with understanding and empathy. Going cross-cultural involves openness to appreciate and enter into each other's gender perspective.

You respect a woman's culture when you understand how much she values relationships and how careful she is about not harming them. So, don't insist that a woman apologize. If you feel hurt by her actions, tell her so. Trust her womanhood to take over from there.

You respect a man's culture when you realize how uncertain and uncomfortable he can be in sharing feelings and vulnerabilities. So don't insist that a man share his feelings, but don't stop telling him how you feel either. He can learn to get in touch with his feelings by listening to you and sharing himself within a non-threatening and supportive environment.

TURN THE GEOGRAPHY AROUND

$\mathcal{S}$ arah collected a few stones herself and joined Matt's attempts at skipping them. "Talk about a change," he said. "I'm 'the guest,' you're 'the hostess.' That analogy is slowly but surely rearranging my sexual world."

"Don't you just hate those paradigm shifts?"

"All but the results," he replied. "One thing it has meant is that I don't have to retreat emotionally from our relationship by succumbing to self-pity. There is no such thing as an entitled guest. Self-pity just doesn't make sense for a guest! At least I know up here," he said, pointing to his head, "that the more grateful a guest I become, the more the trust and love in our relationship will deepen and provide us both with what we want."

"I think you're on to something," she said. "Being a guest is not about being under the domination or control of a woman, it's about being humble. To be successful with a woman, a man should go to the school of humility and learn to be grateful—and not just to get what he wants, but

> *There's a place you can touch a woman that will*
> *drive her crazy. Her heart.*
>
> —Melanie Griffith, Milk Money

as a genuine response to who she is in his life. That attitude will go a long way in opening up my heart to you. And when my heart is open, my body is not far behind."

"So you'd say that humility touches your most sensitive erogenous zone—your heart," he said, reaching down to pick up another stone.

"Definitely," she replied. "You know the saying: 'A man gives love for sex, and a woman gives sex for love.' Maybe it's often true, but that attitude undermines both quality sex and genuine love. Such a tit-for-tat sentiment doesn't lead couples to deeper levels of trust in each other the way unconditional love and acceptance do.

"I'd say a mature relationship would better be described as: 'A man loves a woman without conditions of sexual gratification, and a woman loves a man without conditions of sexual restraint.' Then both feel accepted.

"Given that, I'm sorry for the restraint I've put on our sexual intimacy at times. I can't easily change my hormone levels, but I do think I can increase my level of openness to you and allow my own desires more freedom of expression. Just as you need a study course on what makes me tick, I need the same on what makes you tick."

"I'm really quite simple to figure out," Matt stated, flinging another stone. "Just turn the geography around."

Sarah looked puzzled. "The geography?"

"If it's best for me to focus first on your least sensitive area—up north—it's best for you to concentrate on my most sensitive area—down south, below waist level.

"You know I have a lot of places where I like to be touched. I love it when you rub my feet or caress my inner thighs and bottom or French kiss my ear. You can track my most sensitive places by finding where I'm ticklish—and you've pretty much found all of those!

"Whatever the scientific facts, though, it sure seems like 90 percent of a man's sensory nerves are in a six-inch circumference, the majority being in the last inch or two. For men there is one main erogenous zone. That's it.

"So it's such a thrill when we're watching TV together and your hand drifts down between my legs. If you then slip your hand underneath my briefs, whoa. A hand job is not quite as breathtaking as the oral version, but it's right up there. Manual stimulation provides a big dose of affirmation for a guy—anytime and anywhere.

"When you stroke and rub me there, you communicate just how important and special I am to you. My whole body comes alive, and if you bring me to a climax, it increases that feeling dramatically. I could do it myself but, believe me, there's no comparison to the feminine touch."

"Like trying to tickle yourself versus having someone else tickle you," she said, spying a smooth stone.

"You got it. A lot more work for a lot less pleasure!"

"It's also work for me," she replied. "I can get worn out when it takes a while to get you across the finish line."

"I could suggest something to pass the time. Alternate between thinking about how much you love me and thinking about how much you'd love for me to do something useful around the house! I might feel hard, but I'm putty in your hands. So, use the time to drop a few hints!"

"Maybe you should just hang a sign around your neck:

'Will Work for Pleasure,'" she said, tossing the rock.

"Well, as you mentioned, we don't want our sexual experience to turn into an athletic event, rather than a relational experience," he replied. "But, if you want to get me across the finish line, remember to focus on the last couple of inches since they're the most sensitive, and to generously apply lubricant, lotion, or even saliva. Use your whole hand rather than just a couple of fingers. When I'm headed down the home stretch, pour on the gas and become the little piston that could. And there's one more little tiny extra that adds up to a great big rush."

"What's that?" she asked, looking across the water.

"Add points of contact, in all forms of lovemaking."

"Points of contact?" she mused, looking at him.

"It's like this rock," Matt said, as he picked up another smooth stone and prepared to toss it. "How many contact points do you think it can have with the lake?"

"Well, you're good at skipping—I'll say five." Sarah counted as the stone bounced across the water. "Looks like six. Good job."

"Good lovemaking is like good stone-skipping in this regard," he said. "The more points of contact, the better. Like when we're having intercourse and you begin French kissing my ear, or you reach down to grab me with a hand—or two. You know that quickens my breath immediately. Any extra touch brings my whole body into the experience. And adding oral sex brings to bear a pleasurable sensation distinct from intercourse. It won't be long before the music comes to a spectacular crescendo!

"I think this is why I enjoy giving and receiving oral sex at the same time, 69-style, so much. It's more work than just receiving it, but it is one of those labors of love—

with lots of contact points. My personal favorite is you on top, me on bottom but I'm certainly not picky!

"One more thing I really like is when you squeeze your vagina, particularly at the moment of climax. It's just another point of contact—right at the center of the action—like an invisible hand gripping me. Whoa!"

"Maybe it's time to do those Kegel exercises again."

"Anything I can help with?"

"No such luck. They exercise muscles inside the pelvic area—the ones I clench when I want to stop urinating. Rather unique. In the past Kegels helped me tighten those muscles to better feel you inside."

"Now, that's my kind of workout! Here's another secret you can file away. When you are 'handsy' I cannot be angry or defensive. It's just not possible. So if you have something that you know will be hard for me to hear, start touching and holding me down south and then tell me whatever is on your mind. I promise you I will be incredibly open to anything you say. And why not? I'm feeling totally accepted and affirmed.

"Contrary to the old saying, the way to a man's heart is not through his stomach. It's six inches lower! I'd much rather have you flirting with me than fixing food."

"If I spend more time in the bedroom than the kitchen, we'll have to switch to TV dinners!" she exclaimed.

"Believe me, I'm quite glad you're into both the culinary arts and the sensual arts. But if it came down to choosing one over the other, most men would want their women to master the art of making love long before the art of making pot roast. It's just how it is for us—men would rather women make whoopee than make cookies."

"Actually, making a meal and making love can have a

Kegel exercises strengthen the pubococcygeus, or PC, muscle which can also play a significant role in a woman's orgasmic response. Often, the stronger the PC muscle is, the more likely and easily a woman will come to an orgasm. Kegel exercises can be done as follows: Identify the muscle used to stop the flow of urine. Contract and relax the muscle for 10 second intervals—up to 150 times a day. Continue on a regular basis.

lot in common," she said. "It's all about perspective."

"We do share a lot of love around the dinner table," he agreed. "I'm just saying, setting the table for a great meal is wonderful, but setting the bedroom for great sex is more wonderful. It's like having Thanksgiving dinner on a Monday! When sex is involved, men count it as a cause for great celebration, like it's our birthday or something."

"I guess that means," she said, "if I go naked on your birthday, I'm wearing your birthday suit!"

"Well, I can get presents from plenty of sources but I can only get a naked body from one source, right?! So, if you can't find the perfect gift, skip the shopping, rest up, and invite me to a party for two. That's my idea of a special occasion. And the more unexpected, the better."

"Making love as a lifestyle is my paradigm shift."

"I'll trade your paradigm shift for mine!" he said. "What do you think is the biggest sexual mistake men make? I'd guess, it's going too fast and being insensitive."

"That, and not seeing sex as a product of the emotional connection we share in our relationship as a whole. Now, your turn: what do you see as the biggest mistake women make—being too timid and conservative?"

"That, and not making sex a primary focus of attention. To sum it up, it's this: the more interest you can direct toward me as your sexual partner, the better. When you focus your attention and energy down south I feel loved. Frighteningly straightforward, huh? But I can assure you I didn't invent this orientation. I just inherited it!"

"It never ceases to amaze me...Hey, I'll race you to our sitting log," Sarah said, as she took off running.

Matt watched her briefly, then he took off, too.

A Picture Is Worth 100,000 Words!

How do you react to this image? Is it helpful or not?

_____

Some have entitled this *The Awful Truth!* Do you concur with this title? What title would you give it?

_____

Could the image contribute positively to your thinking?

_____

How Passion Works for Him

A guy has nearly 50 miles of pleasure pathways running through his ears, neck, chest, thighs and feet. Most of those sensory nerves end up in a six-inch circumference, particularly at the tip of his penis. So, whenever appropriate—or not!—treat him with lots of affectionate strokes.

Increase the intensity of sensation by adding points of contact during lovemaking. Use a hand—or, better yet, two hands, breasts, and mouth—particularly in the southern region! It can double and triple his pleasure and bring him to an explosive climax.

Many men and women consider oral sex the most breathtaking gift they can receive: anytime, anywhere, any way, and unexpectedly! Also, many love mutual, "69 style" oral sex. Now, what day would you imagine is observed as Kinky Sex Day? You guessed it: June 9th. And it's a day worth celebrating all year long!

If It's Not Working for Him

Factors such as stress, emotional barriers, and medication can inhibit a man's sex drive and/or prevent him from having or maintaining an erection. This lack of performance leads to inner turmoil and is experienced by as much as 40% of men sometime in their life.

Drugs such as Viagra and Cialis close off blood flow from the penis which can eliminate this problem. Openness by both partners along with advice from a doctor is important to help resolve these issues.

Dressed to Thrill

*F*or as long as they could remember, the couple had called the log their sitting log. After catching her breath, Sarah asked, "Men come at sex from such a different place. How could I ever think like a man?"

"You don't have to think like a man. Consider how women think who make their livelihood pleasing men."

"Prostitutes and strippers know how to exploit men's weaknesses, not how to give them what they need," Sarah interjected.

"True," he agreed. "That's why men aren't drawn to sex workers as marriage partners, even though they may know how to be sexy. More than anything, a man wants to feel special, and a woman who sells her charms to every man has little chance of making any one man feel special. Now, I'm just talking about technique here. I still want my loyal, loving wife and mother of my children."

"Yeah, who has a Masters in Sexology from the University of Sunset Strip. Whoever it was that said, 'You can't have it all'—you certainly never listened to him!"

"Oh, if I had it all," he mused, "I'd have us in Las Vegas working together on a Ph.D. in Sexology. For your part of the doctoral dissertation you'd interview the most popular call girls to document their best techniques."

"And for your part? I assume you'd want me to come back to our hotel room to practice on you, right?!"

"Well, sure. We wouldn't want all that knowledge going to waste! Hey, I'd promise to call you Doctor!" he teased.

"Instead of earning a degree in Vegas, let's say I took a home study course, and you were the professor. What else would you put in your syllabus on male sexuality?"

He paused and said, "Now, I thought you disliked objectifying sex as an act apart from our relationship."

"I do, and I may have to wave off this conversation. But I love you and our relationship, so I want to learn."

"Well thanks for the honor," Matt replied. "Eager students are the best! One thing strippers and prostitutes have figured out is how to get men's attention. Just look at how they dress. And consider why porn sites, adult videos, and men's magazines appeal to so many guys.

"As a young man my secret desire was to be a photographer for Playboy. Fortunately, reality came knocking early and steered me clear of my first ambition.

"Women know men are turned on visually, but they could do more to take advantage of it. Now, I'm not suggesting that you flaunt yourself, because modesty increases your feminine allure. Actually, I'm glad you don't parade yourself around in front of me naked. Explicitness and overexposure dull sex appeal, but it's a thrill watching you get ready for bed and seeing you shed your natural modesty by putting on one of your cute little nighties."

"I know you like that," Sarah smiled warmly.

"I do. And any time you like, feel free to go for broke and do a strip tease—just a little to-do about taking off your clothes in front of me—or with my help."

"Look, I have no illusions here. Maybe it worked a half a lifetime ago, but I'm not one of the women you'd do a photo shoot on for your fantasy Playboy job."

"I'm no Don Juan either," he replied with a smile.

"What I'm saying is that I'm too self-conscious to be parading myself in front of you. It's no secret that I've put on weight in the last few years, and I'm not particularly in love with my body. It's okay, but far from a 10," she admitted.

"Honey, please understand. Wearing a provocative nightie or doing a strip tease is about being vulnerable. Men aren't attracted to bodies as much as to a message of openness to sex. Such availability and willingness is a lot more of a turn-on than any particular body size or shape.

"I've read that unless money or fame are involved, men and women hook up with those who are very comparable in appearance. In our case, I did better! So what can I say—whatever number you are, it's higher than mine, and much closer to a 10 than a 1. But regardless, let's just say that you were a 1. You'd still be the only oasis this thirsty man has and in the desert, an oasis is an oasis! The plainest of women have a feminine form, a feminine scent, and a feminine mystique men find attractive.

"It's not like you've never played up those charms. On occasion you vacuum our home in a tight sweater and lacy underwear. One time I noticed you wearing my dress shirt with nothing underneath. That's what I'd call dressed to thrill. I'm not looking for a nightly bump and grind, or for you to lose yourself in the weird world of male debauchery, but those simple enticements communicate a mysterious feminine charm and sensuality. And the more femininity you project, the more I feel like—I'm the man!"

"You don't need much extra enticement, do you?"

"Well, you're right. Maybe some men do, but I don't. What I do need, however, is your affirmation. Maybe I don't say it very often, or very clearly, but I yearn for you to like me and to want me. As funny as it may sound, what you wear communicates those things to me."

"Or, what I don't wear," she said, looking at him.

"I like that you value modesty, which I think is actually the opposite of being prudish. Prudishness gives out the same non-erotic message as promiscuity; the first says, 'I'm impossible,' the other says 'I'm easy.' Modesty carries the real erotic message. It says, 'I just may be available.' It conveys a sensual, 'catch me if you can' coyness.

"Even the smallest displays of modesty can be incredibly appealing. During my brief fantasy of becoming a Playboy photographer I noticed what works in a woman's favor at least from a male point of view. The most basic observation is that the models are usually photographed wearing something. They dress for sex, drawing attention to their most sensual body parts. Their skimpy clothing and enticing look says it all: 'I'm ready, willing, and able.'

"I've heard it said that if clothing is meant to conceal, alluring underwear is meant to fail miserably as clothing. You are the gift, and your choice of undies is the pretty bow and ribbon. It's great unwrapping the package, although not necessarily every last piece.

"Now, if you're the hostess, it's not my place to tell you how to decorate, but it's not demeaning to dress like a sex object if you are the object of desire to the man who loves you. It reminds me that you are not just my wife, but a sensual woman who I'd better do well by or she just might stray! So, feel free to turn loose all that considerable feminine charm of yours and dress to thrill me."

She smiled and said, "You're making my point about how important subtleness is. If I can learn better how to exploit male sexuality for our mutual enjoyment, I'm for it. I'm looking for the best experience we can have together and if that includes skimpy outfits, then bring them on."

"But," he said, smiling, "I don't imagine you're going to pick up a Playboy as study material any time soon."

"Probably not," she said, glancing his way, "but I do want your fantasy world and my fantasy world to shape our lovemaking into a shared experience of pleasure. That takes understanding. So, imagine me at a magazine rack. I just picked up a men's magazine; what do I see?"

"I'll bet the first thing you'd notice is not the bodies, but the eyes. They're filled with a message of willing surrender. That sums up fantasy for a guy. What these women wear, or what they've taken off and are holding—garter belts, see-through bras, g-strings—serves to back up that message. You'd be surprised how many wear shoes, usually high heels. I even like sneakers. Either way, wearing nothing but shoes to bed is a big turn-on."

"So, you have a thing for shoes?" she said.

"Hey, that's your thing. You're shoe collection may not be the stuff of legends, but you're well on your way!"

"Yes, but I don't have a sexual interest in them, only a fashion interest," she continued with a smile.

"Oh, you're talking about getting turned on by shoes or leather, or who knows what—a fetish. And yes, if you're insinuating that fetishes are mostly a male obsession, I'd have to agree. Like I said, men's sexuality can be wild and weird, but I assure you, I'm not turned on by the things you're wearing. I'm turned on by you.

"You do know those skimpy outfits I've given you are in fact compliments, right? I don't see them as making you beautiful, they simply enhance your beauty—to me. Erotic underwear decorates those parts of your body I find so intriguing and exciting. And it's just plain fun.

"Men love to unhook, unsnap, and untie, or watch their women make a production out of it themselves. It's not the lingerie that turns us on, it's the attitude behind it; lingerie acts as a bold declaration of your sexuality. That's why I like scarlet and purple. It's as if you're producing a mini-drama for our own enjoyment: The Sex of Our Lives.

"So what do you think of all this? Pretty strange?"

"Not really," she replied. "Woman love the pretty paper and bows that veils a gift. It's fun to look good for you because you like it so much, and I see it enhancing our mutual pleasure. Although scarlet and purple are not my first choice of colors, I do enjoy the feeling of wearing sexy underwear like lace-topped bras and panties—as long as they're soft and comfortable.

"So should I take your interest in lingerie as a green light as far as our budget is concerned?" she asked.

"Hey," he replied, "there are two of your expenditures I will never question. One is getting your hair done and the other is your underwear collection."

"And how about your underwear collection?"

"Well, I'd be glad to wear whatever you bring home—at least once. You've never really gotten me anything except some silk boxers with hearts on them for Valentine's Day. Do you have something else in mind?"

"I've looked up sex toys on the web but that's it. I'm not so good at this enticing stuff," she admitted.

"Wait a minute. You're very good—much better than you let on. Do you remember when we were newly in love? You'd come up to me, put your hand around my back, and casually push your breast into my arm."

"No. You mean when we were dating?" she asked. "Are you saying I was flirting with you?"

"Men love compliments, and flirting is the granddaddy of compliments, especially if it carries on after marriage! Figuring out whether you were flirting or not is all part of the allure and fun. It's the best seduction of all, seemingly innocent—the girl-next-door type—but also a bit sly. Men get a thrill when their women appear sexually naive and yet they are able to break down their resistance.

"You played the seduction game so well during our honeymoon. At one point you were doing stretching exercises in your shorts. You laid back on the floor and sighed, 'Can't a girl get any action around here?' Then you looked at me and said, 'Right here, right now!' Wow.

"The most memorable event of our honeymoon for me wasn't the first night, it was the last night, at that restaurant. There you were, sitting so pretty and innocent in a white, flowered dress. Then, under the table you passed me your lacy, black panties and whispered, 'Can you hang on to these, I won't be needing them tonight.' The contrast of doing something a little naughty in such a formal setting—that was so unexpected and hot. WOW!"

"I didn't think that up myself," she said, smiling. "It came from one of those women's magazine articles. You know, '20 Ways to Put More Sizzle in Your Honeymoon.'"

He looked over at her and said, "I know, you told me,

and my offer still stands. I'd be happy to buy you a lifetime subscription to whatever magazine that was! Maybe this was an offhanded comment but do you recall mentioning a few months ago that it was so warm you weren't going to wear panties under your sundress?"

Sarah thought for a moment and replied, "I did?"

"Again, I have an excellent memory for such things. That 'I'm not wearing panties' routine is a surefire turn-on! I think it's another vulnerability thing. See, you're already doing it—at least subconsciously. Just think how good you'd be with some conscious planning!"

"It's not so much the effort as the orientation," Sarah said. "As I look back on our relationship, a major shift took place when we went from being a couple to being a family. My primary identity changed from wife to mom—from husband-pleaser to kid-pleaser. I became more concerned about how to fit our growing family into the van than how to fit sex and romance into our busy schedule.

"Besides the time and energy drain of little kids, they provided me with a large dose of physical closeness, re-placing the cuddles and hugging that I used to only get from you. I remember thinking that my breasts were jugs, all right: milk jugs! I got 'touch tired.'

"Turning away from sex was a way—albeit not a good way—to reclaim my body as my own. It gave me back a sense of control in my emotionally frayed world. What I didn't realize is that making sex such a low priority also meant cutting out the most important emotional under-pinning of my life—you.

"So, unfortunately, as my emotional and physical energy for the kids went up, my sexual energy for us went down. Instead of a way to connect with myself and with

What Gets a Man's Attention?...Passion
Think two words:
Willing Surrender

Naked is nice, but a woman who wears a little something knows that naughty is even nicer! It's not the apparel itself; it's the attitude behind it. *Lingerie* acts as a bold declaration of feminine sexuality. Self-confident vulnerability is the turn-on. If clothing is meant to conceal, alluring underwear is meant to fail miserably as clothing! A phrase like, "I'm not wearing any underwear," means something very different to men and women. Men think of lechery, while women think of laundry!

What Gets a Woman's Attention?...Intimacy
Think two words:
Nurturing Connection

What could be considered the masculine equivalent to lingerie? It's *listening*. Men are turned on by what they see, but women are turned on by what they feel. Expressing interest and listening with empathy, tenderness, respect, and concern turns a woman on. If you're looking for technique, skip the Las Vegas tutorial and get one of Lou Paget's books instead:

For Her: *How to Be a Great Lover.*
For Him: *How to Give Her Absolute Pleasure.*

What Gets Your Attention?

you, sex became just something more I needed to do for someone in the family, for you."

"We both got tired," he sighed. "Making love used to provide us the way to emotional completeness with each other. As life got busier, passion became like a spoke in the wheel rather than the hub. As that happened my emotional center with you drifted—mainly to work related stuff. But it's passion that makes marriage unique. Any two-some can talk about potty training or politics!"

She looked up and said, "It's been helpful to reassert the place of lovemaking by making our bedroom 'non-kid territory' and by setting up other boundaries for time alone from 'kid intrusion.' Giving them some real work to do, like folding laundry and washing the dishes, has also given us more time as well. It may be a small thing, but when we stopped calling each other 'Dad' and 'Mom' it helped reaffirm our basic identity as husband and wife.

"I do recall the challenge to rethink my primary identity, to turn from mom back to wife. A turning point came from a quote I read: 'The best way to love your children is to love their mom.' I realized that the reverse was also true. To provide my children with a caring and stable home I needed to make loving their dad my utmost priority. That meant moving back from mother to lover."

He paused and replied, "Nothing contributes more to

After kids, everything changes. We're having sex about every three months. If I have sex, I know my quarterly estimated taxes must be due. And if it's oral sex, I know it's time to renew my driver's license.

—Ray Romano (married, with four kids)

a child's sense of hope than having a safe harbor where his or her parents honor and love each other. Growing up in that kind of home instills in a child the belief that one day he or she can build a successful marriage as well.

"Also, the determination to set 'kid boundaries' in order to focus on us just makes good sense. You and I live together for a lifetime. As far as our children are concerned, we give them life and have them close for only a short while. Right now it just seems like a lifetime!"

"All this is to say that it has been a struggle for me to think of myself as a mom and a wife at the same time without the mom role taking over. It's just such an all-encompassing job description. I know, though, if I think like a wife, the mom role naturally falls into place."

"Or maybe go a little more daring and think of yourself as a mistress and me as your lover! To think of ourselves as husband and wife, or worse, dad and mom, takes all the pizzazz out and replaces it with a function," he said.

"Our marriage didn't start out boring," she agreed. "So, why should it have to end up that way?"

"You know, seduction does not have to be bold or brazen. Sometimes you'll walk around the bedroom topless in your jeans or you'll wear a stretch top with no bra."

"I'm just trying to be comfortable," she stated.

"Then it works for us both! Seeing your nipples through your shirt communicates to me, 'I just might be available.' It's like you're showing off at a wet T-shirt contest, except I'm the only one ogling. For you it may be about comfort, but for me it's a form of seduction."

"What is it about men and breasts?" she asked.

"What is it about women and butts?" Matt retorted.

"No comparison, but I asked first," she asserted.

"Fair enough. I don't really know, to be honest. I've heard that a woman's curves subconsciously let ancient man know she met his criteria as a suitable mother. What modern men see in them, I'm not sure, but they're pretty irresistible on the deepest level—heck, on every level!

"I suppose our sexuality offers what we subconsciously need from each other. Women look to men for their toughness and hardness and that's represented by what men have during sex: an erection. Men look to women for their sensitivity, tenderness, and softness.

"The sight of rounded feminine shapes—rear ends, breasts, hips, legs—stops traffic and wins wars. Those curves give a woman an air of mystery and fill a man with a sense of awe on par with any beautiful sunset. I'd say half the male population fixates at breast level a good part of the day. I hate to admit it, but sometimes it does take a sheer act of will to only look in a woman's eyes."

"So are you in the 50 percent walking around all day looking at other women's breasts?" she asked.

"You're just not going to give me a free pass on this one, are you! I'll try to answer that question with an illustration, if you'll be patient with me."

"Oh, I've got all the time in the world!"

"I've mentioned this before," he began slowly. "A few years ago I was looking at a single guy's house to buy as a rental and as I entered, the real estate agent warned me about the master bedroom. When I got there I realized why. On the ceiling and walls hung one Playboy centerfold after another, carefully fastened together like wallpaper. It looked like he had been a subscriber for a very long while!

"More recently I was looking at a house being sold because the woman was moving to a nursing home. Some of her possessions hadn't been moved yet, and an incredible 500-volume romance novel collection still filled the bookshelves lining her bedroom walls.

"The similarities between the two scenes struck me. These people were both living off fantasy: His turn-on came from visual images and hers, from romantic images. They had settled on a poor substitute for an actual, flesh-and-blood relationship with a real person."

"That fellow was living your fantasy Playboy job."

"Yeah, more than I ever did," he replied.

"Maybe it's just because I'm a woman, I can appreciate the desire to read about the inner workings of relationships, but I still don't understand pornography's allure. What kind of satisfaction is there in looking at women you'll never even meet, much less get to know?"

"Probably a satisfaction similar to what women get out of fairy tale romance with men who don't exist. These men give off an aura of success and security, guaranteeing a lifetime full of romantic pleasure. Wouldn't you say that could become a woman's version of porn?" he asked.

"Unless you're defining porn in the very broadest of terms, comparing the world of fantasy romance with pornography is like equating soap operas with reality TV. Porn displays real people in blatantly sexual ways. That world is a multi-billion dollar industry—like gambling—that has a dark and ugly side, but I would agree that romance novels can move from a pastime to pornographic if a woman gets addicted to them and some certainly do."

"That's interesting," he said, "but whatever form it comes in, pornography devalues people because it rates them for their entertainment value instead of their intrinsic value. Rather than people to love, they are objects to desire. A man's version of porn treats women as sex objects and a woman's version of it treats men as success objects.

"So, now I'll also answer my own question to you of why women are always looking at men's butts."

"And why is that?" she said, raising her eyebrows.

"They're not just sizing up how tight their rear ends are. They're checking out how thick their wallets are!"

"You are so clever, dear—a real expert on women!"

He smiled and said, "Maybe we should change the saying. Instead of 'Men give love for sex and women give sex for love,' it's: 'Women give sex for success.'"

"Or, more accurately, women give sex for security— which includes elements of both success and love," she replied.

"I've got a question," he said. "Some people make the case that pornographic images help couples fantasize, and thereby enhance their sex life. What do you think?" he asked.

"I know some people use porn like that, but if you're looking at another woman, the fact is, you're not thinking about me. I can, however, warm up sexually watching a romantic comedy or an erotic love story," she explained.

"You likely don't follow my reading list very closely, but I've read and reread sections of romantic novels to get myself in the mood. But watching some silicone-bosomed woman strut her stuff is more of a turn-off than a turn-on for me. I'm not into a three-way with you, me, and Ms. Perfect Body. Two is a pair. Three is a triangle, the Bermuda Triangle! I don't want a third party driving a wedge between us rather than bringing us closer together. Would you agree?" she asked, looking over to him.

"I've told you that as a teenager I was exposed to a

considerable amount of pornography. If anything, porn served to warp my view of sexuality and relating to women. It took an unsure guy and made him into an insecure guy, unable to discipline his intake. Quickly I learned what a powerful, addictive force it can be. Like smoking, once you've acquired the taste, it's difficult to break away. And often the soft stuff leads to harder, weirder stuff. The thrill threshold gets steeper.

"That's not to say that there's anything wrong with fantasy. Fantasies give expression to legitimate desires. They act as a counterbalance to our everyday lives, but there are much better things to do to alleviate boredom and loneliness than looking at accommodating, artificial, airbrushed models. Those women seemingly offer the best of all worlds—they get naked for you and yet make none of the demands that come with a real relationship. You can feel intimate without creating real intimacy."

Sarah paused and said, "Yeah, if you're only relating to images, you never have to do the hard work of learning to listen, respect, forgive, support, and encourage."

"Sure, and isn't it similar for women?" Matt asked. "Don't women love the thought of being taken care of by a strong, compassionate man? Don't the romantic images of novels, soaps, and movies tap into those longings? And yet, like the lady with the big collection of romance novels, those images won't ultimately meet a woman's need for nurture and emotional connection. Instead, they end up warping her expectations of what a real man should be."

"Yes. That's another problem with pornography," she agreed. "Whether it comes in a man's version or a woman's version, porn holds out the illusion that life can rise to the level of a flawless fantasy that denies the realities of paying a mortgage, cooking dinner, and changing diapers, not to mention working through differences or bad habits, dealing with sickness, and growing older.

"It's that perfection that makes porn so threatening to a woman. I'm aging each day, but she isn't. How can I compete for my husband's affection with some slender, surgically enhanced woman who never gets any older?"

"You can't, and neither can I compete with Prince Charming. What I find interesting is that most men do not like to be seen looking at pornographic magazines or websites. We know inherently that it's a weakness and we're embarrassed by it. It's like stealing; we're stealing the sexual energy that should go to our real lover and giving it over to someone or something else—an image.

"I'm sure many use porn to alleviate boredom, but the danger is that it creates a kind of artificial intimacy, sidetracking us from taking on our real issues. There's no need for a guy to confront his selfishness and pride—or a woman, her pettiness and manipulation—if we indulge in 'relationships' with people who look or act perfect."

"We'll always end up disappointed if we compare our real relationship with perfection," she agreed. "No wonder it's more than a little confusing figuring out the difference between healthy and unhealthy fantasy."

He paused and said, "I'd say healthy fantasy comes out of a committed relationship and seeks to enhance it. Healthy fantasy expands the possibilities and pleasures in a relationship, rather than looking for ways to escape the hard work that goes into making that relationship good. In my experience, porn is simply a form of escapism that promises a lot more than it delivers. Unlike porn, which steals sexual energy from our relationship with our mate, fantasy increases sexual energy for our mate."

Sarah looked up and said, "Speaking of escapism, let me ask you a question. Do you think that sex, and maybe even sex with your spouse, can become an effort to escape problems in your life rather than confront them?"

"I suppose anything can be used as an escape."

She continued, "Fantasy and sex open up powerful emotions. It seems to me that we either appreciate sex as a foretaste of heaven and leave it at that, or we make it a substitute for something more than it is—an ultimate need meeter. Nothing, not even the best life offers, is meant to compete with the Creator of those things for meeting our needs. Otherwise we're just chasing another addiction."

"I don't know what it's like being a woman, but as a man I'd agree with that. When sex becomes our first priority, it's no different than the misuse of alcohol or drugs. Sex was never meant to fill up the emptiness inside. That's something only a relationship with God does," Matt said.

"If we appreciate sex as a gift from God, we will enjoy it for what it is—wonderful, pleasurable, bonding—but not, as you said, our ultimate need meeter. I know first-hand that a focus on porn-oriented sexual fantasy comes at a price. Ultimately, such indulgence becomes a distraction, even a substitute, from cultivating a deeper unity with you and a deeper trust in God. I want God and you to be the objects of my fascination and love.

"All this is not to say I don't find porn enticing. If you've grown up with a fascination for it, it's very hard to totally break free of it. Ultimately I know it offers only an illusion of intimacy rather than the real thing."

"What has helped you stay away from it?" she asked.

"I try reminding myself of the long-term value of real

love rather than the short-term rush of excitement that porn brings. Erotic sex or super-charged romance—whatever form it comes in—is just not the end-all of life."

"It's a relief to hear you say that. I worry when you talk so much about sex, like it's all there is to life, but I would like to see passion as the hub of our life together again rather than a spoke. By the way, did you ever answer my question about looking at other women's breasts?"

Por•nog•ra•phy

Printed or visual material containing the explicit description or display of sexual organs or activity. Intended to stimulate erotic rather than aesthetic or emotional feelings.

I know it when I see it.
—Justice Potter Stewart (from a 1964 ruling)

Porn is more addictive than cocaine or alcohol. Porn sends its tentacles in deep. It wraps itself around a basic physical need (sex), entwines itself in a basic emotional need (to be in control) and enmeshes itself with a basic spiritual need (for intimacy).

—Laurie Hall, An Affair of the Mind

The Case Against Pornography

A man's version of porn views women as sex objects. A woman's version views men as success objects. When people are objectified, they get rated rather than loved, and everyone loses a degree of dignity. Love, in contrast to the impulse to objectify, views our mate subjectively—blinding us to his or her imperfections.

Playmates and Princes foster artificial intimacy. They hold out the illusion of perfection, which leads to dissatisfaction and insecurity. Porn makes women feel used and men feel controlled. It sidetracks us from building a deeper passion with our spouse and a deeper trust in God.

Porn acts as a cheap substitute for intimacy. As such, it bears similarity to prostitution (purchased intimacy) and to adultery (duplicitous intimacy). Porn steals sexual energy from our relationship as an end in itself, but fantasy directs energy into our relationship as a means to make it better.

It's amazing how sexually appealing your wife becomes when she's the only woman you look at with sex in mind.

Whatever is true, whatever is honorable, whatever is just, whatever is pure, whatever is lovely, whatever is commendable, if there is any excellence, if there is anything worthy of praise, think about these things.

—Paul, Philippians 4:8

The Case for Fantasy

Fantasy counterbalances the routine with novelty. It can turn perfunctory sex into dynamite sex. Fantasy enhances the attraction a couple feels for each other and makes marriage an illicit affair!

Strict monogamy is constraint enough. Inhibition and prudishness bring no value to a marriage. So, lust after, seduce, and sin with your spouse! And why not? The 10th Commandment says, "Do not covet another man's wife." The unstated implication: get busy coveting your own wife!

"Autopilot sex" is the natural, instinctive norm, but as long as both freely consent, "fantasy sex" can add a fresh, often planned, erotic twist. Sexual devices, toys, games and role playing give couples opportunities to enhance sexual play.

The most important way to love your daughters and sons is to permanently, passionately, and playfully love their mom and their dad. One of the best predictors of a successful marriage is the ongoing quality of passionate sex. Why? Because it helps couples deal with conflict and yet stay connected despite their differences.

Staying connected defines a successful marriage, and it is the magnetism of attraction that keeps drawing two people back for more—of each other.

Passion keeps the 'ability' in compatibility!

What kind of fantasy could you plan?

_____

_____

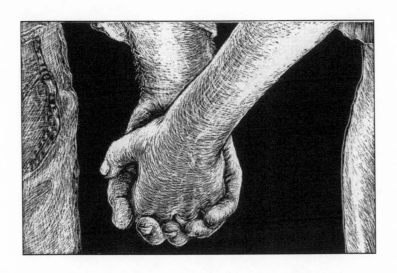

Fantasy: Frustration or Fulfillment?

> **Fan•ta•sy**
>
> The free play of creative imagination;
> a pleasant, exciting or unusual experience;
> a fanciful design or invention; an imagined
> extravagant and unrestrained event or sequence.

Getting up from the log, the couple started walking back to the cabin. Matt began, "Cultivating a man's fantasy life is a key answer to the temptation all around us, whether it's on-line or at work."

"Yes, and 'Diamonds are a girl's best friend,'" Sarah replied.

"What do you mean?" Matt asked.

"Romance and love relieve the temptation women have all around them. Affair-proofing a marriage involves regular attention to both spouses' needs. Or is it just the woman's job to keep men on the straight and narrow?"

"No, it's a mutual effort. But I want to think of you as my secret lover as much as my best friend. I feel that compatibility in marriage is somewhat overrated. Marriage is more about passion than compatibility. After all, when we first met we didn't know each other at all, and when we got to know each other, we realized we were very different people. Yet there was a definite chemistry between us. It was all a little mysterious. Nothing mundane about it.

"It's sad we ever substituted complacency for chemmistry. You may be my wife, but I never want to be able to fully possess you. I always want to think of you as a woman—attractive and sexually desirable. If I think other men wouldn't fall for you, why should I? When I see other men noticing you, however, it gets my attention!"

"I've never told you this," she said, "but it relates to what you're talking about. A few years back I overheard two ladies at a restaurant talking. One of them was complaining about her husband looking at other women. The other one made a comment that shocked her friend—and it shocked me as well. She said that when she notices her husband checking out another woman she asks him, 'Is there something about her look that you especially like?'

"I couldn't believe her self-confidence. Then she explained to her companion that arousal in its most basic form is simply about sex. It's not personal. She said that being happily married hadn't stopped her from liking men. 'I notice men,' she said, 'and I expect my husband to notice women. If he didn't, then I'd wonder.'

"She then said that one of the best ways to understand what men think is sexy is to catch them looking. Her attitude was, 'That woman might draw his attention, but I'm going to find out why, and our relationship will reap the benefits.' I was so floored I had to ask her myself what her husband thought about that kind of attitude."

"And what did she say?" he asked, looking at her.

"She said that when she takes that approach he treats her like a princess. He gets even more intrigued and focused on her. The wandering eye wanders all over her."

"Such self-confidence is impressive," he said, "but it makes sense. What kind of compliment is it if a husband stays faithful because he is never tempted? But it is a great compliment that, with other beautiful women all around, he keeps choosing his wife because to him she is the most special and beautiful of them all, and he tells her so."

"Well said," she replied, reaching out for a branch. "Marriage is a continual process of choosing to love your spouse in the way he or she best feels loved."

"Yes, and guys consider any initiative taken by a woman on a physical level to be an act of love. When you sexualize your orientation toward me, I feel loved—a lot."

"That's still foreign to someone who feels loved through an emotional dimension," she said. "You don't happen to have a manual on seduction made easy?"

"Oh, it's not that tough! Just enjoy being with me, tease me, smile, wink at me, or play footsies underneath the table. Find the most inappropriate places—like when family is around or we're out in public—and flirt with me. Like I said, flirting is the king of compliments to a man.

"It's all about going a step further than expected—a pat on the bottom turns into a massage, which turns into a full-body rub that you do just with your hair and breasts! I'm not unique here. Most men love to be touched—all the time—in all kinds of places.

"A few times you've awakened me with stroking or

kissing in the southern region. That's one great wake up call! Really though, just reaching out to hold me around the waist or putting your hand on my shoulder is reassuring—whether in the bedroom or at the movies.

"I'd love it if some morning you'd get my opinion on which bra to wear for the day. Then that night ask me to undo your bra, turn around, give me a big hug and say, 'Good choice' as you drop it on the floor.

"If you really want to turn my crank, call me at the office and tell me that you've been thinking about sex all morning and I have to come home right now for lunch!

"Unexpected and out-of-the-ordinary seduction goes a long way. It's a guy's version of being romanced. That's why I love it when you express any interest in a change of location from the bedroom. I've got great memories of going for it in the family room and the backyard.

He paused and said, "I've talked about me plenty."

"How about you? You've said you also have fantasies."

"They come and go, occasionally."

"Well, give me an example, Sarah," he insisted.

"Okay, I'll let you in on a fun one. Remember that city concert we went to last year? We sat really close to the orchestra, particularly the bass player. Besides being a great musician, what he really had going for him was his hands! I don't know if it was the wine from dinner or what, but I ended up going on a little mind trip; envisioning my body as that bass and the bass player's fingers playing me. His left hand stroked my breasts and his right, well, you know where it went! That night the fantasy continued as I let you play me to a great orgasm."

"Whoa. You never told me about that. Any others?"

"A few, but fantasies for me generally revolve around

a romantic connection, hopefully involving you—having a fun adventure together, reminiscing, sharing ourselves with each other—you know, 'feeling talk.'

"It's really too bad that many of our wild and crazy ideas and encounters died out after a few years of marriage. We used to do some pretty brazen stuff. I haven't thought about this for awhile, but remember when I met you at the airport after you came back from your first business trip? I led you into a corner, opened up my coat, and gave you a hug. All I had on underneath my overcoat was a lacy white teddy! Then we spent the night in an airport hotel."

"Oh, yeah!" he stated. "That was so unexpected and great. Here's another one in the locket of sexual delights. You announced to me at one of our anniversary celebrations—I think it was our second or third—that later your dress was staying on, but your panties were coming off and the rest was up to me. Then came the real thrill: the next day I found those panties draped over my rear view mirror like a trophy! You can bet I felt like a winner."

She paused and said, "I know it would be wonderful to see some of those memories become reality again. It's just hard to imagine, at this point in our lives, whether they would be fun and enjoyable or just embarrassing."

"Oh, they'd be fun—don't you think?" he asked.

"Again," she said, squeezing his hand, "it's not so much the effort as the orientation. Actually, in my younger days the initial fear of doing some of those crazy things used to be a real turn-on for me."

"All I know is that going to such lengths in becoming vulnerable communicates love to me, then and now."

"Here's something we could consider," she said. "It's

much less dramatic, but surely worthwhile. I've noticed that when you get home from work or when I come in late, we barely acknowledge each other. I must admit, sometimes I've stored up a 'bitch list,' and the first things out of my mouth are more gripey than gracious. But I'd like to start the habit of stopping what I'm doing, even if I'm on the phone, and taking time to greet each other.

"You've noticed the rather lengthy rituals women go through when saying hello and good-bye. Men often express impatience with the time this takes. You don't understand, though, that what's really going on is a mini-celebration of the friendship we share with the other person. We are, in effect, speaking a blessing to each other. As husband and wife, you and I seem to take our 'Good mornings,' 'Good-byes,' and 'Good nights' so much for granted. Why not take those moments as opportunities to celebrate the gift we are to each other?

"I don't know about meeting you at the front door in a teddy, but I could see going into an extra-long kiss just to say, 'Whatever your day was like, I'm so glad you're home with me now.'"

He smiled and said, "I like the sound of those words—spoken or not. They're in my love frame."

She paused briefly and replied, "Your love frame?"

"I heard someone use that term once. It has to do with our particular frame of reference when it comes to feeling loved. My love frame includes the particular things you do for me that communicate love to me. Your love frame includes things I do that make you feel loved. Our two love frames overlap, but they are also very different."

In that moment, Matt looked around for a sandy place. He ushered Sarah to an open spot and picked up a long stick. He then drew a rectangle in the dirt and asked, "Okay, Sarah, what is something I do for you that is normally experienced by you as being loved?"

"When you take me on a walk and hold my hand."

"Bingo," he said, spearing the stick into the ground inside the rectangle. "I've hit inside your love frame."

Sarah looked over to him and said, "I think I've just heard plenty about what's in your love frame."

"Yes, like when you become vulnerable to me in a sexual way," he said, as he pulled the stick out of the sand and speared it again. "You hit inside my love frame. Even when you just let me turn you on—you're in there," he continued, moving the point of the stick back and forth.

"I hate to interrupt you here, but you do know that it doesn't work the same way for me, right?"

"What doesn't work the same way?" he asked.

"I don't get turned on by turning you on," she continued. "I don't sit up nights thinking about new ways to get your motor running. It's just too easy and too automatic! Other women, whose men are uninterested in sex, may envy me. Their love frames are probably different. So, I'm very pleased you're interested, but..."

"But, your husband's motor is always running!" he interjected.

"Exactly," she agreed. "Given the alternative, I'm glad. Remember, though, I don't get the same thrill from turning you on as you do from turning me on. I think that's why it's so challenging for me to enter into your male fantasy world, or do things like talking dirty."

He slowed their walk and replied, "Hey, I wasn't the one who mentioned 'getting into your pants' earlier."

"I can say it about me, and I also don't mind you saying some mild stuff in the heat of the moment."

"Mild stuff?" he exclaimed, looking over to her.

"You've said things like, 'you've got a great ass' or described ways you want to 'get it on' with me. Maybe I could get comfortable with more of that, as long as it's not too crude. Any graphic, four-letter stuff feels demeaning to me and ends up being more of a turn-off than a turn-on. Like any action, our talk needs to be consensual."

"I agree," he replied. "But we weren't given a sexual manual or dictionary when we got married, so we have to make it up as we go along. For men, using those terms is more about expressing passion than about being rude and crude. If I do use them, they're certainly not meant to demean. Actually, you've talked to me that way yourself, maybe without even knowing it.

"I'm sure you remember going to the intramural championship baseball game that year I lost my job. I was surprised you went braless, which is unusual for you. But it was what you said to me right before the game started that really got to me. You told me, 'I've got a proposal that is meant to either motivate you to victory or soothe you in defeat. But you can only choose one option. Which would you prefer?' We both knew exactly what you meant."

"Yes," she agreed, "a hot time in bed and you chose to be motivated. Then you promptly lost the game!"

"Well, baseball is a team sport, but I guarantee you, I played my heart out! Whatever the outcome, your boldness in making such a proposal absolutely thrilled me and I haven't forgotten how you expressed it. You said, 'I'm your game trophy. If your team wins, you get a second reward. You can have me right after the game.' Not, 'we'll make love,' but a more brazen version, 'you can have me.'"

"Yes, and I offered myself to you despite your loss, but you said men prefer a real bet to a 'pretend one,' so it wouldn't be right to change the rules after the fact."

"That's right, and I didn't really care that I lost—twice—because I was so enamored by this sex-crazed wife of mine. I think we ended up going to a movie instead and having a fun evening together. That day was a special treat—all because of your seductive proposal. I love it when we're free to 'think outside the bedroom!'

"Now, I know a lot of time has passed since our early years, but could you see yourself resurrecting the same kind of sultry talk to express desire?"

"Like this?" she replied, making her voice husky.

"Sure. Let's say, for example, we're pretty much figuring on having sex some evening. You can just go along with it, or you can make things really interesting by whispering something rather naughty like, 'I wouldn't mind getting laid tonight.' Now, all of sudden, there's that shot of electricity in the air, an invisible passion, even a little hot marital lust. I'm walking tall and thinking to myself, 'This woman is a sex goddess and it's up to you, Bucko. She likes sex, she wants sex, and she's looking to you for satisfaction. Do your best—be all you can be!' Is that kind of approach possible, or is it too big a hurdle for you?"

"That language is 'male-speak,'" she stated. "To me terms like 'getting laid' have a low-class, raunchy feel to them that can make sexuality feel cheapened rather than precious. It's like using a chain saw to carve a turkey! Or think of the hostess–guest analogy again. As the hostess, I'm inviting you to a lovemaking party. Now it doesn't necessarily have to look like 'high tea,' but it certainly won't look like some backstreet orgy either."

"I'm envisioning this party being an orgy?" he asked defensively.

"Using a certain kind of language gives it that kind of edge—unsafe and scary. Now, if our relationship is full of trust and nurturing, these 'parties' will likely get pretty wild, or at least reflect more of what you're describing. But even so, I'm most likely going to invite you with 'female-speak'—something more tender, like, 'I want you close to me,' or possibly, 'I want you inside me.'

"What you're describing is more like how you used to talk when we first got married. As you toned it down and went from dirty to endearing I've felt more relaxed and honored, which turned the heat up between us! We're at a different place now, and what you're requesting is not off the charts, but it's more 'in your face' than I'm used to."

"If I can be honest, that's why I'd enjoy it. I realize you're crossing a big divide when you speak the language of passion so assertively. Hey, I love it when you write a little come-on in a Valentine's Day card. Once you even tried a little long-distance phone sex. It didn't last long, but I appreciated the effort. How about if we call this whole thing 'pillow talk' rather than 'talking dirty'?" he suggested.

"A change of description is not going to change how daunting these things are for me. Whether it's phone sex and pillow talk or passing my panties and meeting you half-naked, these are not ideas I normally dream up.

"Now I'm not saying they're not fun. Early on I loved the thrill of planning and carrying out some of those silly escapades. I figured our marriage license was all the license I needed to be naughty, but they also could be pretty darn awkward and scary. Down deep inside I'm really more Ms. Etiquette than Ms. Sex Goddess, and I wonder

Living in a Fantasy World and Having Fun with It!

- Work late at the office and play later
- Skinny dip • Have (almost) fully clothed sex
- Make up and play out some fantasy roles like: boss/secretary, student/professor, doctor/patient. One plays innocent, the other experienced, then switch roles
- Play Spin the Bottle • Find a hay barn—take a blanket
- Write a poem/song about how he/she turns you on
- Tie hands (& feet) loosely with scarf/necktie
- Show up as the massage therapist
- Act out a movie love scene
- After some practice, do a striptease
- Pretend to have a marital affair for a week
- Get a copy of the Kama Sutra and read together
- Be a genie and grant him/her three 'whoopee wishes'
- Tell a story about a magical sexual or nonsexual place
- Give each other a bath and dry each other off slowly
- Sit in his lap and make out • Sit in the backseat and...
- Visit Climax, KS, PA, CO, MN, OH, NY, NM, NC, TX. Also while traveling, don't forget Intercourse, PA
- Make a meal of your partner using whipped cream
- "I've got a vibrator and I know how to use it!"
- Play midnight golf, leave the clubs at home
- And remember what Ann Alrich says: "If the psyche is willing, no lack of technique will dissuade it."
- Think "outside the bedroom" by reading Laura Corn. Start with *The Great American Sex Diet*, or *101 Nights of Grrreat Sex*.

> *There are a number of mechanical devices that increase sexual arousal, particularly in women. Chief among these is the Mercedes-Benz 380SL convertible.*
>
> —P. J. O'Rourke

whether a good girl like me ought to even try to become the bad girl we're describing!

"How about this as a compromise? You work on talking with terms of endearment, and I work on being crude and naughty. That will offset our natural bents."

"Honey," he mused, "your personality is more on the naughty side than mine! I do love the thought, though, of recapturing those fun, playful times. Maybe that's naughty, but in a nice sort of way! We both want our marriage to be secure and sensuous, always adding to the experiences tucked away in that locket of sexual delights."

"Well, I have no doubt my efforts to add sizzle fall into your love frame. I do appreciate your desire to improve our love life rather than let it atrophy. Talk to me; tell me what you want and how you want it. Just be careful that your requests come within the context of an interest to improve our relationship as a whole. I need to see the higher purpose in learning the ways of a playmate. Don't get pushy, though. I need to be comfortable with it.

"What I get out of these experiences is the special bond of closeness they create between us. If they deepen that bond, I'm glad to take a walk on the wild side," Sarah said.

"Like so many things," he said, "how we feel loved is unique to us. You ignite my emotional fire when you pursue me sexually, and I get you going sexually when I nurture you on an emotional level. Our love frames will have things in common, but mostly they're opposites!"

Matt looked at his watch, "We have an hour before lunch. Let's take some time to write down things that the other person does that come within our love frame."

Sarah looked at him and said, "One item that falls in my love frame is when you do the things I like without being told. So the very act of giving you a list is a bit outside of my love frame but I know it's not fair to play, 'Guess what's on my mind.'"

"That's the purpose of listing them," he said. "Even though it's unlikely that anything on either list will surprise us, we could always use a reminder of what the other person likes. I know I find lists more helpful than you do but having these things down in black and white makes them more likely to become a reality."

"How many items should we include?" Sarah asked. "I might go on all day!"

His hand released hers and found its way around her shoulder. "I think I'll go for a dozen."

"Well, then I think I'll do twelve," she replied with a squeeze to his waist. "Ready to go back?"

"I think so. It sure is peaceful out here. I'd like to extend our time here for, oh, about a month!"

"That's something we can both agree on," she said.

They walked back in silence. Soon their cabin came into view. Once there they made coffee, settled into their own spaces with notebooks and pens, and began to write.

> *Sexual fantasy: Fairy tales for adults.*
> —Gregory Godek

Lubricants, Vibrators, Etc.

If lubricants have not been part of your lovemaking routine, consider using them. Some women experience excessive wetness, but many, as they age, find vaginal dryness the problem. Need some handy slickness? Warm up coconut oil. Its health benefits can go far beyond the kitchen! Many couples appreciate a silicone base lubricant, such as Pjur (pronounced pure: see pjurusa.com).

Like lubricants, vibrators can make sex more pleasurable, especially for women. Men love tools to fix and improve things, right? Then here's yet another addition to their tool set. If this tool—a vibrator—can help bring your woman to a mind-blowing orgasm, well, enough said! Beyond vibrators, the consensual use of a wide variety of sex toys and games (see adameve.com, for examples) allow for fun, experimentation and mutual enjoyment.

Whatever you do to spice up your love life, and you can do a lot, don't forget to work hard at playing hard. Your number one priority: To become a skilled love maker for the sake of your partner's pleasure!

All Sexual Activity Must be Consensual

It's not unusual for one partner to like creativity, experimentation, risk-taking, games, different positions, and places, toys...you name it...more than the other partner. This difference must be dealt with openness and respect—openess from the more conservative partner to consider new and different techniques, respect from the less conservative partner to never override their mate's sensitivities.

When such openness and sensitivity is extended, enormous trust and security will follow. If intimate conversation was ever called for, it is here.

Interlude on Modesty and Spirituality

> My dictionary defines...modesty as "the damping down of one's allure." [But]...Why did so many women dress modestly for thousands of years if this is all modesty is about? What woman wants to damp down her allure?...
>
> Certainly sexual modesty may damp down superficial allure, the kind of allure that inspires a one-night stand. But the kind of allure that lasts—that is what modesty protects and inspires.
>
> Modesty is prudery's true opposite, because it admits that I can be moved and issues an invitation for one man to try.
>
> —Wendy Shalit, *A Return to Modesty*

While the couple spends time writing, it would be helpful to highlight how to enhance attraction. A wise person exercises restraint and shyness at some times in order to enjoy sexual abandon at other times. Ultimately this mystery of intimacy has a deeper, spiritual dimension.

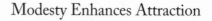

Modesty Enhances Attraction

Pre-marriage sexual abstinence can make post-marriage sexual liberation that much more meaningful. Modesty involves a personal choice to live within certain "sexual boundaries." Such boundaries recognize sexual experiences as a unique gift for strengthening one's future marriage. This valuable goal makes exercising the difficult discipline of restraint worthwhile.

Once married, familiarity can dull passion, but the dynamics of modesty help counteract this. Modesty keeps our sexual embers smoldering until conditions are right for a raging forest fire to ignite and burn.

- Go back and forth between two extremes: Be the sexually shy, naively reserved type, then the sensually seductive, experienced aggressor type.

- Don't parade around each other naked. But do emphasize masculine/feminine qualities in dress.

- Use the erotic elements of anticipation and surprise, constantly tempting each other. Produce a secret video, photo album or clandestine fantasy.

- Practice always looking your best for your mate. Try a sexual escapade in an "inappropriate place."

- How might you use modesty to counteract familiarity and increase your "allure factor?"

How could you use modesty to increase your attracation? _____

_____

_____

Sexuality & Spirituality

Our sexuality arises out of a sense of incompleteness [being only male or female] and is manifested by an urge toward wholeness and a yearning for the godhead. But what is our spirituality if not the same thing?

Sexuality and spirituality are not, of course, exactly the same thing. They are not identical twins, but they are kissing cousins, and they arise out of the same kind of ground, not only in myth but in actual human experience.

The fact is that sex is the closest that many people ever come to a spiritual experience. Indeed, it is because it is a spiritual experience of sorts that so many chase after it with a repetitive, desperate kind of abandon.

Often, whether they know it or not, they are searching for God. It is no accident that even atheists and agnostics will, at the moment of orgasm, routinely cry out, "Oh God!"

At that brief peak point [of orgasm], we forget who and where we are. And in a very real sense, I think, this is because we have left this earth and entered God's country.

Excerpts from *Further Along the Road Less Traveled*
—by Scott Peck

What do you think about Peck's perspective?

_____

_____

Romance & Spirituality

[Anyone] who believes that permanent romance in a relationship is a perpetual possibility is doomed to perpetual disappointment.

In fact, it is the search for God in human romantic relationships that is, I think, one of the greatest problems we have in this and other cultures.

What we do is to look to our spouse or lover to be a god unto us. We look to our spouse or lover to meet all of our needs, to fulfill us, to bring us a lasting Heaven on earth. And it never works. And among the reasons it never works—whether or not we're aware when we do this—is that we are violating the First Commandment, which says, "I am the Lord thy God, and thou shalt not have any other gods before me."

It is, however, also very natural that we should do this. It is very natural to want to have a tangible God, one whom we can not only see and touch but also hold and embrace and sleep with and perhaps even possess. So, we keep looking to our spouse or lover to be a god unto us, and in the process we forget about the true God.

Excerpts from *Further Along the Road Less Traveled*
—by Scott Peck

Intimacy is not heaven.
But it gives us a foretaste of heaven—
like dawn's first light ushering in the new day.

Saturday Lunch

ON THE DOMESTIC FRONT

*T*he clatter of dishes in the kitchen broke his concentration. Matt set his pen aside, satisfied that he had written enough, and joined Sarah's effort to make lunch.

"You must have cheated and looked at my paper," she said, as she passed him lettuce for the sandwiches. "You obviously saw that sharing the workload is in my love frame," she said, giving him a nudge.

"Hey, I might not be Mr. Clean, but at least I'm Mr. Helpful," he said, arranging the plates.

"Yes, and therein lies a problem we can never seem to solve. As a newlywed, I envisioned sharing the work at home 50/50. Your efforts came close to that during the first couple of years, when we both had full-time jobs, no kids, and life was simple. After we started our family and I cut my hours down to part-time, we realized that arrangement wasn't feasible. It didn't take long for me to gravitate to the home track, and you to the career track.

"I know that your job takes a lot out of you and that you need recovery time, but when do I get some recovery time? I realize, given our situation, a 50/50 partnership at home is not feasible—or even fair to you—but I want you to see yourself as more than just my assistant who occasionally pitches in to help. Too often it seems you are home in body, but not in soul. I long for more of a partnership in managing the house and raising our kids.

"I'm not saying I'm ungrateful for what you do, but most of the home and family chores fall on me—even if I enlist your help. We're not really sharing the work; you're just helping out once in a while with little sense of responsibility. That's the Mr. Helpful mind-set."

"We've talked and argued about this a lot."

"Yes," she agreed, "and the reason our 'chore wars' have been so intense is because, for me, they raise the issue of how much you want to be involved at home. Sharing the workload communicates a desire to be a mutual and supportive partner. Setting down the remote and picking up the vacuum tells me you want to be a giver, and that's right in the middle of my love frame. It's not so much about the work as it is about the involvement, and this is true for a lot of other areas in our life together."

"For instance?" he asked.

"Oh, I don't know, let's take a pretty neutral example. How about shopping?"

"Okay," he said, grimacing, "now you're hitting below the belt—given my severe case of mall-o-phobia."

"Sounds pretty bad. The fear of malls?"

"I don't actually fear malls," he said, smiling, "I fear what happens in malls. I can handle a store, but a mall is a bunch of stores. It's the cumulative effect."

"So, as categories of fears go, your condition is in the retail-phobia family," she said, cutting a sandwich.

"All I know is that any time I get within 100 yards of a mall I start getting the shakes," he replied.

"That's because you view shopping like you view housework, somewhere between a total waste of time and a necessary evil. Unless you're at an electronics store, you drop in like a dive bomber, target what you need, and make a fast retreat. If we linger somewhere, like a clothes shop, your eyes begin to glaze over and you become a walking store zombie in search of the nearest bench."

"Hey, more often than not, you don't want me to go shopping with you, you want me to go not-shopping. There are the blouses you're not going to buy, the toaster ovens you're not going to buy, and the bedsheets you're not going to buy. And then there is that perennial hunt for the elusive perfect swimsuit. There's so much looking, touching, contemplating. You don't have to marry that jacket. You just have to purchase it!" he exclaimed.

Sarah smiled. "I'm not assuming you want to go shopping with me any more than I want to watch hours of football and then the interminable sports drivel that follows. I'd just like you to understand that for me shopping is not merely an act of commerce. It's like football for you, a form of entertainment, and maybe even therapy. I get to take my female side out and indulge it for a while. If you do come along, and bring a positive attitude, I love sharing the experience together. To take the sports motif a little further, it's a major league turn-on."

"Weren't we talking about housework? In lieu of more arguing, tell me what you'd like to see happen."

She looked over to him and said, "I recognize that given your full-time job, we've settled into fairly traditional marriage roles, and that's okay with me. When it comes to the workload at home, I'm not looking for equality of time so much as assurance that you see yourself as a full partner in what goes on inside the walls of our house."

"Are we talking about managing our home or raising

the kids?" he asked.

"Well, both, but if I had to choose between the two—having a good father for my children or a good house-keeper for my home—I'd pick having a good father in a heartbeat. Anyone can do housework, but being a parent is like exercise. It's one of those things you can't delegate or hire out. We're it. I'm our kids' one and only mom, and you're their one and only dad.

"I'll admit that becoming a mom triggered a lot of expectations in me about being a family and raising kids. I've pretty much adopted the parenting style I grew up with, or at least idealized, and so have you. Your dad was not much on nurturing. You've made a conscious effort to break the mold, but I see you still struggling, often allowing your work to consume you.

"As a mom, with all of those famous motherly instincts, it's so important for me to see my kids well cared for. And a key component of that includes how well you father them. In lots of ways you're a great dad; I really mean that. You cheerlead their successes, and you dispense a lot of good humor and grace around the home."

"But I'm not their emotional center."

"That's true," she replied. "What I'd like to see is both of us providing more of that emotional center, in different ways. Neither of us should be the default parent, but partners in co-parenting. So, I'd love it if you'd get more involved as their personal mentor. The more you give your

The sexiest thing about my husband is that he is a wonderful father. After 10 years, he's still the one!

—Kimberly, interviewed
by Laurence Roy Stains & Stefan Bechtel

time and energy to them—their interests, their schooling, their development—the more I feel appreciation for you as my husband. It just works that way."

"This morning you said that you are 'hormonally challenged' when it comes to a sex drive, and that I am more 'hormonally charged.' So, I need to provide an environment for your hormones to kick in. Well, the same is true here. I'm relationally challenged, and you're the expert. I need you to provide some creativity in planning and carrying out things that nurture our family along. As you do, it really helps me to engage as a father. So tell me, how do you think I could get more involved?"

She looked at him and said, "Being better parents would make a great topic for another weekend. We can even make 'parenting frames!' What I'd like to say now is that I'm thrilled when I see you reaching into our kids' lives and meeting their needs in ways that I can't. It makes me proud of you and so appreciative of your fathering. And yes, it even attracts me to you sexually."

"Interesting," he mused. "Earlier you said that you are trying to limit the dominance that mothering has over you in order to be a better wife. Now you're saying that the more I give myself to fathering, the better husband I become. It does make sense, in a strange sort of way: You focus on being a great wife and the mothering naturally takes care of itself. If I focus on being a better father, I get a big dose of appreciation from you as your husband."

"Yes, it boils down to finding our satisfaction in the right places: you, inside the home rather than just at work, and me, with you rather than just with the kids, my friendships, work, and all the other priorities in my life."

After a pause to collect her thoughts, she asked, "Do

you really want to talk about the housework now?"

"Sure. Why not?"

"Then let's discuss a purely hypothetical situation," she continued slowly. "Think of yourself as a wife trying to get your husband to pull his weight in sharing the workload around the house. What would you do?"

"Ideally, I'd hire the house cleaning out," he stated.

"Which a family like ours could easily afford when I worked full-time, but not so easily now," she replied.

"I thought this was a hypothetical situation."

"Just adding a touch of realism," she said, smiling.

"You vetoed this before, but why don't we pay someone once a month to come in for a day?" he asked. "We could afford that, and at least it's some relief."

"I'm open to that, but I find it takes so much out of me just getting ready for the cleaning service."

Matt sighed and continued, "We've discussed this before. You don't have to clean up before a housekeeper comes. That's what they're coming to do!"

"It's hard to convey why this is so difficult. Before it's worth having someone come in, the house needs to be picked up, but it's hard to get even that far ahead, particularly when it's just once a month. Let's say it's an option I'll consider. Getting back to our hypothetical situation: How can a woman get a man to think he's more than an occasional helper, but a partner who shares the load?"

"Maybe one way is to free her from the tyranny of thinking she has to be so prepared before having a professional come in—even if it's just once a month! A little reality check on perfectionist tendencies could go a long way here. Beyond that, I'd want to help her understand the male mind-set. Most men view the work world as their

All in the Family

On a scale of 1-100 percent, who does the following
with your children and at what percentage?

Disciplines them	W_____	M_____
Nurtures self-esteem	W_____	M_____
Helps with homework	W_____	M_____
Initiates activities	W_____	M_____
Gets emotionally involved	W_____	M_____
Encourages value-building	W_____	M_____
Organizes baby-sitting	W_____	M_____
Oversees their friends	W_____	M_____
Encourages spirituality	W_____	M_____
Shuttles them around	W_____	M_____

Others:_____

How would you like to see your husband's/wife's involvement with your kids change or develop?

_____

How may this alter your feelings toward him/her?

_____

In It All—Keep the Main Thing the Main Thing

*If you fail to meet each other's needs, your marriage, which
is your source of strength in achieving all your other objec-
tives, will weaken. And if your marriage suffers, everything else you value will suffer along with it.*

—Willard F. Harley, Jr.

Check out his helpful website: MarriageBuilders.com

domain and the home front as their wife's domain."

"Even if the wife works full-time?!" she exclaimed.

"Yes," he said. "I'm sure it's less true than a generation ago, but, as unfair as it sounds, yes."

"It doesn't just sound unfair, it is. From what I've read, even in two-career homes, women still do more than 75 percent of the household chores. If a man cooks it's usually because he wants to. If a woman cooks, it's because she has to—no one else will. Where's the justice?"

"I hope a wife can realize it's nothing personal. She's not battling a recalcitrant, couch potato husband so much as thousands of years of male genetic programming. It's a hunter–gatherer thing. Men gravitate toward outside work—at least I do, but I realize mowing the lawn is more sporadic, less involved. Regular, day-to-day housework just doesn't naturally flow out of the male gene pool.

"I'd also want the lady of the house to understand that a typical man has a different definition of 'clean' than she does. When was the last time you visited a dorm room or fraternity? Been a while, right? What to a casual observer looks like a pigsty, a guy may very well consider his private version of the Taj Mahal. Right or wrong, men's standards of clean are just not as high as women's."

"Now who's talking stereotypes?" she asked.

"Well, sure, there are exceptions, but most guys can tolerate a lot of clutter. And when it comes to dirt, well, something must have happened at birth with the optic nerve. Even when the eyes see dirt, no signals travel to the brain that something is not right with the world."

"Again, my desire is not that a man has to see the dirt, or even clean 50% of it up, so much as he sees himself as a full partner in what's going on. I'm sure most husbands

> The three words that, said regularly, can save your marriage. No, it's not "I love you." It's "Let's eat out." (Or even better, "I'll cook tonight.")

don't want to saddle their wives with all the burden, but last time I checked, the tooth fairy isn't doing double duty. Someone has to do it. So what does the wife do? She's running out of options and getting upset."

He thought for a moment and said, "We've been down this road so many times. It's helpful to hear you express how interested you are in partnering rather than just considering me 'unhired help.' I need to have the larger vision reinforced of how meaningful this is to you. Even with that, though, I don't really know how to interject myself into what I think we both consider your turf."

"It's not my turf; it's just dirty turf," she replied.

"That's not how I see it. In most ways you are the one who has the final say in what we buy for the house, how we arrange it, and what goes on there. You really do see it as your territory, and that's understandable since you have more expertise with our homemaking."

"You tend to come in and out more as a guest than a co-owner," she stated. "That's the problem."

He paused and said. "If what we want is a partnership, could you see yourself as the 'head among equals'?"

"And how would that work?" she asked.

"I'm sure this kind of setup wouldn't work for all couples, but it might work for us," he said. "You don't do all the work yourself, but you oversee getting it done. You have me, the kids, and even a little outside help at your disposal. If we were a business, you wouldn't be the sole owner but a senior partner, with me as the junior partner.

"Like any senior partner you'd size up your junior partner—my abilities, interests, and energy—and brainstorm on how you and I can best serve the company. Who's good at what, who hates something less, who's got the time. Go ahead, what's your assessment of me?"

"Of all the chores, those you tolerate best are the left-brained, three-step ones like doing the dishes, vacuuming, and basic laundry. If there are power tools involved, like a chain saw, you turn into Super Fix-It Man. You're just not detail-oriented, so you miss all the small stuff like mildewed shower curtains and dirty ovens."

Putting the plates on the table, he said, "I do like chores with a few clearly defined steps that I can see through from beginning to end. If they're more complicated, I'll usually need you to line up supplies and review what should happen. Either way, it's important that you let me run my own operation from there. If I have to do it your way or you get on me later about missing something, it's more like you're my boss than my partner."

"You do realize that overseeing you becomes one of the chores on my list. You hate it when I nag and sometimes you hear my requests as nagging. So, you need to have a good attitude about responding when I ask."

"Yes," he said, "you've mentioned that I often start with a grumble. If that continues, you have the right to point out my 'bad work attitude,' but try not to wait until you're fed up to make your requests or you won't be nearly as diplomatic about getting me involved!"

"Agreed," she replied, "but being a junior partner doesn't mean you wait around like an employee who always has to be told what to do. Instead, you seek to an-

> Besides "I love you," what three words does a
> woman want to hear most? "I'll fix it."
> (Or even better, "I'll take care of it.")

ticipate needs. Looking for ways to get involved is so supportive; it's definitely in my love frame. Finally, as senior partner, I have the right to set the standards of cleanliness for this company—with your input, of course.

"Maybe now would be the time to bring up a topic I postponed earlier," she said, as she set two glasses on the dining room table to finish off their lunch preparations. "You know, sex and money."

"Sounds intriguing," he said, taking a seat by her.

"When we first got married I earned more than you did, and yet I automatically considered you the primary provider. I think this is true in many marriages—women look to men to provide for them financially. Similarly, men look to women to provide for them sexually. That's where the money and sex connection starts.

"From the beginning, you were pretty tight-fisted about spending. First you said you were like your dad—as if it were a genetic defect. Later, as we became more financially secure, you talked about the need to save for a car or a house or make some investments for the future. At times you've even taken control of the pocketbook and I had to ask for money, or you put me on an allowance."

"You weren't happy with those arrangements, and we ended those little experiments pretty quickly."

"Yes," she said, "because I saw you as free to spend money any way you wanted, particularly when it came to big-ticket items, like a new raft or a high-end laptop. At

Our Daily Chores

On a scale of 1-100%, who does the following
and at what percentage?

Do the laundry	W_____	M_____
Clean the house	W_____	M_____
Mow the lawn	W_____	M_____
Cook the meals	W_____	M_____
Wash the dishes	W_____	M_____
Oversee schedules	W_____	M_____
Vehicle maintenance	W_____	M_____
Vacuum/Picking up	W_____	M_____
House maintenance	W_____	M_____
Home accounting	W_____	M_____

Others:_____

_____

How do you feel about your arrangements?

_____

Can you hire out or delegate any tasks to kids?

_____

How could you become a "housework team?"

_____

The Predictable Grumble Factor

Ladies, men want to be heroes and save the day—or, at least,
wash the dishes! BUT before we do, we often have to shake
ourselves out of our natural self-focus with a grumble. That
grumble may feel intimidating but don't let it stop you from
unapologetically asking for help. Hearing the need helps
men realize something you've known all along— the workload is uneven! Requests, instead of demands, give space to
say "no," which frees us up to say "yes."

the same time you'd get on me for spending too much for needed household items or things for the kids, not to mention birthday presents or gifts for friends.

"I know that women generally buy the consumables and gifts; that's why those types of advertisers focus on us. I've seen that men tend to think long-term and buy items that have resale or investment value. There is a reason, though, why women spend on the here-and-now that you should understand. We spend according to our priorities, which are relationally based. That's why I put lots of thought into what the kids need or which pictures and knick-knacks will adorn and beautify our home."

"So, how does all of this relate to sex?" he asked.

"I'm getting to that," she replied. "If a wife sees her husband as the provider, but also senses he is holding out on her with the money, or criticizing her spending habits, or making her beg for it by putting her on some kind of allowance, well, can you see where I'm going with this?

"When a wife feels her husband is stingy with his pocketbook, she is likely to be tight-fisted with her sexual generosity in the marriage. When, on the other hand, she sees him seeking to understand why she views money the way she does, and communicating appreciation for her values, she will feel quite nurtured by his attitude.

"You mentioned you'd like me to see myself as your mistress, right? Well, think about the way a man treats his mistress. He never chides her for 'frivolous spending.' As a matter of fact, he is the one who spends on her—like there's no tomorrow! A man who generously opens his pocketbook up to a woman will find a woman who more freely opens herself up to him sexually."

"So, I should never take you for granted as a wife, in

any area, including, especially, how we spend money, but always keep wooing you as my mistress."

"Definitely," she said. "Marriage is not a state so much as a process, a process of wooing, if you will. The more I feel like you understand me and appreciate what I bring to our life as a woman and your wife, then, yes, the more likely you are to get frequent and adventurous sex. For a woman, it's all about feeling understood, appreciated, and nurtured. It frees us up, and turns us sexual.

"In the last few years you've lightened up considerably about the way I spend money—even thanking me for how I make our family, friends, and home such high priorities. I'd say that has contributed to deepening the trust level between us and acted as an invisible hand of support, increasing the freedom of my sexual passion."

"Did you put that on your love frame list?" Matt asked, peering over at her notebook.

"It's in there," Sarah replied, tearing out the page.

> We do ourselves a great disservice when we fail to understand how much making a home and making love have in common. A man, in particular would do his relationship a world of good to think of housework in a new, and likely more motivating way, as *choreplay*.

Identifying Love Frames

*W*ith sandwiches in hand, Matt and Sarah exchanged their love frame lists. "Ah, relief," she said.

"What's that?" Matt asked, taking a bite.

"Well, let's just say these may broaden out the subject matter of our discussion," Sarah replied, smiling.

"Don't get your hopes up! Actually, I'm amazed that you haven't waved us off from talking about some of this yet, but I really have appreciated your patience."

"I keep reminding myself that we're here to learn. That is what's happening, right?"

"Definitely," he replied, taking a look at her list.

Write Down Your Love Frame

On page 156 and 157 write out your love frame. Ask your partner to do the same on pages 158 and 159 and then create final versions to exchange and talk about.

Here's the question when writing out your love frames:

What are things my partner does,
or could do, that make me feel loved?

Sarah's Love Frame

1. Listen to me with understanding, empathy, and eye contact! Let me be a woman and vent my frustration, anger, and hurt safely—without becoming judgmental or defensive or giving advice.

2. Tell me that you love me often—and with feeling! Then show me love by coming up with new ways to spend time together. Act a little jealous every so often, even if you're not.

3. Tell me what your hassles and struggles are. Include me in your world and your fears. Let me in on your goals and your inner life.

4. Share family resources freely with me. We make financial decisions together. Take my saving and spending priorities seriously.

5. Let me know you are on my side by being willing to back me up or defend me when necessary. Provide the security of being trustworthy and honest as well as a responsible provider and planner.

6. Do little things that show me I'm special to you: give me a hug and kiss when leaving or coming home, read to me, leave me a note, take me on a walk, put your arm around me, hold hands. Call and text me regularly, particularly when plans change. Keep me informed.

7. Initiate conversations and spend time with me talking about anything and anybody. Spend time reminiscing—recounting our history with photos, talking about our kids, our experiences.

8. Take lots of time and energy to be engaged in the kids' lives as a loving father and mentor. Also plan for family activities. Be interested in how we can parent each one of them better.

9. Tell me what you like about my mothering of our children in specific terms and that you appreciate my work at home.

10. Partner with me on housework and other projects and occasionally surprise me by doing something unexpected.

11. Sincerely say "I'm sorry" or "Will you forgive me?" or "I was inconsiderate" when appropriate, and don't seek to justify or defend your actions when you know you're wrong.

12. Take care of things for me when I'm hurried or overwhelmed.

Matt's Love Frame

1. Express admiration. Let me know that I'm your hero for my efforts to support the family and to be a good father and husband. Compliment me even if I don't seem to care. Boast about my accomplishments. Let me know you feel safe and secure with me around.

2. Show me you're happy to be with me by doing things I enjoy with me, like rafting, bike rides, or even watching football on TV.

3. Give me time to unwind and space to work out problems on my own. Understand that this is not about you, but my need to process stress in my day. Encourage me to go out with the guys once in a while and pursue my interests with friends.

4. Flirt with me, tease me, and tempt me in any creative way. Initiate intimate touching while we're casually sitting together.

5. Tell me, verbally or non-verbally, that you really enjoy me and having sex with me—that I'm a big strong guy and a great lover. Be open to talking about sex, like you have been this weekend!

6. Make our sex life a high priority. Be open to my advances. Make love with me frequently, including morning quickies, afternoon delight and oral sex.

7. Take initiative with me sexually. Show me that you want me and my body, even 'beg' me for sex! Though I'm easy, seduce me by what you wear, what you say, and how you act toward me.

8. Be open once in a while to something in my "fantasy love frame."

9. Express your trust in our relationship by sharing your intimate thoughts and secrets. Allow me to see your vulnerability and be the one who can help you as no one else can.

10. Show you care about looking good for me by taking care of yourself. Be active and physically fit. Keep yourself intellectually challenged and willing to discuss issues and ideas.

11. When I make a mistake, even in parenting, act as if you didn't notice or correct me in a casual way as if it's no big deal.

12. Be as happy as you can be. Let me know your negative feelings aren't criticisms of me; it's other things that have you so upset.

My Love Frame (rough draft)
Write Down Your Love Frame

I feel loved when you:_____

_____

_____

_____

_____

_____

_____

_____

_____

_____

_____

_____

_____

_____

_____

_____

_____

_____

_____

_____

_____

_____

_____

_____

_____

_____

For more information on Love Frames...

My Love Frame (revision)
Write Down Your Love Frame

I feel loved when you:_____

_____

_____

_____

_____

_____

_____

_____

_____

_____

_____

_____

_____

_____

_____

_____

_____

_____

_____

_____

_____

_____

_____

_____

_____

_____

...see guide at IntimateConversations.com.

Ask Your Partner (rough draft)
To Write Down His/Her Love Frame

I feel loved when you:_____

_____

_____

_____

_____

_____

_____

_____

_____

_____

_____

_____

_____

_____

_____

_____

_____

_____

_____

_____

_____

_____

_____

_____

_____

_____

_____

_____

Once written out, both partners should then...

Ask Your Partner (revision)
To Write Down His/Her Love Frame

I feel loved when you:_____

_____

_____

_____

_____

_____

_____

_____

_____

_____

_____

_____

_____

_____

_____

_____

_____

_____

_____

_____

_____

_____

_____

_____

_____

_____

_____

_____

...complete a final revision to give each other.

Sarah spoke first. "So what do we do with the lists?"

"I'm going to keep yours in my planner as a reminder. For now, I do see an interesting pattern," Matt replied.

"So do I! You mentioned something having to do with sex five times—40 percent of your items. That's a lot, given the fact it makes up maybe 5 percent of our time together."

"Well, what I observed was the opposite. You mention touching several times but making love is a no-show. Please tell me you just forgot about it!" he pleaded.

"You know, that's funny. I didn't even think about putting sex in my love frame. It isn't because I don't feel loved by sex, I do. I guess it's just because sex is the end result of being loved for me. It's the culmination and celebration of our love. When the act is over, I often bask in a warm afterglow, knowing we really care for each other.

"So, I guess sex didn't make my list because, for me, it's more about us loving each other than about you making me feel loved. If my love frame is empty, sex has no positive meaning, but if it's full, sex is an expression of joy. It's the gold frame around my list—no, it's the gold frame around our combined love frames. In broad terms, my love frame is built around experiencing your affection."

"That's interesting," he noted. "You don't use that word either, but the idea shows up all over the place on your list. As much as you like affection, it would be smart for us to draw up a solid plan to make it happen. You know how I like the good old three-step approach."

"Well, if it's an affection plan you want," she said, with an air of drama, "it's an affection plan you'll get." She then snatched her list out of his hand, turned the sheet over and began writing. The earnestness and speed of her writing brought with it a feeling of anticipation. He sat quietly, waiting for her to complete the task.

A few moments later, she began to read:

> ### Affection Plan for My Man
>
> - Three times a day, hug me, kiss me, or tell me you love me in the morning, when you come home, and at bedtime.
>
> - Twice a day, give me a compliment about how I look, what I'm wearing, or something I've accomplished.
>
> - Once a day, partner with me on something like fixing a meal, working in the garden, or going shopping together at least.
>
> - At least every other day, check in with a text or call me to see how I'm doing and share how you're doing.
>
> - Once a week, do something special for me like leave a note, buy a little gift, or bring home flowers.
>
> - Once a month, surprise me with an extra-thoughtful gesture.
>
> - On special occasions, put some thought into events and gifts for my birthday, our anniversary, Mother's Day, Christmas, Valentine's Day.
>
> - Double or triple it all when I'm having a bad day or week.

"Now," Sarah summarized, "you've got a plan to shower me with affection!"

"Another helpful reminder to keep in my calendar," he replied in a surprisingly serious tone.

"Now, don't get all 'scheduled' about it," she said, nudging him. "As much as you like lovemaking to be wild and crazy, or at least spontaneous, I like your affection toward me to be just as wild, crazy, and spontaneous."

"You know me, I've got to plan to be spontaneous. Any

habit, including the habit of affection, takes a fair amount of determination and discipline to master. I know in the past I've delivered up plenty of good intentions."

"No comment," she said, obviously pleased with his comment. "Just remember, for you, affection may be a part of sexual foreplay, but I love affection for its own sake. So, in general, keep your touches and embraces on a nonsexual level. You can be sure that as my love frame fills up, affection will turn to passion, which turns to sex.

"And please consider that last line closely. 'When I'm having a bad day or week, double or triple it all.' You can count on it—once a month I'll have a few difficult days, and one or two bad days."

"You mean when you're having your period."

"PMS doesn't mean Premenstrual Syndrome to me," she continued, "it means Physical Misery and Stress. The stress comes first. One moment I'm doing fine, on top of the world, and the next I begin feeling touchy and claustrophobic. The world around me feels like it's closing in. If I seem like I've gone a little berserk, it's because I have. It's like something turned the dial of my feelings up from a 3 to an 8 or 9. Instead of living, I just start coping.

"Then, on top of all that, a couple of days later I get bloated and crampy, often have a headache, and sometimes even suffer a little dizziness or nausea. Like I said— Physical Misery and Stress. If there's any good news, it's that the best sex we have consistently happens right after the cramps stop, even while the bleeding continues. Although it's messy, I feel so much more relaxed. Then comes a couple of weeks of emotional and physical equilibrium before it all starts up again."

"You know," he replied, "it's too bad that the physical

discomfort doesn't come first, before the emotional difficulty. Then we'd both be clued in before your feelings take a nose dive. As it is, often we're both taken by surprise."

"You mean by my grouchiness," she admitted.

"Well, maybe I should just ask, 'How do you want me to respond when you go into a PMS funk?'"

"That's really a no-brainer," she said, shifting in her seat, "with tenderness. Give me space, but don't leave me. If ever I need your empathy and emotional support, it's during these times. Make it okay for me to overreact. Let me be irrational and illogical. Too often you try to correct me or balance me out by saying something like, 'You seem touchy,' or worse, 'Aren't you overreacting?' or the very worst, 'Are you having your period?' Those kinds of comments—and the attitudes behind them—will just set me off more. Check out your 'Plan.'"

"I know there are lots of times you've 'ramped up' your tenderness toward me. I really want to be there for you in the same way. It's just those times sneak up on me, and before I know it, I find myself reacting to you either with a nasty comment or by withdrawing emotionally.

"Is there any way you could signal me by saying something like, 'I'm having a tough day' or 'I think I'm starting my period'?" he asked, looking over to her.

"Maybe, but I can't guarantee it. My period usually comes every 28 days, so put it in your planner if you want. Otherwise, realize I'm a woman who will overreact at times, whether it's due to PMS or something else.

"If you make it safe for me to 'lose it' emotionally, and respond to me with kindness and understanding, I can guarantee that over time you will generate lots of affection for yourself. You may have to love me on some bad days

Top 10 Other Things PMS Stands For:

10. Pass My Shotgun
9. Psychotic Mood Shift
8. Perpetual Munching Spree
7. Puffy Mid-Section
6. People Make Me Sick
5. Pardon My Sobbing
4. Pimples May Surface
3. Pissy Mood Syndrome
2. Pack My Stuff
And the number-one thing PMS stands for:
1. Plainly Men Suck

And Now, For the Rest of the Story

Every woman with PMS suffers some kind of physical and emotional symptoms, but intensity levels can vary greatly from woman to woman and from month to month. Symptoms begin after ovulation and intensify as menstruation approaches. Then they cease. PMS symptoms include the following:

Physical Symptoms: dizziness, headaches, bloating, increased appetite, constipation, weight gain, breast tenderness, muscle/joint pain

Emotional Symptoms: irritability, anxiety, depression, loss of motivation, nervous tension, fatigue, memory loss, loss of concentration

but if you can do that, you will certainly be loved by me on many good days.

"Or, let me put it this way: The more you shower me with affection, the more I'll be inclined to shower with you and show you my affection. That kind of thing fits into your love frame, doesn't it?"

"Honey, you've always been able to turn a phrase. Any other issues?" Matt asked, reaching for his glass.

"Since you asked, I do have one other issue that we've talked about before; you getting a vasectomy. According to my watch, it's past time to do it. In our first few years we worried about getting pregnant. Then, we tried to have a baby, which really freed up our sex life."

"Which was great," he said, "with the added bonus that we were actually trying to create a little life."

"Yes, but now, since we're not planning on more kids, I'm not sure what you're waiting for—for me to go through menopause? That's soon, but still a ways off."

"I don't know. I realize we're not looking to have more kids. But the whole idea makes me a little nervous."

"Too nervous to improve our sex life? As you know, sperm only accounts for about one percent of what's in semen, so you're not going to lose out there. Birth control has done nothing to enhance our lovemaking experience, so we certainly won't lose out there.

"Actually, it's been a hassle most of our married life. We started out with condoms, went to timing, then the pill, and recently a diaphragm with spermicide. They all have their pros and cons, but none of them takes the spontaneity out of foreplay, at least for me, as much as the diaphragm. It starts lovemaking with a chore."

"We've talked about you putting it in earlier in the day,

but I know you're not fond of that either," he said.

"I don't mind it that much, but all such 'strategy' could be easily ended with a small cut of the knife."

Matt flinched. "You did have to mention the c-word."

"Hey, this is probably the single easiest thing you could do that would lead to more sex," she added.

"Actually, I've been thinking about this too, and your little 'it's-in-our-best-interest' pep talk confirms what I should do. I guess you noticed, sex is in my love frame."

"I did note that sex made it on to your list!" she said.

"You know, it's funny, because when I started my list, I tried to think of nonsexual ways I feel loved by you, but it wasn't long before my thoughts brought me right back to it. It's hard for me to conceive of feeling loved in our relationship without sex being a part of the equation."

"Well, then maybe the good news is that it isn't the only item in your love frame!" she stated. "I spotted a few other things you want from me, like some personal space, companionship, admiration, and acceptance."

"I'd say admiration tops that group," he said, looking over the list. "If sex provides my most nurturing event, admiration provides my most nurturing environment. I get a lot of my sense of identity from what you—the human being closest to me on the planet—think of me.

"Your criticism cuts deep even if I don't act like it, but when you're happy, and happy with me in particular, it brightens my world like the sunrise. I know you've struggled with disappointment regarding the time I've put into my career, so it's very touching when you tell me how much you appreciate the way I provide for us.

"Words of praise lift me way up. When you back off from trying to control me, I feel affirmed. Knowing you respect me, like me, trust me, and appreciate me is such a source of strength. When you tell me I'm a great handyman or a great friend or a great dad, well, that's almost as good as telling me I'm a great lover. And, you know, the more you tell me those things, the more I'm going to want to become them, and probably will.

"A few months ago I heard someone else singing your praise of me second-hand, and that had a multiplying affect, like getting a triple shot of self-esteem."

"Your love frame list is quite clear, but you could expand on your meaning of admiration," she said, "and write me a plan for it just like I wrote you for affection."

"I'll start with a definition of love from our wedding bulletin," he said, shifting through his notebook. "It's from First Corinthians 13. I'd say it best describes the kind of admiration and respect that I'm looking for. I brought the bulletin along because of this passage."

Finding his place, he read: "'Love is patient, love is kind. It does not envy, it does not boast, it is not proud. It is not rude, it is not self-seeking, it is not easily angered, it keeps no record of wrongs. Love does not delight in evil, but rejoices in the truth. It always protects, always trusts, always hopes, always perseveres. Love never fails.'"

"It's been a while since I've seen that," Sarah said, taking the folder out of his hands to look.

"A couple of lines, in particular, describe admiration and respect." He pointed to it and reread: "'Love is not easily angered, it keeps no record of wrongs. It always protects, always trusts, always hopes, always perseveres.' I'd say the key word here is 'always.' When I think of being admired, I think of knowing I'm always special to you. With so much going on in your life—your projects, and friends, the house, our kids—when I see you drop other things for me, I know, when it's all said and done, I'm the most important one and that means a lot to me.

"So, when you greet me at home with a hug and a kiss, when you put your hand on my shoulder, when you create a special romantic time together, when you say you're proud of me, or thank me, when you express your happiness with me, I feel appreciated and admired.

"Last year, for a few weeks after Valentine's Day, you wore a button which said 'I love' and over the heart you wrote Matt. I didn't tell you at the time, but that little gesture kept me walking tall and feeling special."

"You are special to me," she said, touching his arm.

He covered her hand with his, "Actually, one of the best ways you communicate that is by what you don't do. When you, as this line says, 'keep no record of wrongs.' It all goes back to acceptance. When I make an obvious mistake or mess something up and yet you treat it casually, like it's not that big a deal, I feel very loved.

"Like when I forgot to pick up our youngest from the baby sitter a few weeks ago. Don't think for a second that I didn't notice that you let me off the hook. You said something about how I must have had a tough day. I was embarrassed and defensive. I barely even acknowledged your graciousness, but, be assured, I appreciated it!

"We all need to establish boundaries so that people treat us respectfully. At the same time we all also have our hot buttons, struggles, and blind spots that necessitate giving each other the freedom to be imperfect and to fail."

"Which doesn't mean," she replied, "that we lower the bar of responsible behavior, only that we raise the bar of acceptance. Acceptance never provides an excuse for bad

Love Frame Quiz
What's #1-5 on your lists?

#1 Answer For Many:

- Men feel loved through sex.
- Women feel loved when being cherished.

But obviously there's more to a relationship than sex and being cherished. Men are generally more physically-oriented and women are generally more emotionally-oriented.

#2 Answer For Many:

- Men love recreational pursuits/hobbies (which include watching sports on TV)
- Women love conversation (especially concerning their relationships)

Now to get personal: In a nutshell what are your partner's and your top five love frame items?*

You	Your partner
1. _____	1. _____
2. _____	2. _____
3. _____	3. _____
4. _____	4. _____
5. _____	5. _____

What some people consider love, others do not. They may even dislike it because it just doesn't meet their particular need or desire. So, it is also helpful to learn what is not in your partner's "love frame."

*In *His Needs, Her Needs* by Willard F. Harley, Jr. and *The Five Love Languages* by Gary Chapman, the authors identify five love frame categories common to most couples.

behavior, and it doesn't mean either of us should sweep conflicts or hurt feelings under the rug for the sake of harmony. I need reassurance that you are sincere about our relationship, which means to me that you're willing to talk out conflicts and genuinely apologize, if necessary."

"Are you saying I have difficulty apologizing?!"

"I am far more touched," she said, "by a heartfelt 'I'm sorry' or 'I apologize' or 'I was wrong...hurtful...insensitive...inconsiderate...'—take your pick—than the most romantic 'I love you' you can muster. Maybe it's because they are not emotionally based. Or maybe it's just because I know how tough it is for a guy to admit he's wrong. It's even harder than asking for directions! It must be hard to admit failure if you're nearly perfect."

"What do you mean, 'nearly perfect'? Okay, I'll admit that I have a little difficulty apologizing. So, I apologize for my lack of apology! How's that?"

"A typical 'male-pology,'" she replied. "Thank you for making my point for me."

"Seriously," he continued, "it seems that when I do apologize, you typically withhold your acceptance of my apology. I'm in the doghouse and you've got the key. Until I grovel, whip myself, and make a dramatic, remorseful statement of wrongdoing, you're unwilling to let me out."

"I'm not insisting that you grovel, but you are in such a hurry to get everything back to right immediately. I just can't gloss over bad feelings that quickly. I'm wounded, shut down, closed off. You've got to allow time for my hurt to heal and my heart to open up again. The less defensive you are and the more sincerely apologetic, the less time it takes. You like math, so I'll put it in an equation."

"So," he said, looking at her, "what you're saying, if I

can put it in 'male-speak,' is that I win by losing."

"Maybe. Could you be more specific?" she asked.

"As a man, I'm geared up to go into battle and win. Men have done it for centuries. Obviously, though, that's a flawed strategy when it comes to relating to a woman. So, I need to define winning not as being the most logical, but rather as being the most agreeable or gracious. Do I want to be right or do I want to be happy?"

"You get points for being humble and honest."

He paused and said, "At times, I feel like I have to sacrifice logic or truth, even go to the edge of compromising myself, for the sake of harmony in our relationship."

"So, my feelings are based on irrational responses?"

"No," he replied. "I'm just saying it's a struggle. I get in trouble when I forget your equation and try to defend or justify my position. I have learned—even though it isn't always apparent—that your orientation toward intuition and feelings is just as valid as my leanings toward judgment and logic. Whether that's true or not in any given situation, I'd be wise to always act as if it were."

"What you're losing in youth, you're gaining in wisdom! The first item on my love frame list is to 'Let me be a woman and vent my frustration, anger, and hurt safely—without becoming judgmental or defensive or giving advice.' Why win an argument's logic battle and yet lose the war of keeping a loving connection? In my feminine world view, that makes no logical sense!

"I've heard that women are more feeling and intuition oriented than men—60 percent to 40 percent. It only makes sense that we are more sensitive to relational nuances since we are the ones who give birth, tend children, and handle the social agenda. So, maybe we can get nit-picky. Add to

My hurt feelings

+

your defensiveness and justification
of your actions

=

days to get over it.

~ or ~

My hurt feelings

+

your lack of defensiveness and justification

=

hours to get over it.

~ or ~

My hurt feelings

+

your lack of defensiveness and justification

+

your effort to sincerely apologize

=

minutes, possibly seconds to get over it.

that the fact that women get negative feelings out of our systems by verbalizing them. Given all this, you've got to give me chances to let the steam out of the kettle by talking out negative feelings and hurts. Once the steam is out, I feel better and regain a more balanced perspective."

"In the heat of that kettle steam, I can just plain forget all that, particularly if I start to feel your negative feelings are about me. Then I begin feeling defensive and start shoring up my side of the argument with reasons which, to you, sound like a growing pile of justifications."

"Or," she cut in, "you might say, 'It's no big deal.' That hurts just as much because you invalidate my feelings.

The more I sense I'm not being taken seriously or not being heard, the more our tension rises and trust drops. And each time that happens it's harder to come back from feeling angry to feeling affectionate again."

"So, how can I build up more trust with you?" he asked.

"That's a great question. Trust is built as we take each other's feelings seriously. As that happens, over time we create an vast supply of 'blue sky' between us."

"I'd like to do something on paper that we talked through during counseling a few years back," Matt said.

"What's that?" Sarah asked.

"Let's graph out our trust level during the course of our relationship," he said, looking for his notebook.

"You mean the way we each have perceived the level of trust in our relationship change over time."

"Right," he replied, as he reached for a piece of notebook paper. "We both know there have been some rocky times in our history, but I think it would help to get the overall picture in place. So how about this—take the short end of the paper and make the vertical axis the level of trust, say 0 to 100 percent, and the horizontal axis becomes the years of our relationship. Like so:

"For history," he continued, "you can put in year one, year two, etc., or maybe some key events in our relationship like dating, engagement, honeymoon, our first child, job changes, etc. Whatever you want."

"I'd need a roll of paper to do this justice," she mused

"True," he said, "but just focus on some of the main events that have shaped our trust level with each other."

"Like turning points?" she asked, meeting his gaze.

"Sure. Place dots on the graph between 0 and 100 for those events and then draw a line between them. You can even go under 0 percent, into negative territory."

She looked over the page and said, "You mean when we've gone from trust to mistrust, from being intimate allies to intimate adversaries."

He thought for a moment and then said, "That's a better idea. I should redraw the graph to more accurately portray what you're describing. It's not at all unusual to move from trusting each other into mistrusting each other.

"For whatever reason—real or imagined—we begin to believe that our partner is not out for our best interest but is indifferent to our needs or worse, using us to get what he or she wants. When we feel disrespected or neglected or manipulated, trust changes to mistrust and the sky between us turns from blue to dark and threatening."

She looked over his new graph and said, "Relation-

100%	Intimate Allies
Trust Level	- - - - - -History of our Relationship - - - - - -
-100%	Intimate Adversaries

ships are complex, but it's critical to stop a negative trend with a ready supply of forgiveness because feelings of mistrust are so damaging. We've both felt unappreciated at times, like we aren't really partners at all, just two individuals who happen to live within the same four walls."

He continued, "I guess this is a type of 'relationship assessment tool.' At least it should help us make an honest assessment—the good, the bad, and the ugly."

"This is a little scary because it's very subjective, but I do appreciate your openness to talk about things more in depth," she said, looking up from the paper. "How long do we have for this exercise? I'm going to need some alone time this afternoon to think about it. Shall we meet around three o'clock on the...veranda?"

"So, that's what we're calling the porch? We're living in such high-class accommodations," he joked. "Then I'll see you at three—on the veranda."

Love's Long-Term Equation

Intimacy
Openness, Support, Trust, Connectedness

+

Passion
Attaction, Sexual Desire, Romance

+

Commitment
Loyalty, Devotion, Dependability, Faithfulness

=

a Lifelong Love Affair

A Message for Him

A woman thrives on your tenderness when she is struggling. Track her monthly cycle, empathize with her emotional let-downs and validate her feelings. Sow seeds of renewal by abstaining—letting your sexual life "lay fallow" for 5–7 days while you focus on a nurturing connection with her. About the time her period begins, sensual desires also re-emerge and you will both reap an abundant harvest of sexual passion.

A Message for Her

A man needs your affirmation, respect, and appreciation to live up to his own ideals, not to mention yours. Since it takes over ten positive compliments to outweigh one negative comment, you certainly have your work cut out for you. So, keep a running log of specific things about him and his actions that you appreciate, and tell him one each day. Then go out bragging about him to your friends.

An Exercise for All

100%

Draw a horizontal and vertical axis on paper. Chart out how you view your relationship's *Trust Level Time Line*. Share your findings together.

Trust
Level

History of Our Relationship

-100%

Saturday Afternoon

PASSAGES, HONESTY, AND OPPOSITES

*T*hree o'clock came, and the couple reunited, ready to talk about their history.

Sarah began, "In charting the trust level between us, it helped me to identify other things going on in our lives at the time. We haven't had just one marriage, we've had four or five different ones! About the time we start getting comfortable in one phase, we start another. So, I divided my chart into five stages, one for each of our five marriages."

"Any particular reason for five?" Matt asked.

"Five major periods came to mind: dating/first years, getting established, young family, serious struggles, and full house. Soon we'll go through some other stages, such as older kids and empty house, and then our kids will get married and start a relational history of their own."

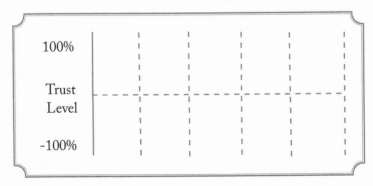

"Yeah, with us in the grandparents stage!"

"And we'll ask," she said, "Where did the time go?' I'm sure I'd never notice it going by so quickly without seeing our kids grow up. It won't be that long before our oldest will be the age we were when we first met!"

"Whoa, scary. Weren't we a lot more mature?" After a lengthy pause he smiled, "Okay, maybe not!"

Finding her place again, she continued. "The word that comes to mind for dating and the first few years is bubble. The problems and conflicts that would later surface largely stayed outside the bubble of our new love. Trust ran high as the feelings of newness allowed us to give each other the benefit of the doubt. We were wide open about things.

"I remember some of our early discussions about in-laws, money, sex, and the division of labor. Lots of things seemed so flexible and open for discussion. But at the same time, it seemed all too easy to slip into doing things the way we'd seen them done by our parents."

"At times we accused each other of acting just like your mom or my dad," he replied, "and hated it. In hindsight those assessments were closer to the mark than we'd like to admit. We sure carried lots of preconceived notions of what we should be as a couple—as a husband and as a wife—rather than making a new way for ourselves based on who we are and what's important to us."

She nodded. "It took time, and more than a little counseling, to see we were playing out our parents' roles in our relationship—the positives and negatives—mimicking how they treated each other and ran the family."

"I think," he began slowly, "the real problem was, we weren't being us. We were reliving their lives and their values with a few superficial changes."

"I identified the second stage of our relationship as getting established," she said. "This is when we began to get serious about growing up—finding real jobs, buying a house, making decisions about money and trying to change each other! With all the transitions came plenty of excitement, but also bickering and tension. Infatuation gave way to a power struggle. I wasn't all you had hoped for and you weren't all I had hoped for. The honeymoon became 'honey-why-don't-you.'"

"It seems that we took on both the role of reformer—seeking to mold the other in our image, and the role of conformer—suppressing our true self in order to please the other and be loved. But that kind of back and forth reform/conform strategy only served to reveal our immaturity, not to mention our lack of respect for each other's differences. We were left with a kind of dysfunctional love that depleted the passion we once felt for each other."

"I actually remember debating with myself," she said, "whether I could accept you the way you were instead of trying to change you into what I felt a good husband should be. Changing you won out, I'm sad to say!"

A woman often marries a man for his potential. If women married men for who they actually were, there would be far fewer marriages. When a woman loves a man, she says to herself, 'I could improve him. Once we're together, things will be different.'...[But men] tend to resist change...When a woman begins to encourage a man to live up to his potential, he misunderstands that as her overall dissatisfaction with him.

—Jay Carter, O, *The Oprah Magazine*, June 2003

Don't Conform and Don't Reform

When partners do not respect and appreciate their complementary differences they lose their electricity, i.e., they are no longer turned on by each other. Without the polarity, they lose the attraction.

This loss of attraction can happen in two ways. We either suppress our true inner self in an attempt to please our partner, or we try to mold them into our own image. Either strategy—to repress ourselves or to change our partners—will sabotage the relationship.

Every time you suppress, repress, or deny yourself in order to be loved, you are not loving yourself. You are giving yourself the message that you are not good enough the way you are. And every time you try to alter, fix, or improve your partner, you are sending him the message that he does not deserve to be loved for who he is. Under these conditions love dies.

The good news is that this process can be reversed; we can learn to find ourselves again [and rekindle love] without always having to change partners.

Excerpts from *Men, Women and Relationships,*
—John Gray

"You didn't want me to just play 'follow the leader,' did you? A wimp for a husband is hardly appealing!" he exclaimed.

"I know the argument," she said, "but unconditional acceptance is so scary. If I let you be who you are—rather than a better husband—who would meet my needs? Would those needs ever get met? How could I just let you be, when happiness itself seemed to be at stake?

"Then came stages three and four, pretty much mixed together. Our young family encountered some serious struggles. Starting a family brought a new set of expectations—that I'd be like your mother in her idealized state, and you'd be like the father I wished I had. We certainly brought in a lot of expectations that were not evaluated very realistically or critically."

"You went from lover to mother," he replied, "and started setting out some well-defined expectations of what I needed to do to be a better father. But instead of getting more involved, I started to back out emotionally. You turned into a child-rearing machine and I went into workaholic overdrive. Then the serious struggles began."

At that point, the tone of their conversation became more solemn. He began again, "I know we've talked about it many times but one reason I wanted to do this exercise was to bring up this period of our life again.

"Trust-wise, our marriage reached its low point when I became emotionally involved with, well, you know who. Besides the attraction itself, I said some awful things comparing you with her that I really regret. My dissatisfaction in our relationship at the time was a reflection of my dissatisfaction with my life in general. We've been down the road of counseling and talking and healing, and I think you have forgiven me."

"I have forgiven you," Sarah cut in, "and I'm so thankful the attraction didn't turn into a full-blown affair and give us a lot more trouble to work through."

"I presume it's naive to think that situation doesn't continue to affect your trust in me?" he questioned.

"I don't know, maybe it does somewhat. Forgiveness does not erase memory. When I drive by your old office

I still find my mind wandering back over some of those events. I was deeply wounded by the things you said—maybe as much as if you actually had had an affair.

"You know that women are fierce protectors of our love relationships. We can sense it when sexual energy is being directed toward our man, long before he is prepared to even acknowledge it. You initially turned a deaf ear to my concerns about a couple of the women at your office. Your defensiveness was hard for me to cope with. I know I'm not the jealous type, but you acted like I was the one with the problem because I was overreacting. Then my worst nightmare came true as one of them became quite attracted to you—and you responded in kind.

"It's interesting, though—on my chart I put a large spike in my level of trust in you at that time. For one thing, it was a relief to get things out on the table and find out I wasn't overreacting. When you finally did tell me you were taking an interest in her as well, I felt so betrayed. Even in that dark time, though, I felt encouraged because you didn't use her as leverage against me."

"You mean that I was willing to go to counseling with you and break off the relationship?" Matt asked.

"Yes, but beyond that, you didn't hold that relationship—and, the potential of ending ours—over my head. If you'd said that I had to change or else you were 'out of here,' I think our relationship would have moved toward divorce but after the big blowup, you took a large share of the responsibility for it—maybe more than you deserved. You told me that you weren't sure our marriage would work but that you were willing to try and, from that moment on, you would be completely honest with me about everything—there would be no sneaking around behind my back, even if it didn't work out between us.

"I still felt quite insecure, but what caught me off guard was your level of honesty—honesty plus a measure of acceptance, even empathy, for me. It was a watershed experience in our relationship, and it helped me to begin to take responsibility for how I was driving you away.

"I know that serious temptation often arises when complacency, boredom, and neglect exist in a marriage. Just knowing there was another woman 'waiting in line' for my husband provided quite a wake-up call for me."

He reached out and touched her hand, "We both need to be reminded of how important it is to fan the fires of attraction for each other—it's our number one priority. Being best friends is hardly a substitute for passion. A marriage requires ongoing passion to survive and thrive."

"You know," she said, "it was your commitment to be truthful that reminded me just how important honesty is. It's fundamental if I'm going to find out what you need and for you to know what I need from this relationship. In many ways, that crisis experience laid the groundwork for this straight-talking weekend. I guess the best reason to always be honest is that the alternative is worse!"

"Yes," he replied, "but there is a difference between privacy and secrecy. I keep some things to myself, as do you. You know, for instance, that I often struggle with making decisions and then regretting how they turn out. You can get pretty darn frustrated with me when I verbalize those regrets. It's an area of my personality you can find hard to love. So I pick and choose which regrets I verbalize and which I keep to myself. I only share a few of them—the ones I can't contain! The rest, I keep private."

"I agree. Privacy is legitimate except when it affects

Don't Trust Your Wife's Vow, Trust Her Nature

I wouldn't trust my wife for a second! We went through a ceremony some years back and she said, "I do." But that makes little difference to me. Maybe other guys think, "Hey, I married this woman. It's not a matter of how I treat her now. She's not going anywhere. End of story."

I can't afford to think that way though. Why? Because my wife is not a vow. She's a woman, a desirable, sexy creature who has emotional and erotic needs. Her heart burns with a fire, looking for love and sexual satisfaction wherever she can find it. W-h-e-r-e-v-e-r that may be.

Am I foolish not to trust in her commitment to be faithful to me? I don't think so. You see, I rely on something far more secure—I trust in her nature. Why would a woman who is treated with kindness and respect, who is cherished and accepted for who she is, ever stray? I suppose it's possible—anything is—and yet her feminine nature rules her. Unless I take her for granted, that nature will prompt her to keep looking to the one who provides love, romance and sexual adventure. That's me!

Do you think my wife is different, that she trusts my vow to stay faithful? Hardly. What I know about her, she also knows about me. There are many women (okay, more like a few) who would gladly take up residence with me.

So, I don't trust my wife and she doesn't trust me; which is another way of saying we do not take each other for granted. Instead, we work hard at bestowing affection and attention in keeping with each other's needs. Such sentiment provides the ultimate in compliments. Although we are both desirable to others, we keep choosing to come back home because it is so very satisfying.

our partner's well-being. Then we're responsible for telling him or her pertinent information. Otherwise, we cross the line into secrecy, which is a form of lying and deceit.

"I remember how hard it was to tell you about the many sexual experiences I had had when the time came. I appreciated the fact that you just wanted the general facts and not a bunch of specifics. Neither one of us saw how those past details were going to enhance our present relationship. But when you asked about something, I decided I would not shade the truth. Nothing erodes trust more— even when it's about something seemingly small."

"How small is 'small'?" he asked.

"I was actually thinking about last summer when you wanted to drop by your parents' house on our vacation. I felt another stop added too much to our itinerary, and yet I wasn't really clear about my feelings until after you told them we were coming. Remember that?"

"Oh yes," he said. "And after brooding over it for a few days, you unloaded on me because I didn't—at least you said I didn't—give you a chance to voice your opinion. That led to the worst fight we've had in a while."

"I realize, as I later told you, that I communicated my feelings in a vague way, like: 'It would be nice to see your parents if we have the time.' I was torn between what I wanted to do and what I felt I should do. Then, when you told them that we were coming, I felt betrayed, like you pulled a fast one on me and cut off my freedom to choose."

"But," he replied, "you wanted to play both sides of that fence. Time was moving on, and we had to do one thing or the other. We had to come to some decision, and then you blamed me for what I decided."

"I'm not trying to say I was right," she stated. "I knew

I was rationalizing my indecisiveness with the idea that I didn't want you to be disappointed, but I really knew what I preferred. Keeping those feelings to myself brought us both nothing but grief when they came out."

"As I've said before, you do me no favors when you try to protect me from the truth. I'm a big boy. I can deal with a 'No,' or at least see it as a basis for negotiation. I want both the freedom to come clean with you and the security of knowing you're coming clean with me."

"I know," she agreed. "The best thing would have been to communicate my indecision from the start and say something like: 'I'm feeling caught between what I want to do and want I think you want to do.' And then, when I clearly knew my preference, I should have told you straightforwardly about my choice. I don't blame you for not wanting to play, 'Guess what's on my mind?'"

"I hate that game! I'll tell you, though, any time you communicate your desires or needs with a degree of humility or vulnerability, it draws the empathy right out of me. Men want to help women, especially when we feel like we're the solution rather than the problem. Then we can do what we do best—attempt to fix something!

"We both want truthfulness as the solid foundation of our marriage. I guess my question is, 'How honest is completely honest?' Is it not appropriate to shade the truth at times to cushion the shock of complete honesty? Do we really want to tell each other everything?

"It goes back to privacy versus secrecy. But how do you decide what should be shared for honesty's sake, and what should not be shared, for harmony's sake?"

She thought for a moment and replied, "I'd say the answer depends on what you are trying to protect by being less than honest, and why. So much lying is justified for the sake of harmony, but each little lie cuts into intimacy and frays our trust. If we err, we should do so on the side of honesty to have a more authentic relationship."

"So, you want to be told exactly what I think each time you ask me how a new dress looks on you?"

"Sure, I want your honest opinion," she said. "Just be careful about how you say it. I have touchy issues, too."

"What if I have a fleeting attraction to a woman or you to a man? That's potentially a lot more threatening."

She paused and said, "It would be better, as you mentioned, for you to work on reminding yourself how attractive I am and 'make yourself jealous' by noticing other men checking me out, and that I do the same toward you. We'd both be better off noticing others eyeing our spouse! A touch of jealousy goes a long way to remind us that we can never fully possess each other. We are both attractive people with many of potential would-be suitors out there. So, we'd be wise to keep each other happy!"

"I agree with that, but we're talking about a different issue here: how honest do you really want to be? Should I say something if I'm attracted to another woman's body? You don't want to hear about that, do you?"

"Well not if it's some kind of subtle commentary about my body," she replied, "rather than a commentary about your struggle with self-discipline. Can't you just be honest and pure as the driven snow at the same time?"

"I wish! But it's not an issue of being pure so much as being a guy with millions of years of biological conditioning working against me. When I promised to be faithful to you I didn't vow to stop liking cookies, just that I'd make you the only cookie jar. Men are turned on by the sight of shapely women—that's biology. What we do after that point is character. We might initially react like Pavlov's dog, but we don't have to drool! At least we can exercise control over the second reaction.

"How about this proposal for our pursuit of greater honesty in our relationship: Any time we talk about our use of money we are completely honest with each other, because I think we'd both agree that finances are critical to the running of our household. No secrecy at all there.

"As a matter of fact, when asked directly about any-thing, we come completely clean with each other—no shading the truth, like you mentioned before. This means we're careful about what we ask each other directly. When not asked directly, we can keep things to ourselves that do not pose a risk to our relationship or partner.

"If I have a fleeting attraction to another woman or you to a man, for instance, why should that require creating unnecessary insecurities by telling each other? It stays pri-vate unless it leads to a change in behavior."

She looked over to him and asked, "Such as?"

"Going out of our way to cross paths with that par-ticular person, or spending time alone with him or her. If thoughts turn into actions, truthfulness cannot be compro-mised. Fantasies of naked bodies come and go without re-sulting in an action. If, however, I began renting X-rated movies or squirreling away pornography or surfing inter-net porn sites, the thought has become an action.

"When we carry through with our thoughts to an ac-tion, we then need to be completely honest with each other. That level of honesty might threaten our marital harmony, but it also leads to a more authentic relationship. And I can assure you, the idea of telling you what I'm doing will

> How do you decide what should be disclosed, for honesty's sake, and what shouldn't be shared, for harmony's sake?
>
> The answer depends on what you are trying to protect and why. Privacy is legitimate—it withholds information that is of no real benefit to our partner.
>
> But secrecy destroys trust—it withholds information that affects our partner's well-being or our relationship.
>
> The time to be completely honest in a relationship: when a questionable thought moves toward or becomes a questionable action.
>
> *Infidelity is not whom you lie with. It's whom you lie to.*
>
> —Frank Pittman

provide additional self-discipline for me.

"It goes back to what you said about honesty mixed with acceptance. If I feel that you won't come unglued over an impulse I have, say, to watch an adult movie, then I will be able to tell you about it and talk it through.

"Would you be open to another issue I have concerning trust?" Matt asked.

"Go ahead," she said, moving her paper to the side.

"This may sound mundane to you, but when you need to talk, your women friends seem to get your trust automatically. I'm often held at arm's length with suspicion. Maybe it's because they're proven listeners."

"Women want more than just information trading or 'report talk.' We yearn for back-and-forth, self-revealing 'rapport talk' that connects friends on a deep level. Talking like that gets us there," she said emphatically.

"I know women like to connect and it's starts early. Whether it's going out for coffee or drinks, shopping, or texting, girls are busy communicating with each other even it's just to talk. Now, when have you heard a boy call another boy, "Just to talk?" It just doesn't happen in the male world.

"We don't naturally communicate our feelings or talk about relationships. We keep to the important topics, like who won the football game! Given this, I'm very glad that your women friends can take the pressure off our relationship by supplying a lot of the kind of interaction you want and need. But it's not that uncommon for you to assume that I won't understand some issue or problem and then close yourself off from me."

"That's surprising. From my perspective, you go inside yourself much more than I do, and then I feel shut out. My hesitancy to share things with you does not come because I don't want to talk; I love to talk! That's why, as you said, the good Lord created girlfriends—he knew how much we need to talk things out. But I don't think it's healthy for our relationship if I get all my conversational needs met by women. I really want to talk to you. I'm just not always sure you want to listen or talk back," she replied.

He paused briefly and said, "You know that men tend to process things internally and women process verbally. So, if I'm going through a problem, I don't go to my friends and leave you out—I leave everyone out of it!"

"But I don't want to be left out of it. If you don't share your feelings with me—whether I provide any kind of help or not—how can our love grow? When I ask, 'What's wrong?' it's not because I want something to be wrong, it's because, like most women, I have an early warning radar system for trouble, and I want to steer our relationship around it. I care a lot about you and about us.

"Sometimes when I say, 'Let's talk,' you respond, 'About what?' like I must be grumpy or unsatisfied for no reason. That's so frustrating! It's like you saying, 'Let's make love,' and me saying, 'What's the point? We already have all the kids we want.' As much as you like sex for its own sake, I like talking for its own sake. Talking connects us emotionally, just as making love connects us physically.

"Sometimes I see you trying to listen but getting uncomfortable when there's too much emotional energy behind the words. Or if what I'm saying doesn't completely add up logically, you might dismiss it as an irrational tangent but you're listening only with your head. My women friends listen for why I'm feeling the way I am. Are you willing to listen like that—not just to what I'm saying, but to why I'm saying it? I know you love me, but do you really want to understand and know me?"

"I do," Matt said emphatically, "but so often I feel out of my league with all of this."

"I actually think there's something a bit more subtle that frustrates our relationship here," she replied. "Opposites often attract, right? I was attracted to you as a life partner because you have personality qualities I lack in my

Often men can not keep up with the same amount of conversation, but they can work at "pitching back"; Something like, "that's interesting—tell me more" is a sincere acknowledgement that can help as much as talking.

For ways to encourage more conversation, see Paul Coleman's book, *How to Say It for Couples* (pp. 47-53). His book suggests and illustrates the very best ways of talking with each other.

life, and vice versa. I wanted the security of a partner with more direction, common sense, and stability. You wanted someone more emotionally alive, colorful, and spontaneous. We both got what we wanted, right?"

"Apparently so," he replied, smiling. "We should have been been looking on eHarmony but instead we ended up finding each other on OppositesAttract.com!"

"Think of the packing process we went through to get here this weekend," she reminded him. "My style amounts to a stress-free, wait-till-the-last-minute-and-toss-it-in attitude. You're Mr. Thorough, with your lists of what to take for every occasion.

"I don't particularly like your means of packing, but I do like the result. We almost never leave something we wanted to bring, which leads to a stress-free vacation! I'd say there's an upside and a downside to every personality style. It just gets difficult because now we live every day with an opposite personality type. So, the very things which attracted us to each other—the traits that add balance to our lives—easily become irritants."

"Or sources of outright conflict," he said.

"Right," she replied, nodding. "I'm not attracted to women friends in the same way I'm attracted to you as a life partner. I don't tend to look for friends who complete me, but rather for those who understand me. Those women often have personality types similar to mine.

"Our relationship, if it doesn't blow up along the way, will be so much more complementary and effective because as opposites we bring the strength of different perspectives, abilities, and personalities into the mix."

"I've heard it said that we marry one parent and become the other," he said, searching for words. "You're saying something similar: We marry someone who will help make up for our deficiencies, and we befriend those who will empathize with our deficiencies."

"Right, but how does the parent thing fit in?"

"It's just another example of being drawn to both an opposite and a similar personality type. You're saying it's easier for you to talk to your women friends because they have an innate understanding of where you're coming from, gender-wise and personality-wise.

"Then let's talk about the different personalities we bring into this relationship. If being opposites helps us compensate for each other's weaknesses, then shouldn't that add to the trust level rather than detract from it?"

"It makes us stronger," she said, "if those opposite traits become complementary, rather than sources of conflict. Too often we have let them be the latter, and that has only decreased the trust level. Blue sky turns gray."

"For me it's an issue of attitude. If I can appreciate and honor the differences you bring, then your flint and my steel create a warm fire, not just a bunch of sparks. Shall we explore those differences in a positive way?" he offered.

"Sure," Sarah agreed, "let's do that but I think I've had my fill of 'exercises' for one day. You like categories and graphs, but I'm too right-brained for much of that."

"There's the first difference," Matt declared as he put pen to paper, "I'm left-brained, you're right-brained."

"Yes, and as a right-brained person, I'm going to confiscate your chart," she said, whisking away his paper. "I'll come up with a right-brained way to talk about this."

"Now, maybe that should be interesting."

"It will be. Meet me in the kitchen in half an hour to make dinner. By then I'll have something figured out."

The Magnificence of Magnetism

At some point parental love is no longer enough because parents "have to love us" and thus cannot truly convince us that we are special. That's where the wonderment of attraction between a young man and woman takes center stage. These "strangers" don't have to love us but freely choose to do so. In so doing, they recognize in us a unique beauty that compels them to "forsake all others" for us! We may be loved by our parents, but we are special to our spouse.

We tend to befriend people who understand us—our similars, and marry people who complete us—our opposites. After marriage those opposite qualities will either stir up contention or, if valued with respect and appreciation, provide the spark for ongoing solidarity and passion.

Our lives are shaped by those who love us and
by those who refuse to love us.

—Anonymous

In what ways are you and your partner opposites?

At present, is your oppositeness more complementary, contentious, or both?

What would improve your relationship right now?

Interlude on Boundaries and Forgiveness

Boundaries define who we are and who we aren't. They foster an internal resolve to take responsibility for the things we should—our feelings, attitudes, and behaviors—and to avoid taking responsibility for the things we shouldn't—other people's feelings, attitudes, and behaviors.

Boundary-less people are whoever they think others need them to be. They take on responsibilities, disappointments, and consequences that are not theirs. On the other hand, boundary busters seek to avoid responsibilities, disappointments, and consequences by imposing them on others.

Boundaries are not a means to control others or make demands. They are self-disciplined perimeters, helping us to identify ways to express genuine love, acceptance, and forgiveness. Boundaries help us know the difference between being used and freely giving.

As the couple gets ready to "celebrate their differences," it would be good to identify how boundaries can help us stay connected to, and reconciled with, each other.

Know Your Boundaries but...

Remember that a boundary always deals with yourself, not the other person. You are not demanding that your spouse do something—even respect your boundaries. You are setting boundaries to say what you will do or will not do. Only these kinds of boundaries are enforceable, for you do have control over yourself. Do not confuse boundaries with a new way to control a spouse. It is the opposite. It is giving up control and beginning to love. You are giving up trying to control your spouse and allowing him to take responsibility for his own behavior.

In a marriage, as in no other relationship, the need for revealing your boundaries is important. Passive boundaries, such as withdrawal, triangulation, pouting, affairs, and passive-aggressive behavior, are extremely destructive to a relationship. Passive ways of showing people that they do not have control over you never lead to intimacy. They never educate the other on who you really are; they only estrange.

Boundaries need to be communicated first verbally and then with actions. They need to be clear...

—Henry Cloud & John Townsend, *Boundaries*

Boundaries show us where our yard begins and ends. When someone violates our property—when they disrespect or wrong us—we can identify where the starting point is for reconciliation. Appropriate boundaries thus lead to extending forgiveness appropriately. They also raise our awareness of our own need to seek forgiveness.

How might this apply to you right now?

...Always Pursue Reconciliation

Forgiving someone does not lower the bar of responsibility or excuse bad behavior; rather it raises the bar of acceptance and love. Forgiveness does not dismiss a wrong as if it never happened. It releases the guilty party, even if he or she fails to apologize or show contrition. In so doing, forgiveness sets aside injustice for the sake of something more important—freedom from the consequences of ongoing estrangement and our own inner turmoil.

It may take a while to forgive—surrender our right to get even and wish the other person well—especially if there is no acknowledgement of the offense. But ongoing resentment and bitterness are toxic to our relationships and to our inner life and the only antidote for these poisons is forgiveness.

> *When we forgive, we set a prisoner free*
> *and discover that the person we set free is us.*
> —Lewis Smedes

Asking for forgiveness takes humble maturity, but it is more valuable than the longest chorus of "I love you's" we could string together. Ultimately, our apology communicates, "I need you to help me be the best person I can be, and reconciliation with you is vital to my growth and to our harmony."

Establishing boundaries of respect is critical. But mutual vulnerability, humility, and forgiveness will produce respect better than any boundary. So, compete for "first place in humility." The couple with the most-reconciled partners wins!

Love seeks the best, forgives the worst, and finds a
way to wisely live with the difference.

Looking for the Best Scriptural Text for a Wedding Homily?

Consider Matthew 5:44:

Love your enemies and pray for those who persecute you.

Granted, this is not the Bible's most endearing passage, but it may be the most helpful and here's why. Our enemy is seldom some stranger out there who we've never meant. Our enemy and persecutor is most often the one closest to us, who can hurt us most deeply: Our spouse.

Marriage has a way of bringing us to our knees, and this can be a good thing. Coming to the end of our rope reminds us that we are not the end all in this Universe. We must look elsewhere for help: ultimately to the One who created us, who knows us best and who loves us most deeply.

Such a need is readily exposed when it comes to loving that best friend of ours who has, all of a sudden, become our worst enemy, that lover of ours who has, all of a sudden, become our greatest persecutor.

It is in these terrible, gut-wrenching moments that makes or breaks so many marriages. Will we be there for our partner when they are at their worst and when we may be at our most vulnerable? Will we reach out for a power beyond ourselves to help keep ourselves together?

This one verse can stand in the gap for us, can remind us to embrace humility, to fight fair, to offer forgiveness, to return to each other's side, to live and love yet another day. So, while saying, "I Do," to each other, also say, "I Will," to Matthew 5:44 and to the One who can help you fulfill both vows.

Admiration and Respect

Sarah looked up from the table as Matt entered the kitchen. "I'm confident this meal will accommodate our conversation."

Matt stopped momentarily and considered the arrangement. "Looks tasty."

"I've spread out everything we'll need on the table," Sarah continued, looking over the ingredients.

Matt looked at her and said, "Need for what?"

"For spaghetti and salad. This meal should give us more than enough varied foods to help us describe each other's personality."

"So that's your right-brained proposal?" he mused.

"Yes. Choose a food and tell me how it illustrates an aspect of my personality. Then I'll do the same for you."

"Okay," he said, as he picked up the cheese close by. "You remind me of Parmesan cheese, not to mention garlic. You add such an interesting and creative flavor to our life together—like what we're doing right now. Without you I'd find that proverbial rut and stay there."

"Then you're the hamburger," she said, as she emptied a small package into the pan. "Some may think it bland, but I consider it a consistent, reliable staple—the stuff that holds our life together."

"Wait a minute," he protested. "If I'm the left-brained, hamburger type, I'm going to have to organize this little free-for-all a bit more."

She looked at him with bewilderment and said, "I've got a question: How do you organize a free-for-all?"

"By organizing it! Now you pick up half the ingredients, and I'll pick out half and, as we add our particular food into the meal, we'll give our little speeches."

"I'm supposed to be positive. So instead of saying you come across like a close-minded, uptight, control freak, I'm actually going to say I admire your desire to make a difference. You're such a take-charge kind of guy."

He looked at her and smiled, "Where I'm from, they call that a back-handed compliment."

"Hey, a compliment is a compliment," she noted, "but for the sake of this experiment in cooking, I'm going to be absolutely, 100 percent positive."

"Here then," he began, as he picked up the bottle, "you take the wine because I think you've already been into it! And I'll take..." The room fell silent as they began to pluck various items off the table and place them on their respective sides of the kitchen table in front of the stove.

"Ah, don't you just love the symbolism," she said after they completed their task. "From two different sides of life we come, mixing our ingredients together to make one delicious meal."

"Sounds a bit melodramatic, don't you think?"

"Work with me here," she said, arranging her items.

"Well, the hamburger's frying, the water's boiling, and I have the noodles," he said, placing a handful into the pot. "This ingredient reflects both our personalities. I tend to be the rigid, conservative, and cautious one."

"That has a wild and crazy streak," she added.

"Yes, but it's just a streak. You, however, have only a streak of cautiousness," he said, putting in a few more noodles. "You're more like the noodles after ten minutes of boiling: flexible, spontaneous, easy-going, energetic."

"How are cooked noodles 'energetic'?" she asked.

"Hey, work with me here," he replied, plucking out one of the noodles from the pot and tossing it at her. "How many of these things do you put in here anyway?"

"I never know but probably a few more than that," she answered, as she looked for the tomato sauce. Holding the jar up she pointed to it and said, "You're like this sauce."

"Rich!" Matt exclaimed.

"I wish," she replied, pouring the jar into the pan. "More like thorough and detail-oriented. You have a knack of getting into everything around you and getting something out. I appreciate your intellect, how well-read you are, your curiosity about so many things. You challenge me to think through the issues."

"Thanks. You're like the onion," he continued.

"I make you cry?" Sarah said, touching his eyes.

"No, you make me laugh. You're sweet, charismatic, vivacious, on the wild side. You do a great job mothering our children and guiding them into new experiences. After all these years I'm still amazed at how accepting and loving you are toward people. You've helped me change from my naturally cynical and judgmental self."

"We do make one fine mutual admiration society, don't we!" she said, looking at the table. "Let's see, I've got the mushrooms and croutons—this is a bit of challenge. How about if I swap them for your margarine and bread."

"Okay, mushrooms and croutons," he repeated. "You're earthy—how's that?"

"Mushrooms are earthy, but croutons are from..."

"My point still stands," he broke in. "I'm results-oriented and practical. You like to experience things, get your hands dirty, enjoy the process. You're a dreamer. You paint with broad strokes and like to see the big picture."

"I guess that works," she said, beginning to cut and butter the bread. "This is going to take a little thought here. Okay, you rise to the occasion like bread.

"Hey," she continued, protesting his questioning look, "your last one was at least this 'iffy.' You persevere and endure when the going gets tough. I can be a 'doom and gloomer,' but you're an optimist and hardly ever get discouraged or depressed."

"And how about the margarine?" he asked.

"Well, you're made of chemicals. No, I've got it. You've got an opinion about everything, and you're not afraid to spread it around. No, it's this. You're very self-confident and a hard worker. And I do think you provide our kids with a great deal of self-esteem and a sense that they can accomplish anything they put their minds to."

"I think it's time to take back that wine now," he said, pretending to reach for it. "Okay, let's see what I have left. Tomatoes. Tomatoes are easy. You are soft and on the delicate side. You're a giver; easygoing, pleasant, and humorous. I really do love being a—round you."

"That's sweet," she replied as she added some lettuce

to the salad. "Here's the cucumber. You've got the knife, why don't you cut it up."

"No, go ahead. Here, I'll give you the carrots, too."

"Okay," she said taking the knife. "Whether it's cucumber or carrots, you're straight and true. You come from hearty stock. You're reliable, with strong convictions and a strong character. I admire the way you communicate your opinions and ideas with such clarity."

After a few more minutes of bantering, Matt announced with finality, "The salad is finished, the noodles are done, and I must say that's the most unusual personality test I've ever taken."

"Oh, I've got one more observation to make," Sarah exclaimed, as she scooped up a handful of salad, "you're a very understanding man." With that she launched her hand over his head and released a fistful of salad, which cascaded over his face to his neck and shoulders below.

"Oh I am, am I!" he said, reaching for her arm as she tried to make her escape. Straining to hold her, he spotted the colander in the sink and grabbed a fistful of noodles. "Remember how I said you're like these noodles?" he asked, dangling them in front of her face.

With her free hand, she found the bowl of salad and reached back to pour its entire contents on him, but before she could lift it high enough, he intercepted the bowl in mid-flight and declared, "Food fight!"

Between fits of laughter and screams, the kitchen descended into a whirl of spaghetti and salad chaos.

Finally, Matt lifted Sarah up and laid her on the living room area rug, but let her roll on top of him as victor.

"So, what did we learn from all that?" Sarah asked as the action subsided. "I guess you're not such an under-

> *Chains do not hold a marriage together. It is*
> *threads [or noodles!], hundreds of tiny threads, which*
> *sew people together through the years.*
>
> —Simone Signoret

standing man," she said, pinning his arms to the floor.

"No, I'm very understanding," Matt replied as he surveyed the mess. "It's just that my wife apparently did not want to eat spaghetti in the normal way tonight."

"So, I am having an influence on you with all my creativity," she replied, standing up, a little out of breath.

"Haven't we proved the adage once again? Opposites attract," he said, picking up croutons from the floor.

"Like magnets," she smiled as she rearranged plates.

"I guess the challenge is to not let one of the magnets get turned around so they repel each other. How can we make sure that doesn't happen?" he asked.

"To me, the answer is spelled: r-e-s-p-e-c-t," she began. "If we grow to genuinely appreciate each other's differences—me being the minus and you being the plus or vice versa—then we will keep finding ourselves attracted to each other as intimate allies. If we lose that respect for each other's differences, attraction turns to rejection.

"More than any other relationship, marriage tests a person's ability to respect another human being. And respect sees differences as adding something to our lives rather than taking something away. If we can build respect and stay attracted, we will be a positive force for ourselves, our family, and others. Have I stretched this analogy about as far as it will go?"

"You're definitely pulling me in!" he said. "I'd say I'm

attracted to you because there is no one I'd rather have a food fight with than you."

She looked at him and replied, "Thank you, honey. I can't think of anyone I'd rather roll around in spaghetti with either. Did we need a little tension reliever or what?"

"Oh, so that's your excuse," he said with a grin.

"Here, things are arranged as well as they can be. How about we gather what's left of our dinner and do some vegging out in front of the TV?" she proposed.

"Sure," he replied. "Oh, and did I mention when I was being so nice—before you became so naughty—that you have a great way with words?"

"No, but you said that this morning. What do you want to watch? It's very basic cable out here."

"You choose," he said, tossing her the remote. "I'm actually surprised they even put TVs in places like this at all. You just can't get away from it."

"You know, I am really glad about something and this is another compliment to you. When we recarpeted our bedroom and rearranged the furniture, you insisted we not bring the TV back in."

"While we're passing out compliments," he said, "I must tell you, honey, you give really good compliments."

"Thank you. How so?" she asked.

"For one thing, they're frequent, and they're also very specific. You must know they're in my love frame. You don't just say I'm a good husband, you tell me very specifically what you appreciate about me as a husband—like that I suggested we take the TV out of our bedroom. You do know how to give a really great compliment."

"Well," she replied, "you didn't do such a bad job yourself in giving me a very specific, very sweet compliment about my compliments! Thanks."

"So, as we're watching TV, tell me, what do you like most about not having a TV in our bedroom at home?" he asked, as he reached over to the remote to mute the volume.

"I'd say, if you're looking for what stole half the conversations from families and couples, you don't have to look any further than that rectangle in the corner. I've heard the average person spends 28 hours a week watching TV. That translates into 13 solid years of his or her life. Just think of the dialogue not happening because of all the monologue it produces. I think removing it from our bedroom has increased our talk time quite a bit."

"Actually, it was you who suddenly had the vision for a 'love chamber' instead of a bedroom," he continued. "As I remember, the mantra was, 'If it doesn't relate to sleep or sex, it's gone.' So out went the treadmill, bill desk, and those old family photos and in went the mood lighting, music, candles, massage oil, and even occasional flowers—not that I'm in any way complaining!"

"I love the change," she said, "but I couldn't handle it when you replaced our light bulbs with red ones that one night. That had all the charm of a red light district."

"Hey, they were left over from Christmas. Not every idea is a winner," he sighed.

"What has been just as helpful as taking the TV out of our bedroom and planning to watch just certain shows without commercials. No live TV. Now, how about taking the batteries out of the remote control?"

"Hey, evolution destined that ancient man turn into modern channel surfer man! That would be frustrating."

"Yes," she said, poking him. "I'll take frustration if I

can also get more conversation. Conversation is all about words, TV is all about images. The remote control multiplies those images a hundredfold. No wonder people struggle with impatience, isolation, and loneliness. It makes me depressed just thinking about it."

"Boy, aren't we the preachers tonight," he said. "How about I use the remote to channel surf while you come up with some more deep thoughts on the subject."

"Here's a not-so-deep question: Why do guys have such a love for the remote? I'd say if you're looking for the phallic symbol for the modern man, that's it!"

"I don't know about all your 'psychologizing.' I do know, though, that men love action. The remote provides the ultimate action-enhancing tool. Women love stories, so they have less interest in flipping through the channels."

"You're saying men are more superficial," she said.

"Did I say that?" he asked with a nudge.

"I'm just interpreting for you," she exclaimed, as she took the device and clicked off the power. "Let's not debate anymore. How about snuggling?"

"Sounds kind of superficial, don't you think?"

"It sounds relaxing," Sarah said, sliding her arm around his back and putting her head on Matt's chest.

How would you best describe a great marriage?

- A Two-Member Mutual Admiration Society
- A Love Affair Between Best Friends
- Intimate Allies in the Journey of Life
- A Long Love in the Same Direction
- _____

Turn a Negative into a Positive

He is argumentative	—	has strong convictions
She talks too much	—	is friendly and outgoing
He's a "know it all"	—	is quite intelligent
She is so conceited	—	has personal confidence
He's too easygoing	—	puts everyone at ease
She spends too much	—	seeks to improve our life
He's so stingy	—	is trying to save for us
She's too rigid	—	is very organized
He never sits still	—	has so much energy
She's too emotional	—	is so sensitive

Love isn't blind. It's just quick to put on blinders!

What Women (and Men) Want Most

Turn-offs	vs	Turn-ons	Improvements
Low-esteem		Confidence	_____
Laziness		Industriousness	_____
Lack of humor		Sense of humor	_____
Self-centeredness		Sensitivity	_____
Little understanding		Imagination	_____
Lack of tenderness		Compassion	_____
Negativity		Positive outlook	_____
Dependence		Interdependence	_____
Extreme jealousy		Commitment	_____
Insecurity		Decisiveness	_____
Self-pity		Courage	_____
Dishonesty		Integrity	_____
Little ambition		Goals	_____
Overbearing		Supportive	_____

—Adapted from *Light Her Fire*, by Ellen Kreidman
Also highly recommended, *Light His Fire*.

Hello Talk, Head Talk, Heart Talk

Getting up from the couch, Sarah exclaimed, "It's been such a nice day. How about we take in some fresh air on our veranda before the sun sets. Would you like dessert?"

"Depends on what you mean by dessert. How about a naked lady covered with whipped cream?"

"I'll take that as a request for a beverage—of my choice—hot tea for me, cold tea for you," she said, disappearing into the kitchen. Upon her return she asked him, "How often do you think about sex on any given day?"

"It depends. Less often than I used to," he replied.

"Which was what, about every 15 minutes?"

"Probably so when I was 15 or 16," he agreed.

She paused and said, "You're exaggerating, right?"

"Not by much. My first memories of getting turned on came right after puberty, at about age 14. A rather large-busted dental assistant was working on my braces, and she kept using her breasts as leverage against my shoulder.

The sensation was so unusual and so pleasing. Not long after that, a cousin invited me over to his college apartment for an evening. He wasn't much for art, but he sure had a collection of centerfolds. I was fascinated—so that's what those things look like!

"When I got to high school the fascination grew. On an occasion or two I got to find out first-hand what those things looked like—and felt like. I remember taking a life-saving class and at one point the most well-endowed girl in the class needed 'saving.' The instructor chose me to go out and get her, to the envy of all the other guys in the class. I don't remember a thing about my technique other than having my arm over her chest as I 'rescued' her. Of course, that barely made up for then being chosen to give mouth-to-mouth resuscitation to one of the guys!"

"Life does have its little trade-offs," she mused.

"The group of guys I hung around with fed my natural interest in girls," he continued. "They never failed to brag about how far they were getting."

"That's disgusting," she said.

"Maybe so, but it's more stupid than sinister. When you mix a little male hormone with a little male bravado you're bound to get more than a little male preening."

"Sounds like the animal world," she stated.

"Or the boy's locker room, as the case may be. Granted, locker room boasting is more about insecurity than truth. Many of us joined in to fit in. I actually felt rather awkward and self-conscious around girls. You know that, but no one could get me to admit that my virginity remained securely intact throughout high school.

"A few of my friends valued abstinence out of principle. Others of us weren't quite so noble. We valued it out of lack of opportunity or lack of daring, or both.

"Either way, now I'm glad for what didn't happen. I don't have any memories of having sex with other women to contend with. As you mentioned, growing up is confusing enough without the kind of emotional bonding that sex brings. You were my first and only. Before you, the furthest I ever got was to second base."

"Second base? You mean being handsy," she said.

"First base is kissing; second, fondling up top; third, going down below; and home base—you score."

"No, what young men don't understand is, that's just running the bases! Scoring starts at first base, when embraces turn into the mutual pleasure of kissing. It continues as you get to second and a woman invites you to enter her heart by feeling and kissing her breasts. Then third base comes when she willingly opens up and welcomes your presence inside her. That's when you both score. So, you never went all the way, but you thought about it."

"Non-stop. Still do—with you, of course," he said, smiling. "Please understand, since my late teens things have cooled off considerably. The time from one sexual thought to the next has increased substantially."

"Like how much?" she asked, leaning back.

"I don't know. At least a minute for each year older I've become."

"So, now you go as long as 40 minutes without thinking about sex!" she exclaimed.

"Even longer! Back in my 20s, I'd get an erection just watching you undress. I could make love several times a day with no problem, and as you recall, sometimes we did. After a climax I could wait awhile, then go for it again. My problem was never coming too slowly, just coming too quickly.

"But age mellows a fellow. In my 30s I noticed that I increasingly needed direct stimulation to get and keep an erection. The good news was that premature ejaculation became less of a problem, and I began to focus more on your pleasure. At least, I think I did.

"Now, in my 40s, I notice that direct manual or oral stimulation is even more important and it takes quite a while after climaxing for me to be capable, not to mention interested, in another one. And one more thing—even given everything I've said, I'm not nearly as desirous of the 'wild and crazy stuff' as I was when I was younger."

"I've heard that after 40, men start to become women," Sarah said, smiling. "I'm waiting for that."

"What does that mean?" Matt asked, taking a drink.

"I don't know, I think it means that nurturing and romance become a higher priority for guys. I'm not sure how much evidence I see of that yet! What do you think?" she inquired.

"Sure, it's true. I realize life is hectic and when we get the chance to focus on romance and lovemaking, more than anything I want it to be a good experience for us as a couple. Better sex isn't wilder and weirder sex. That's just supplemental, to spice things up once in a while. The normal stuff is simply taking the opportunity to celebrate our love by joining our bodies. It's comfortable, affirming sex.

"If sex in my 20s meant getting it on with you as often as possible and pulling out all the stops, creatively speaking, now it has more to do with entering into life's most intimate experience. It's the one thing we do together that is unique to us. No one else on the planet gets to be a part of it—it's that locket of love we share together.

"I guess I just don't want monogamy and monotony to become synonymous, so I keep looking for a degree of novelty, whether it's a new position or location or whatever. If we're not done exploring the depths of our love for each other, why would we be done exploring the depths of our lovemaking with each other?"

"That's a nice way to put it," she said, nodding.

"Thanks. Now, how about you—as a girl, didn't you have some fantasies?" he asked.

"I was caught up—fascinated, as you put it—by some of the guys in teen magazines, rock bands, and movies. I followed them and talked about them with my girlfriends. Sometimes fascination turned to fantasizing. At times those thoughts turned sexual, but generally they were relationally based, much like they are for me today."

"And how are they for you today?" he asked. "If you were to have your wildest dream come true, in terms of our relationship, what would it look like?"

"That's a great question," she replied. "You're catching on to that seductive thing! My greatest fantasies probably involve being taken care of.

"Women can so easily have relationship anxiety, and moms have an added mothering anxiety. Anytime I take on something new, or our kids confront a risk or challenge, I can get pretty worked up about it. My fantasy is wishing someone would come along and make it okay.

"You fulfill that fantasy when you pick up on my worries and come into my world with understanding. I love it when you lend support in the form of a listening ear, and we talk through my anxiety together. It relieves those worries as I share with you on a 'heart talk' level."

He looked intrigued. "Heart talk?"

"You may remember," she continued, "in college I read a book identifying various stages of communication: hello talk, head talk, and heart talk. Hello talk amounts to what people say in an elevator. It's pleasantries. For a couple like us, it amounts to information sharing."

"You mean," he interjected, "like who's taking the kids to school, what's for dinner, where are the keys, when are your parents coming, how did the grades turn out?"

"That's right, the five basic questions of life—who, what, where, when, and how. This level of communication is necessary to keep the domestic front going, but it's hardly the stuff passionate, fulfilling relationships are made of.

"Head talk goes deeper. When we share our opinions and ideas we engage in head talk. A good example is when I said, 'I think this weekend would be good for us.' 'I think' statements characterize this level of communication, where we share our viewpoints.

"A particular perspective on which laptop to buy, how much money should go to savings, or even what we believe about the afterlife may be very important to us, but those viewpoints are not really personal ones that reveal our uniqueness. The same belief may very well be shared by thousands, or even millions, of others."

"I'll bet that's the level most arguments occur on."

"Probably so," she agreed, "even though very little gets communicated about who we are in personal terms. When I share the way I feel about something, though, it highlights why it is important to me and reveals something distinct about me. When I describe an issue I'm dealing with in terms of how I feel about it, I express my fears, my hopes, my pain, my disappointments, my joys."

"That's heart talk," he replied.

"Right. We may believe the same thing that millions of others believe, but we have our own feelings regarding how and why it's important to us. Heart talk uses the personal pronoun I and links it with our emotions: 'I feel.' We convey our unique feelings with phrases such as: 'I'm anxious about...'; 'I'm grateful for...'; 'I'm hurt when...'; 'I'm frustrated about...'; and 'I'm hoping that...' As we reveal our feelings, we let the other person in on who we are and that's where intimacy begins."

"I do recall you talking to me about that book," he said. "The best part of it for me was the author's explanation of why we often hold back from sharing ourselves. It helped me see why I have difficulty sharing my feelings.

"Fear of rejection holds us back. Sharing feelings opens up our vulnerabilities, as you said. If I share a hurt or an anxiety, I wonder what the other person will think. Won't he or she think less of me, hold it against me, or maybe even reject me because of my struggle? Even with you, those weaknesses are embarrassing. I especially hate expressing anger because it reveals a lack of self-control."

"But how can you deal with feelings such as anger unless you get them out and explore what's behind them? I've heard it said that anger is a secondary emotion we use to help us deal with a primary feeling. Anger acts as a defense mechanism. We actually feel ashamed, belittled, unappreciated, etc., but it's easier to express ourselves through anger than to deal with those other emotions.

"The problem comes when we fail to explore those deeper feelings, keeping them unresolved inside. It's like we keep stuffing them into a gunnysack. Eventually the sack breaks and the results, in such a concentrated form of unresolved anger, can prove to be quite ugly."

"Often I'm not even sure how I feel," Matt said.

"I know, I find myself there, too," she replied, nodding. "The more we can get in touch with those feelings, however, the more we are in touch with our true selves.

"Being able to express our feelings—negative and positive—is so valuable because they are us, in verbal form. They may seem inappropriate or exaggerated or even embarrassing, but they express how we see reality at that moment. Getting them out ultimately keeps us from repressing them, only to have them spill out later in a volcanic eruption of anger.

"When feelings are disclosed and received openly, we can see into each other's world. That's why I want you to share on a heart level with me. When you open up your feelings and talk about your most intimate joys and struggles, you honor me with your trust. You invite me into your world to let me know the real you."

"I understand what you're saying," he said. "That's the point the author made, too. Instead of being rejected for sharing our feelings, the opposite is almost always true. It's rare that people turn against us because they realize they've been given the gift of our trust. So the usual response includes acceptance, even empathy. They actually like us more, not less, because we're more genuine and they now know more about us to like."

"That's so true. Now, I don't mean to browbeat you, but there is a certain etiquette required when people share their feelings. Rule number one: don't give advice.

"When I share my feelings, especially the negative ones, I'm not looking for you to turn into Fix-It Man. I don't want your problem solving or solutions, and I certainly don't want an 'I told you so' lecture or life-lesson

> A certain etiquette is required when people honor us by sharing their feelings, and advice-giving is bad manners. A lecture is the worst form of advice-giving, and saying "I told you so" is the worst possible summation to advice-giving! We appreciate a listening ear, and we treasure the attempt to understand and empathize. Then, advice sounds more like wisdom.

number 85: I'm over-working again and should relax. I just want your support. I'm looking for a knight in shining armor, but he won't be riding an advice-spouting white horse. Instead, he'll be there to listen and empathize. It's Feeling Sensitive Man! He's my hero."

"Sometimes you seem to want my advice," he said.

"If I want your advice, I'll ask for it," she replied. "It's rare that you come up with something I haven't thought of, so even if I ask, you'd be wise to give advice tactfully—in a very non-condescending, soft-spoken way.

"From what I've experienced, the problem with advice-giving is this: It amounts to a head-talk response to a heart-talk expression. Vulnerable feelings are met with non-vulnerable thoughts. It won't take long for that to shut me down, at best, or make me upset with you, at worst. I'm never looking for a lecture, even a nice one!"

"Then the problem becomes how I'm responding to you, instead of the problem itself. I hate that," he stated.

"You can avoid that," Sarah said, sipping her tea, "by providing a listening ear and an understanding attitude. That's often all I need to talk out my negativity."

"Sounds deceptively simple," Matt replied, looking at her. "You're just looking for some sympathy from me."

She set her glass down and said, "Or empathy. I think of sympathy as something expressed on a hospital visit: You feel for the person's pain but empathy feels with the other person. Expressing empathy is such a tall order because we have to lay aside our own view-point, suspend judgment, and come into the other person's world to see what they see and feel what they feel."

He sighed and said, "Yes, even when we think their perspective is skewed!"

"Particularly when we think their perspective is skewed," she stated. "That's why empathy is one of life's greatest gifts. How about an experiment in empathy?"

"Is this another right-brained exercise?" he asked.

"Let's take, for example, the depression I went through right after becoming a mom. Grief comes when we experience a loss and turns to depression when it appears there's no way out. During the first few years of our marriage I racked up a lot of losses that felt hopeless, like losing self-confidence during some difficult job situations, losing stability and friends because of all our moves, and even losing the security of our relationship for a time.

"Your initial response to my depression was to say, 'Don't sweat it, it's no big deal.' Such a response actually added to my losses because it invalidated my feelings and dismissed what I was going through. Then, when you saw that wasn't helping, you went into a fix-it mode."

"I recognize," he said, raising his hand as if being sworn in, "that I'm guilty of responding to your feelings with fix-it advice rather than acceptance and appreciation for your vulnerability. Maybe you can get a little white flag and wave it while you're sharing yourself. It will remind me that your feelings are not a threat to me. I just need to swallow my solutions, listen, and empathize."

She reached over to pick up her napkin and said, "It's white, so will this do?" she asked, waving it.

"Sure," he mused.

"I do appreciate you hearing me out on this," she continued, "because the fix-it attitude, which makes sense in your male world, does not help when you use it in the female world, where I live!

"Feelings—including feelings of depression—just are. They should never be invalidated, because they're not good or bad, appropriate or inappropriate. They're simply a human response to a set of circumstances we face. Of course, how we act on those feelings is another matter.

"Before action is taken, however, the vulnerable position we place ourselves in when we share our feelings should be honored with total acceptance. When you try to fix me, it comes across as a kind of subtle judgment that my feelings are inappropriate. It can seem like you're saying I'm wrong for feeling that way.

"You do know that we women flush negativity out of our systems by expressing those repressed feelings. Once those feelings are verbalized—at least if they're met with acceptance—we feel much better and can come back to a place of balance and a sense of well-being."

"My problem," he replied, "was that when your depression hit some of its lowest points—the times when I

> Feelings are not good or bad—they just are. We can't control how we feel about something, only how we express and act on those emotions. Growing up is all about getting in touch with our feelings so that they are assets, not liabilities. We have feelings; they don't "have us."

should have had the most empathy for you—I felt like I was in danger of being sucked into it, like a black hole. At times I could empathize, but at other times your world seemed so dark that all I could do was back away from it. I don't say this to justify my actions, only to explain them."

"But that's when I felt really abandoned," she said.

"You seemed to think that if you empathized with my depression, you would assume responsibility for it, too. All I really want is someone to be on my side as I try to cope with the loss, whatever it may be. If I'm in a black hole and you follow me in with tenderness and empathy, it will help dissipate all that oppressive pressure, and my positive disposition will emerge much more quickly.

"One way or another, when I share difficult feelings they should not pose a threat to you because I know my feelings are my problem, not yours."

"How about when your feelings do come as a result of my actions?" he asked.

"Like I said," she asserted, "I've still got to take personal responsibility for them. I know it's not appropriate to say 'I feel such and such' and then go on to accuse you of making me feel the way I feel."

He nodded and said, "I wouldn't disagree with that. When such blame shifting happens, instead of bringing me closer through sharing your vulnerabilities, it makes me feel accused and defensive. That's when it's helpful to keep to 'I statements.' They remind us that we're taking personal ownership for our feelings rather than unloading that responsibility onto someone else."

"I know," she said, cupping her mug with both hands, "that sometimes I have unloaded the responsibility for my feelings onto you. But I want you to know that they're not your fault. I do accept responsibility for them.

"Whatever the cause, they're still my feelings. I can't help that I have them, but I am responsible for how I express them. When I say 'I'm disappointed' I want you to know that, whatever caused the disappointment, it is still my disappointment I must deal with—it's a problem stemming from my feelings.

"Here," she said, handing him his napkin. "You can wave the 'flag' when you sense that by sharing my feelings I'm accusing you of being the culprit, the one causing me to feel a certain way. Take it home as a souvenir!"

"Okay," he said, "but this can be such a problem for us. How can we better communicate in non-threatening, non-accusatory ways?" he asked, picking up his napkin.

"Well, I could take us through a simple, left-brained approach for that," she said. "Could you take some notes?"

"Now you're speaking my language," he replied as he placed the napkin back on the end table between them.

"We'll need a pen," Sarah stated.

"Just a minute," Matt said, momentarily disappearing into the house.

Levels of Communication

Hello Talk: "How are you doing" pleasantries.

Head Talk: "This is what I think" information sharing.

Heart Talk: "Here's how I really feel about it" sharing.

Heart-to-Heart: "Let's share ourselves with each other" back and forth.

Your Challenge?_____

If You Have to Fight, Fight Fair.
Better yet, Call It: Discuss with Care!

Anger is a secondary emotion prompted by a primary struggle with feelings of betrayal, shame, helplessness, etc. The problem isn't the anger, it's dealing with it. Instead of denying, nursing, or venting your anger, express it constructively.

Here are some Don'ts:

- Don't Generalize: One mistake does not equal a character flaw. Be specific about your grievance.

- Don't Exaggerate: Stick to the facts of the matter. Remember, you're not trying to win a debate.

- Don't Replay History: Focus on the current issue. Never bring up the past to bolster your case.

- Don't Name Call: This only raises defenses and sabotages any hope of a positive outcome.

- Don't Kitchen-Sink-It: Stick to one problem at a time. Don't throw in another, and then another.

Which of the above helps you to discuss with care?

Often the difference between a successful
marriage and a mediocre one consists of leaving
about three or four things a day unsaid.

—Harlan Miller

Non-Accusatory Communication

Matt came back to the porch with pen in hand, sat down, and asked, "So where do you want to start?"

"With the napkin," she said, carefully unfolding it.

"What I meant was, where do you start when you need to share negative feelings?" he asked again.

Sarah paused for a moment. "I heard a counselor on TV say that she could predict, with something like 80 percent accuracy, whether a couple would divorce by the way they resolved conflict. It became apparent, after 15 minutes of listening to a couple argue, whether they were willing to use basic ground rules to keep their fight from spinning out of control.

"The point is not to resolve every conflict," she said, "because, given our differences, some aren't resolvable. The point is to remain a team instead of taking sides, even though we may still disagree. A successful marriage is not about reaching agreement, but rather about staying connected during the process of disagreeing."

"Or, you could say, to agree to disagree—agreeably.

Conflict comes from lots of sources: personality quirks, gender issues, how-we-were-raised differences, even birth order issues. I've noticed, though, that our conflicts often boil down to the need to control—or the feeling of being controlled. Maybe that's the case because we're both first-child types who grew up being rather bossy. Whose perspective will win out? How do I, or how do you, feel about the other calling the shots about this or that?"

"Sometimes the hardest part is figuring out just what the issue is," she replied. "I know it often takes me a while to identify what's bothering me, so I just start talking and eventually find my way there."

"Okay, good. 'Identify the Problem,'" he said, writing in the upper left corner of the napkin. "Then what?"

"Unless I've lost it emotionally, I avoid getting nasty by taking responsibility for my feelings and using those non-accusatory, 'I feel'–type statements."

"Step two," he replied, as he wrote 'Describe My Feelings Using 'I' Statements' in the upper right corner. "And what happens when you lose it emotionally?"

"You know what happens. I start yelling at you."

"I like the first option better! What's next?"

She paused to think and said, "I make a request about what I want changed in a nice way, of course."

"Of course," he said, as he wrote in the lower left quadrant, 'Request Change in a Positive Way.'

"Anything else? I've got a quarter of the napkin left," he added.

"Sure," she said, taking the pen out of his hand and writing in the remaining quadrant, 'Give Time to Respond'.

"There we have it," he exclaimed, "the non-accusatory method of dialogue. As long as we have this napkin, nothing can go wrong with our conflict resolution."

"Well, we'll see about that," she challenged. "How about working through a struggle I'm having right now—in real time? Do you want me to describe it?" she asked, pointing to the upper left corner of the napkin.

"Let's not get too personal," Matt said, grinning.

"Actually, that's just the point," Sarah replied. "If I use the napkin approach to communication, I can avoid making it too personal, and if it's not personal, you don't need to respond with defensiveness, right?"

"Right," he said, answering with a nod.

"If I wanted to get personal, I'd use an accusatory approach. I'll start in that direction, but don't get defensive because when I'm finished I will change my tune."

"I am a rock, and a rock feels no pain!" he stated.

"Well, rock, meet the rock crusher," she began with an air of determination. "Here it goes. Obviously, we both know you want more frequent, more creative sex, but you always try to get your way by pressuring. Even this weekend you're controlling the conversation through constant repetition, like your dessert comment earlier. You know you can wear me down if you keep at it. So, we never talk about the things I think are important. Everything is always about you. Now, let me ask you, are you open to dialogue?"

"No. I'd rather run and hide!" he replied.

"Or, more likely in your case, stay and fight!"

"The thing that gets me most upset," he said in a serious tone, "is having my motives trashed. How can you or anyone really know why I'm doing what I'm doing? It makes things even harder when you sprinkle the words 'always' or 'never' throughout your comments."

"Obviously," she broke in, "I completely undermine

my goal when I create an accusatory environment for talking through an issue. I know I've been guilty of that."

"Also, using words like 'always' or 'never' incites tension. It amounts to lighting a fuse and waiting for the conversation to blow up. We've talked about this before."

"I agree," she said, pausing briefly, "but consider giving me some latitude on this. When I insert those words in a sentence, I'm using 'woman-speak.' Please don't take it personally. I use 'always' or 'never' for emphasis, to get heard. When they have come out of my mouth, you sometimes point out that technically you don't always or never do anything. But criticizing me for using an extreme word is never helpful. It always leads to tension, right?!"

"Right, but one word I'd like to see us both drop from our vocabulary is 'should.' Saying, 'You should have done this' or 'You should do that,' amounts to punishment for something in the past or demanding something in the future. Either way, it creates resistance and resentment. A simple request, or a recommendation that states the benefits of doing something different, communicates respect and helps ensure our point of view gets heard."

"I've thought a lot about the big difference our choice of words makes," she said. "Instead of putting you on the defensive, I want to make you an ally. I realize that my language can either anger and alienate you, or it can increase your willingness to respond. So, I've tried, in contrast to what I just did, to let you know that my frustration and bad feelings are just that—my frustration and my bad feelings—even if I still use 'never ' or 'always.'"

"I appreciate that because if I become the bad guy, then we can't really work out the issue. Instead of the problem being the problem, my lack of listening or empathy or

> *The words we use in our daily conversations with our partner can make the difference between getting along and getting a lawyer.*
>
> —Paul Coleman, *How to Say It for Couples*

something else becomes the issue. Then I'm the one who's got to change. Whatever circumstances are causing your pain, even a perfect response of empathy from me will not guarantee you a happy result. I am not you. Only you can change you and only I can change me."

"A perfect response of empathy wouldn't hurt!"

"You've got a point," Matt agreed.

"I'll admit that until a few years ago, taking responsibility for my anger, depression, and pain was foreign to me," she said. "There is a certain power that comes from playing the victim: the power of self-pity. But whatever attention I got for being a victim, it didn't make me happy.

"I'm convinced that willingness to take responsibility for our attitudes and actions reveals our maturity level. Happiness requires a choice, and it begins with choosing to be responsible for my unhappiness. Ultimately each of us decide how happy we want to be. It's life's sobering but freeing equation: Happiness is 10 percent what other people and circumstances bring our way and 90 percent how we choose to respond to it."

"You are the Wise One," he said, bowing, "and if I could add anything to your eloquence I'd say happiness is also our gift to those around us. Anything more?"

"Oh, I'm only getting started," she said, with a smile of self-satisfaction. "Watch and learn. Now I'm going to communicate to you the same feelings as before, but with

Responsibility = Response + Ability:
Exercising the ability to choose my response

My State of Happiness Is My Choice

Contentment is a state of mind, not of circumstances. Happiness involves a choice, and it begins with choosing to be responsible for my unhappiness. My parents, my friends, my spouse, my children, and my boss will act as they will, but nothing they do determines how I must react.

Between any circumstance and my reaction comes a moment of choice, my choice. Nobody makes me choose my attitude. Nobody makes me frown or smile through any particular situation.

I determine how content I will be—whether I'll be grumpy or grateful. I make all such decisions.

It's life's sobering but freeing equation: Happiness is 10 percent what other people and circumstances bring my way, and 90 percent how I choose to respond to it.

My State of Happiness Is also My Gift

The more at peace and happy I am, the greater blessing I am to those around me. So, I work hard at choosing to be hopeful, thankful, and joyful every single day.

Test: On a scale of 1 (miserable), to 10 (ecstatic), how happy are you right now within yourself?_____
Around your mate?_____ family?_____others?_____

a non-accusatory approach.

"First," she said, holding up the napkin, "identify the problem: One reason we came here was to talk about our sex life—and we have lots, maybe too much for me.

"Next, I describe my feelings using 'I' statements: I feel drained and overwhelmed by the intensity of the conversation and the constant references to sex. A couple of times I thought about waving my hand to put an end to it, but I wanted to hear you out. Your naked-lady-for-dessert comment, however, put me over the edge.

"Now, I request change positively: I don't mind if sex continues to be a topic of conversation, but I'd like you to be extra sensitive and not talk about it in a flippant manner. I don't want to disengage here or get upset," she paused. "What do you think? Take some time to respond."

"This is a real-life frustration, right?" he asked after a moment of hesitation.

"Yes, it is. So now, I'll wait for your response—and remember, start with empathy!"

"Well," he began slowly, "it sounds like you're frustrated that we keep coming back to sex without getting very far with other issues in our relationship. I'm sure I'd feel the same way if I thought we weren't taking time to talk about the topics I want to discuss. And I'm sorry for my flippant dessert request. You're right, it was over the top.

"I'm fine with not bringing up the 's-word' again this evening," he said, "and I won't even pursue any 's-activity' tonight. I realize I've largely set the agenda so far, and we've talked about it—a lot. I have appreciated your openness. Would you consider discussing it tomorrow if it naturally flows from what we're talking about?"

"Look," Sarah replied, "I'm not seeking a pledge of

celibacy here, but for the evening, I'll take it. As far as any particular subject goes, I don't want to unilaterally exclude something from our discussion.

"I'd be open to continuing to talk about sex as long as it comes up naturally. I just don't want you to bring it up so casually, out of the blue. You know, when I sense that you're making an effort to listen, I'm open to talking about virtually anything you want to discuss."

"Would you call this heart-to-heart talk?" he asked.

"That's a good way to put it. Heart-to-heart talk goes to the deepest level. It's the intimacy level, where feelings shared by one person meet an empathetic response from the another person—back and forth."

"So," he summarized, "there's hello talk, head talk, heart talk, and heart-to-heart talk—the intimacy level."

"This fourth level of communication encourages a two-way connection. It's not just about one person opening up their feelings; it's about both partners alternately sharing themselves and listening, which strengthens the bonds of understanding and acceptance. It's heart-to-heart."

"How about hearing a frustration from my end?"

"Okay, I'm open to that," she replied.

"I'll identify the problem," he began, picking up the napkin. "I don't have any complaint with our time here together. You've been very gracious to talk so much about what I've wanted to talk about, but I would like to vent a frustration regarding how hard it was to get here. We left home late Friday morning because one of us didn't have all her things packed and ready to go on time.

"Now, to describe my feelings using 'I' statements: Yesterday at home I felt put off and irritated. It was frustrating because leaving felt chaotic and disorganized. We ended up getting here later than we had planned. Once we got here, though, it didn't seem like a big deal.

"Since I want to "fight fair," I won't bring up past situations, but it seems that we often run late because it takes so long to get ready. I know there are lots of things for you to take care of, but I'd still like to get going sooner.

"Now to request change in a positive way: I would like to get to places on time. That might mean that you hurry your preparations, or, better yet, begin earlier. Now, do you want some time to respond?"

"Here's my response..." she started.

"Remember the e-word, empathy!" he interjected.

"Oh, yes," she said, nodding. "What I hear you saying is that you find yourself uncomfortable with being late, and frustrated with how long it takes us to get out of the house. You've raised this issue before, and I admit it—I do tend to be last-minute. But I have frustrations of my own because I have so many things to get together that you can be rather oblivious to, especially for the kids.

"In the past we've talked about me giving you a 'to-do' list of ways to help out when I get overwhelmed. If I could get that organized, it might be helpful! Other than that, I can make a stronger effort to start the process earlier. If you could bring up suggestions in a nice way—which means without any hint of a condescending attitude—I'd be very open to hearing them."

"That's a nice response. I know we've both got to get such frustrations out, or they go into a 'simmer mode.' Then, when we can't hold them in any longer, they boil over, making reconciliation that much harder. I really hate it when the process itself produces more conflict."

"That seems to happen fairly often," Sarah said.

"Yes it does," he said. "Sometimes, for instance, during a disagreement I'll be trying to make my point and you interpret what I'm saying as me being insensitive, which leads to more hurt and anger, plus now an additional issue to work out."

"Often all I really want is for you to express an understanding of my point of view. I'm not going to hear anything approaching empathy until you stop arguing your position and begin expressing sensitivity for my feelings. Otherwise, I feel bullied rather than listened to."

"Yes," he replied, "and all of a sudden the resolution of our original conflict is in doubt, and we're upset with each other again—for a different reason."

"Managing conflict is a delicate operation. It's not surprising that secondary conflicts result from trying to resolve a primary conflict. That's when skill and sensitivity are called for. We can always go back to our step-by-step napkin approach. It should help us to identify and deal with any frustrations—including the ones that surface during the reconciliation process. The ultimate goal is not to resolve every issue but to reconcile with each other.

"Remember, early on we had a method to head off day-to-day conflict and to share our thoughts and feelings. Do you remember that? It was BK."

"You mean before kids. Sure. We'd get together after dinner for a few minutes to get a temperature reading on how things were going in our separate worlds. We called it 'touching base,' and it amounted to a condensed version of a weekly date—a quickie date, if you will."

"Do you recall," she asked, leaning back in her chair, "that during one of those touching base sessions you came up with an acronym for what we were doing?"

> Relational success is not about reaching agreement but about staying connected during the process of disagreeing. Given our differences, some conflicts aren't resolvable. But success comes in maintaining a strong connection with each other—and not drawing lines—even though we still may disagree.

"It sounds familiar," he replied, "remind me."

"It was one of those kind of step-by-step guidelines you like so much, meant to create an intimate moment with your mate. The acronym was I-N-T-I-Mate."

"And again, what did that stand for?" he asked.

"The letter 'I' starts it with an 'I love you' statement about something you like or appreciate about your mate. Words of affirmation begin the process, as each of us shares what we appreciate about the other that day. Something like, 'I appreciated your thoughtfulness in shuttling the kids around today,' or 'I loved the way you made dinner so entertaining and fun tonight.'

"'N' stands for news. After sharing some words of appreciation, we give each other a news update on how our day went. This includes basic need-to-know details as well as the people, places, and things that made our day unique. This time isn't just meant for information sharing, but as an opportunity to let each other know who we met, what annoyed us, what brought us joy, what we learned."

"To keep us 'in the know,'" Matt added.

"Exactly. The T represents a target we have: a goal or dream for ourselves, our kids, our career, or our future. Getting to verbalize these on a daily basis, whether it's to lose 20 pounds or remodel the house or write a novel, helps us retain passion for the goal instead of seeing it get buried under life's practicalities. Sharing these regularly also gives our mate a chance to own them and to know if and when there's a change in our thinking or direction.

"'I' ends with irritants. This gives us the chance to share any complaints we have. Instead of letting them build up, we can express them as they arise to keep short accounts with each other.

"And finally, 'I' also brings us back full circle to another 'I love you' statement, which puts a pleasant P. S. on our time of touching base together."

Non-Accusatory Communication

1. Identify the problem at hand	2. Describe feelings with "I statements"
3. Request change in a positive way	4. Give time to respond to my request

Which step(s) do you find yourself most likely to bypass during a heated argument? # _____ # _____
Our fallback position: agree to disagree agreeably.

Using an I-N-T-I-Mate Conversation Plan

I – 'I love you' statements

N – News you can use

T – Target goals and dreams

I – Irritants... and back to 'I love you'

...to share time daily with our Mate

Saturday Evening

A Gentleman and a Soul Mate

As darkness replaced daylight, Matt and Sarah retreated to the kitchen. After loading the dishwasher, they set up a washing brigade for the pans.

"I do have another sex question," Matt said. "May I ask it?"

"Thanks for asking," Sarah replied. "Sure, why not? Just keep it light."

"We've used the phrase 'having sex,' and at other times, 'making love.' Do you see a difference?"

"Having sex or making love? Hmm. I would call what we're doing right now making love."

"Unless I'm missing something, you're stretching definitions rather thin," he protested.

"I like the term 'making love' because it includes the most important body parts. There's a line on my body," she said, drawing an imaginary line across her chest. "Having sex involves everything from the breasts down. Making love involves everything from the heart up. Theoretically you can have great sex with anyone, but great lovemaking comes out of a great relationship."

"Or it helps make a relationship great," he added.

"Yes," she agreed, "but I would never start with sex in defining the quality of our relationship, and I don't think many women would. This morning you waxed eloquently on what having sex does for you. Allow me to describe what making love—or being loved—does for me.

"Love connects—not just our body parts, but our hearts, our longings, our desires, our needs, our values, our dreams, our fears, our futures. When I feel loved I'm safe, as if I were cradled in my mother's arms, and maybe that's the best analogy I can use to describe it. Love is a place where I'm hugged and fussed over, where my needs are understood and made the highest priority. I feel completely accepted for who I am, but even more than being accepted, I feel valued, like daddy's precious little girl.

"When I receive that affection, I then look for a way to express it by caring for others. Maybe you could say men are genetically predisposed to spread their seed far and wide, but women are programmed to nurture that seed. Our genetic code has us looking for a man who is loyal, supportive, and committed to helping us parent the sons and daughters we bear.

"So, it makes sense that a man's fantasy life involves unencumbered sex with as many attractive females as possible, while a woman's fantasy life revolves around finding a strong, devoted, and affectionate male."

"Just like in the 'chick flick' we saw the other night."

"And unlike the action flicks you usually want to watch," she replied. "They're just too violent."

"Hey, where else am I going to learn the finer points of using semi-automatic weapons? Why is it that most women don't get into action movies, anyway?"

"Probably the same reason we don't operate the remote control when men are around," she stated.

"You can't handle the remote," he replied, grinning.

"No, you can't handle the story. Men don't seem to care about what's on, just 'what's next!' The remote allows you to bypass the slow parts, move through the buildup, and keep the action going non-stop—whether it's an action show or not. Women want to get into the story, the characters, how they interact with each other, their concerns, their fears, their hopes. The high point for women is not when the clothes come off, but when a couple makes an emotional connection, when they gaze into each other's eyes and feel a special closeness and oneness.

"That's why daytime TV and romance novels can be so popular with us. You can't just click through these stories. Instead, you get immersed in the experience of a man and a woman finding a way to come together—or not. Anticipation, not action, rules. The buildup is the story.

"Think of Christmas as a kid. The lights, the tree, the music, the family gathering, the presents. The longer you have to wait to open those gifts, the more you want to open them. Then you have 365 days to go through the buildup again. Anticipation makes Christmas that much more special. Opening presents is to the holiday what the 'happily ever after' ending is to some romantic novels. Women are like kids the night before Christmas. We love the buildup."

"I've read drama with some romance in it," he said, "but I've never read an out-and-out romance novel."

"You know, if I can pick up tips from the way women are presented in men's magazines, you can certainly learn a thing or two from romance novels."

"I'm game. Like what?" Matt asked.

"I think there are a few on the living room bookshelf. Let me look," Sarah said, vanishing from the kitchen.

"You found some," he said as she reappeared.

"Yeah, and I'll bet just looking at the covers will prove helpful," she replied, arranging them before him. "Unlike the newer covers that tend to just portray the hunky, shirtless guy, there's quite the variety here. What do you see?"

He reached for one of the books. "A nice-looking guy and a nice-looking girl or, shall I say, woman."

"Actually, you were more correct the first time. She's old enough to be a woman, all right, but the women on these covers speak to the girl inside us."

"The girl inside you?" he mused.

"There are many different types of heroines in these novels, all of them archetypes that appeal to the girl within. Here's the typical Cinderella or Snow White waif type," she said, pointing to one of the books. "And this cover pictures the free spirit type."

"And this one?" he asked, pointing to another book.

"Well, let me mention a few other heroine types, and you match them up with the book covers. Heroines also come as the spunky tomboy, the classic seductress, the nurturer, the crusader, or even a repressed type like the librarian who undergoes self-discovery. Then there is the boss. This kind of woman is as tough as any man, or tougher.

"No matter how take-charge and independent these heroines are, however, they will ultimately melt in the presence of a gentleman whose only goal in life is to cherish, affirm, nurture, and support them."

"That's what this communicates to you," he said, pointing to another cover. "Is this guy that kind of gentleman?"

"Yes, he is, but there are just as many male heroes that women are drawn to as there are female heroines. Being an English major and a movie buff helps here.

"The guy on this cover is your classic chief. He looks

like a prince, or maybe a duke. Chiefs are leader types. Think of John Wayne, or Marlon Brando in *The Godfather*. Similar to the chief is the warrior who saves the damsel in distress. He's the classic knight in shining armor like Orlando Bloom, or Bruce Willis in *Die Hard*. This cover," she continued, picking up another novel, "obviously portrays the bad boy type like Robert Downey, Jr. The title is a dead giveaway here as well: *Forbidden Love*.

"Then there's the swashbuckler like James Bond, Indiana Jones, or Aragorn in *The Lord of the Rings*; your best friend like Hugh Grant or Tom Hanks; a charmer such as Johnny Depp or Sean Connery. There's even a lost soul type, Romeo, or how about the Beast from *Beauty and the Beast*?"

"The beast?" he repeated, looking across the table.

"Well, all this is to say that there is no one type of romantic guy for all of us different types of gals in all the various phases of our lives. But all the men that women are most attracted to do have something in common. They treat us with kindness and respect. Remember, little girls are made of sugar and spice and everything nice, right?"

"Right!" he agreed.

"Women are just taller little girls. We like nice. We value being nice and especially being treated nicely. So, anything that comes across as abuse—mental, emotional, or physical—is like antimatter to a quality relationship as far as a woman is concerned. You're just not going to win over our heart with rude and crude. So, right off the bat, skip the body sounds, nasty gestures, and profanity."

"That's just the testosterone speaking," he replied.

"Whatever it is, keep it in check," she said, looking up. "Make it your aim to be an officer and a gentleman."

"I don't know—sounds like a movie."

The M & M's ®...

Movies Portray Togetherness

Okay, guys, you're desperate for some guidance in the romance department. Well then, start with something simple and visual like a romantic movie: the dreaded "chick flick."

Romantic movies make love the primary subject. Whether it's a drama or a light-hearted comedy, love's perplexing challenges find expression. Even though Hollywood film makers get it wrong as often as they get it right, some of these movies are just plain fun. They provide a safe environment to laugh, cry, relieve stress, set a mood, see a happy ending, lighten up, encourage dialogue, reassess what's important, and learn—together.

Music Enhances Togetherness

Bypass the intellect and move directly into the emotions with music. Music can set a calming tone in the home or a mood that expresses the specialness of your relationship. Songs have a way of speaking words of love from our hearts. Not only that, you can reminisce when "your song" comes on, or take to dancing at a moment's notice. And dancing is an inherently romantic activity!

Beyond listening to your favorite music together, consider a serenade. Sing a favorite song to your lover—with music backing you up, if that helps. The issue isn't the quality of your voice, but the pleasure of your partner.

...of Romantic Togetherness!

Meals Celebrate Togetherness

We have to take time out to cook and eat regularly, right? So why not add a touch of romance to the affair? The dining experience brings with it great potential to relax, share moments of intimacy, and take pleasure in each other's presence. In a busy world, meal time should be a set time to reconnect.

Just think of all the creative connection opportunities: breakfast in bed, picnic lunches, candlelight dinners. Whether at home or in the finest restaurant, sit close, make lots of eye contact, feed each other occasionally, use the same straw or fork, play footsies—whatever makes that moment a fun celebration of your life together.

Memories Reinforce Togetherness

Memories provide invisible yet powerful bonds between us. They help us to continually reconnect with each other by revisiting shared experiences.

What would an hour looking through family scrap books, photo albums, or videos do for a sense of togetherness? What about revisiting a special place or just talking about the "good old days"? Where might it all lead?

For a list of great movies, see Gregory Godek's book, *1001 Ways to be Romantic*, pp. 176–179. For music and songs see pp. 164–175, and his book, *Love,* pp. 379–383.

"Hey, if you want me going with you to Las Vegas to learn a few tricks, so to speak, surely you can come with me to a movie theater for a little romance injection!"

He looked at her with a grin, "I'm definitely going to need a movie guide for this. Take the idea of a gentleman. It seems more remote than romantic."

"Maybe the word 'gentleman' sounds old-fashioned, even aloof to you, but to me the concept conveys the essence of attractive maleness. A gentleman lives by his name; he is a man who is gentle. A gentleman can be counted on to treat you like a lady, to save you when you're overwhelmed or hurt. He will always be there for you. It is his solemn code of honor toward his lady.

"There is another side of a man that a woman yearns for, though, and that's having a partner, a soul mate. A gentleman will be there for you, but a soul mate nurtures you and your dreams. He gets into it with you."

"Gets into it with you?" Matt questioned.

"Yes, he connects with you on an emotional, even on a spiritual level. A gentleman rescues you from calamity, but then a soul mate takes over to empathize with your pain. He feels what you feel, without passing judgment or giving advice. He loves you for who you are and wants to be with you every step of the way. He is the man every woman looks to give herself to—heart, body, and soul.

"My favorite example from the movies is Wesley in the classic, *The Princess Bride*. For him, Buttercup was the woman he would always come back for, even from death. He was a gentleman and they were soul mates."

"I loved *The Princess Bride* too, but Wesley is a little too 'out there' for me. Anyone a little more realistic?"

"Okay, let's go a different direction with this," she said.

"Do you remember that film we saw many years back now, *The Bridges of Madison County*? It was based on a very popular novel about an Iowa farm wife named Francesca. She had a brief encounter with a magazine photographer."

"Right, I somewhat remember it," he said with a nod.

"Francesca's life changed forever when Robert Kincaid crossed her path," she continued, rethinking the story out loud. "Robert was part swashbuckler, part best friend, maybe even part lost soul—the man her heart longed for. Their four-day affair proved to be the watershed experience of her life, as her kids discovered after her death.

"During the couple's last evening together she realized that to go with Robert meant sacrificing the honor of her husband and the love of her children. Her adultery would be compounded by the even crueler act of abandonment. But to stay in Iowa was to sacrifice her girlhood dreams of living life fully with the man of her desire."

"Yes, I remember," he said thoughtfully. "What got me about the movie is that they never saw or spoke to each other again. Even after her husband died they never reconnected. Those four days together carried such meaning throughout their lives—a mixture of sadness for what might have been and hope from what was."

She looked at him and said, "What I found intriguing was what might have been in different way. Many who know the story consider Robert to be Francesca's soul mate. He was humble, winsome, and a bit mysterious. He embraced life with joyful confidence and refused to force himself on a woman—even the one lady he so desperately loved and felt to be his life match."

"What more could a woman want?" he asked.

"I'll answer that question," Sarah said, raising her

hand. "A woman wants that kind of relationship with her husband! Robert and Francesca connected as deeply as any man and woman can in four days, but it was just four days. During that time they experienced all the passionate dynamics of an adulterous affair—great intimacy, great magnetism, great sex. But my question is, 'Why couldn't Francesa and her husband have experienced those kinds of feelings for each other over a lifetime of marriage?'"

Kosher Adultery

An Ingenious Melding of Intimacy and Passion

You will avoid adultery by integrating its passionate dynamics into your own marriage. This is the captivating solution proposed by Shmuley Boteach in his book, *Kosher Adultery: Seduce and Sin with Your Spouse*. The following passages are from pages 40 and 55:

[Although] adultery is one of the most destructive and harmful sins that erodes the foundation of a marriage, the possibility of adultery—a.k.a. kosher adultery—is necessary to sustaining passion and novelty within a marriage. Kosher adultery is the perfect antidote to the greatest problem facing marriage—namely, that husbands [and wives] gradually become complacent.

The principal solution to the loss of passion in marriage is to have an affair with your spouse—to bring adultery into your marriage by cheating with each other. The goal is to see your wife not as a complacent and content woman, but as a sexual adventuress, a seductress, and a potential mistress. Conversely, the aim for a wife is to see her husband as a sexual tiger and her would-be ardent lover. Every wife has the potential ability to dig and unearth the Don Juan that lurks within every husband.

"They could have if they would have integrated the dynamics of that affair into their relationship," he mused.

"That's right," she agreed. "Recovering passion in a marriage involves a change in perspective and in attitude, not in partners."

"So," he said, "all we need to do is make our marriage an ongoing illicit affair. Isn't that why we're here? You become my sex goddess, I become your soul mate."

This Is the Best Brief Advice for Building a Passionate Lifelong Love Affair:

994

Gals: You want more romance? Give him more sex. (Try having sex every night—night after night after night after night—until he begs you to stop! Just try it as a little experiment. It just might transform your ho-hum relationship into a raging love affair!)

995

Guys: You want more sex? Give her more romance. (Romance her like Don Juan. Like Romeo. Like Clark Gable. Romance her every day in every way. Romance her using every single idea in this book—and then think up one thousand more ways to be romantic. And she'll give you all the sex you could ever dream of.)

Excerpts from *1001 Ways to Be Romantic*, p. 343
—Gregory Godek

And now—# 1002

Proceed quickly to your local or online bookstore and buy a book by "America's Romance Coach," Gregory Godek. Start with *1001 Ways to Be Romantic*.

"That may take an additional weekend—or two!" she said, matching his smile. "But we're quick learners."

"Right," he replied, bending down to put away the pot. "Let's see now, how long have we been married? Okay, I'm actually a clueless male," he admitted.

"Now we're starting to get somewhere. You've just entered my little 12-step program for the romantically challenged and taken the first step: admitting your need!"

"Then go ahead, O Enlightened One," he said, bowing slightly, "teach me the finer points of romance."

She paused and then replied, "You've got to see the big picture first. I'm not looking for flowers or chocolate or jewelry; I'm looking for a connection. Being a soul mate starts with a gentleman's mind-set of treating a woman like the lady she is. That doesn't mean I'm more or less your equal. It just means that I'm special, your very special best friend—the apple of your eye.

"Maybe you remember me talking about a husband of a college friend who would open every door for his wife. It got to the point where she would come up to a door, stand there, and wait for him to open it. Some of my friends made jokes about it. They even acted out parodies with such drama and sarcasm. But, deep down, we were all just jealous for that kind of male attention.

"Maybe I'm stuck in the dark ages on this, but I love it when you act gentlemanly toward me—when you open a door or pull out my chair at a restaurant. It means a lot to me when you offer your arm for support, carry items when we're shopping, or come right out to the car to help carry groceries in when I get home from the store.

"Even if I don't need the help, I still love it when you offer. And when I do need the help, my antennae go up to see if you really want to get involved. If I sense you are feeling put out or resistant, I tighten up inside and resolve just to do it myself. If I sense you genuinely want to help, however, I love it, and I love you for it.

"It's not that I can't make it on my own, but I'm looking for the attitude of a gentleman as much as anything. It's like the guy who will lay down his coat on a puddle for his lady to cross over. He's her bodyguard—ready, willing, and able to shield his lady from whatever difficult situations cross her path."

"And how much does this job get paid?" he asked.

"The payback is my affection, and lots of it. I can guarantee you won't regret your efforts. Trust me!"

"I'm ready, willing, and able, but I'm not always sure what your bodyguard job description entails."

"I'm not looking for you to take a bullet for me. I just want you to be on guard for me. Guard me against being overwhelmed by taking over. Guard me against fatigue by making the plans. Guard me against those hard times in my life by listening to me and taking my side. And, guard me, most importantly, against any emotional distance between us by working hard to keep connecting.

"This morning you suggested I sexualize my orientation toward you. I'd suggest you seek to romanticize your orientation toward me—which means be on the lookout for me. Look for ways to take care of me and nurture me, for chances to renew an emotional, even spiritual, connection with me. Communicate your feelings for me in truly personal ways, and not with ulterior motives."

"You mean, 'not to get sex,'" he said, passing a dish.

"Sometimes, but not necessarily. Occasionally you use romantic gestures to make up after a fight. That really gets on my nerves. Use an apology when an apology is appropriate, not romance. It's not about you giving me something so that I'll give you something back. Romance is cheapened when it's used as a bargaining chip to pacify me or get back in my good graces—or get me into bed.

"I guess you'd call that conditional love or, at least, conditional romance. Either way, it devalues a relationship because you're using manipulation to get what you want. If we have to barter things back and forth to get love and affection and sex, where does it end? Much better to freely give and freely receive—particularly when it comes to sex and romance. No strings attached."

Relational Weather & Blue Sky

Relationships go through seasons—fall, winter, spring, summer—and sometimes it's helpful to identify where you are in the cycle. Why? Because like the weather, our relationship can change, but, unlike the weather, we have much more control over those changes.

Some have found the term blue sky a helpful description of where they want to be. When you have blue sky, you've built up a storehouse of goodwill that helps you weather (yes, we'll use that term) the difficulties that might otherwise bring gray skies your way.

How's the weather in your relationship right now? Stormy, partly cloudy, partially sunny, clear and bright—blue sky?

_____

What would it take to see more blue sky appear?

_____

"Now just a minute, earlier you said I could manipulate you for sex all day long by doing nice things!"

"I said that?" Sarah said, hanging up the dish towel.

"Yes you did," Matt challenged.

"And I actually meant it. Use this as a barometer: If you're willing to hear a "not now" to sex and be fine with it then, yes, go ahead and do everything you can to get me into bed. It's all in the attitude. But we weren't talking about sex; we were talking about romance, right?"

"Yes, and I was looking to get a romance job description from an expert on what women want," he said.

"So, now I'm the expert?" she said, looking at him.

"You're a woman. Is there a better authority here?"

"Well, just like each woman looks different, has a different personality, and feels a different set of emotional responses, each is looking for something a little different from her husband or boyfriend."

"Surely there are some universals," he replied.

"Maybe this will help," she said, as she proceeded to take out two tall glasses from the cupboard. "I spotted vanilla ice cream in the freezer and we brought some Dr. Pepper. How about a Dr. Pepper float for dessert tonight?"

"You know I'm always up for that, but what does a float have to do with romance?"

"I'll tell you what," she stated, taking the ice cream out of the freezer. "You make these while I go to the bathroom. In the meantime, take some time to think about what you like about a float—not about the ice cream, but the soda. I'll see you on the porch."

"You mean the veranda. I'll be there."

Soul Mate Romance

Romance is not a once or twice a year thing. It's not reserved for special occasions, holidays, or just to get out of the "dog house." Romance has little to do with jewelry, chocolates, roses, or sex. It doesn't have to be expensive or sap hours from your day.

Man (or woman) is the center of real RoMANce. It's about sharing and giving of yourself. It's a combination of all the little (and big) things you do to say "I love you" and to let someone know how special they are. What is most romantic comes from your heart (and is created by your hands), not from inside your wallet.

Make it a goal to be romantic all year round—starting today.

—Michael Webb
Adapted from his preface to *The RoMANtic's Guide*
Check out Michael Webb's website: TheRomantic.com
Also visit: MarsVenus.com and GarySmalley.com

Ro-MAN-tics and Ro-WOMAN-tics are men who love the femininity of their women, and women who love the masculinity of their men. That love manifests itself in an ever-increasing fascination and fondness for our counterparts. Such magnetism derives its power from being mirrored images—male and female—fashioned from the reflection of the Creator him/herself.

God made man in his own image, in the image of God
he made him; male and female he created them.

—Genesis, 1:27

Soul Mate Sex

Soul mates know that romance is a non-utilitarian act. Its purpose is to make both partners feel special and to strengthen the emotional connection between them. Soul mates know that sex is likewise meant to strengthen that emotional connection.

If you're looking for the best, emotionally connecting "sexual technique," try this:

- Eyes-Wide-Open Foreplay
- Eyes-Wide-Open Intercourse
- Eyes-Wide-Open Orgasm

Even with bodies entirely entwined, sex can be a private encounter with our own pleasure—and all the more so when eyes are closed shut. Eyes-wide-open sex is an invitation to join each other—deep within our inner worlds—as we experience the wonder of passion together.

This is not so much a technique, as a way to deepen the bond that naturally forms between soul mates. When you first try it, you may feel awkward, even embarrassed, but that should dissipate. Keep at it. Sooner or later you will likely break through to a new place—a soul-wedded place.

A man shall be united to his wife, and the two will become one flesh.

—Genesis, 3:24

In his helpful book, *Passionate Marriage*, David Schnarch goes into depth about eyes-wide-open sex. See pp. 187-239.

The Couple Bubble

In his insightful book, *Wired for Love*, Stan Tatkin encourages couples to form a safe place, "a couple bubble," where each partner feels accepted, wanted, protected and cared for—a commitment to be there for each other no matter what.

In contrast to independence and autonomy, the couple bubble promotes interdependence and mutuality. Partners aren't blind to each other's foibles and flaws. But they recognize their "for better or worse" commitment includes the decision to take the partner in all parts, not just the ones most attractive and desirable. The following is an excerpt from *Wired for Love*:

The couple bubble is a term I like to use to describe the mutually constructed membrane, cocoon, or womb that holds a couple together and protects each partner from outside elements. A couple bubble is an intimate environment that the partners create and sustain together and that implicitly guarantees such things as:

- I will never leave you.
- I will never frighten you purposely.
- When you are in distress, I will relieve you, even if I'm the one who is causing the distress.
- Our relationship is more important than my need to be right, your performance, your appearance, what other people think or want, or any other competing value.
- You will be the first to hear about anything and not the second or third, or fourth person I tell.

On a scale of 1 (very little) to 10 (a lot), to what degree is your relationship a "couple bubble?"_____ How could it improve? _____

ROMANCE 101 AND BEYOND

*M*ounds of ice cream scooped into frosty glasses awaited Sarah's return. "I've been thinking about floats and romance," Matt announced as she arrived.

"And what have you come up with?" Sarah asked.

"Absolutely nothing."

"Then let me stimulate your thinking. If there's a universal," she said, "it's this: When it comes to romance, no woman likes it flat any more than uncarbonated soda."

"You mean bland," he said, stirring his ice cream.

"Flat. Unappealing. Tasteless. Lackluster. Dull. Flavorless. Stale. Generic."

"You're a regular walking thesaurus," he declared.

"No, I just know good romance when I see it."

"Or not," he added, taking a sip.

"Precisely. Generic romance amounts to getting a store-bought card with a signature inside: It's impersonal. It's flat. It's dull. No woman wants to hear sweet nothings from some birthday or Valentine's Day card writer!"

"Hey, at least it's something," he said with a grin.

"I suppose, if you're desperately thirsty, even uncarbonated, stale soda—or, in this case, generic romance—is better than nothing. But..."

"But you want it personalized," he interjected.

"Of course. That's what romance is all about: It's a personal expression of your love for me. Even to underline words in a Hallmark card or add one extra sentence personalizes it somewhat."

"I've never claimed to have great intuition, but I've got a feeling that's still not enough," he stated.

"Then you're with me here! The best romance comes with a personal attention to detail. Some women love to go bungee jumping and hang gliding, others prefer the opera and guided museum tours. A romantic begins by studying his lover to know her well and to know what she likes.

"I like red, so you bring me red roses. That's very nice. I'm taken by a blouse I see on a store rack, so later you go back and buy it. That's being attentive. You hear me express that I'd love to read a certain book, and lo and behold, it shows up on my night stand. That's touching.

"It's not about the things you give me or how much those things cost. It's about what they represent. When you pay attention to the details, it means you're thinking of me and want to make me feel special and affirmed.

"You're a list person. Keep a running record of things that catch my fancy and then think up special moments to express your thoughtfulness.

"A great word to add to your romance vocabulary is 'pamper.' Women are constantly giving, and consequently we can end up feeling used up and neglected. I appreciate it when you change the oil in my car, but it's just not the same as indulging me with a bubble bath or taking over all the housework on a Saturday. A few nurturing gestures go a long way in renewing my spirit and reminding me just how great a guy you are.

"Now, how do you like your coffee?" she asked.

"What is this, beverage night? Straight black."

"And how do I like my coffee?" she asked.

Looking puzzled, he said, "With cream and sugar."

"Romance can always be improved with 'cream and sugar'—a little style and flair. Whether they're red, yellow, or pink—one, three, or a dozen—roses are great. But instead of giving them to me in a vase, make a trail of petals leading through the house to the vase, with little notes of appreciation along the way. Or, when you bring home the blouse I like, put it in the closet with a necklace around it for me to discover. Or, with the book I mentioned, insert a little handmade bookmark with a message of love.

"The idea here is to start with a basic romantic concept and then expand it and give it an unusual, personal twist that you think I would appreciate. All of a sudden a good romantic idea becomes a great one."

"Sounds like a little creativity is in order," he said.

"That's the difference between men and women. I know guys like to be romanced and treated special, too—who doesn't? But your version of romance is uncomplicated, like getting tickets to the ball game or a gift certificate for a power tool or a 'get out of jail free' punch card to use when you do something totally insensitive and don't want to suffer the consequences."

"By the way, I really appreciated that card. It was a real life saver. Too bad I used it up so quickly!" he joked.

"What makes guys so easy is that as long as sex is included in a woman's romantic efforts, well, I'll bet I could skip all the other nice gestures, move right to something on your fantasy wish list, and you'd be tickled pink. But romancing a woman is not so simple. A woman's life involves a web of interconnected relationships and interests; great romance for a woman takes that web seriously."

"It does sound a bit complicated," Matt replied.

"Not really. Great romance for a woman isn't especially complicated, but it does invite complications."

"Invite complications?" he mused.

"Let me give you an ideal here. A woman loves it when her man connects various aspects of their lives together. So, let's dream up a girl's fun week. On Monday you ask me to go out for dinner and a movie on Friday. You're thinking ahead. I can prepare myself and look forward to our time together. I love the forethought—and I'm thrilled that you've already line up a baby sitter!

"On Wednesday, I get a phone call, and you mention that you're looking forward to our time together. 'I've got some exciting things to talk about,' you say, knowing how much I love a good buildup. Now you're on a roll!

"Thursday comes and I find sticky notes attached to the bathroom mirror, to one of my favorite coffee mugs, on my purse, and a few other places. The first one says, 'You are delightful,' and then each one adds to how you find me so delightful. I love the praise.

"You also know that I enjoy dressing up once in a while. So you mention, as you get home from work Friday, that it would be nice to dress up and that maybe I could wear a certain dress you like. When we arrive at the restaurant, a little gift—something you clearly wrapped yourself—awaits me. It's that pair of earrings I told a girl-friend I liked. You must have called around to my friends ahead of time. How thoughtful, and so very charming.

"During dinner you 'get into it' with me. We talk and laugh, just like you said we would. We do some reminisc-ing, and you share some feelings about how wonderful it's been to see our little family grow up. In our 'give and take' you listen and ask me attentive questions along the way. The time goes by quickly, and we head off to the theater to see of all things, a romantic comedy.

"Then, to top off the evening, after we get home you have another little gift—a CD featuring the soundtrack of the movie we just watched. You start a fire in the fireplace, pour some wine for us, and put on the music. We listen awhile, and you propose a toast. Then you roll up our area rug in the family room and we slow dance."

He raised his hand. "I must have forgotten to do some-thing on Tuesday for this 'fun week.'"

"No problem, because the following Monday morning you leave a card on the kitchen table that expresses what a great time you had Friday evening. And with that, you've tied it all together—time alone with you, kids taken care of, checking with my friends to see what I might like in a gift, a little dinner, a little sharing, reminiscing and laughter, a touching romantic comedy, a little dancing, and a thank-you note to top it all off! Not all that expensive, not all that time-consuming, but tied wonderfully together with some touching creativity—just what a girl lives for—an absolute lovely week of romance."

"By the way, does lovemaking play any part in this?"

"Oh, absolutely," she stated with a nod.

"Just checking," he replied.

> Being consistently romantic produces a cumulative effect: Your life will be revitalized, your spirit will blossom, your partner will fall in love with you again.
>
> A pretty good payoff for a little togetherness, wouldn't you say! This cumulative effect of romance counterbalances the negative effect of 'relationship entropy,' which is the natural tendency of couples to drift apart unless they actively work on their relationship.
>
> —Gregory Godek

"To be more specific—the mind-blowing, multiple-orgasm type. What would fun week be without a fireworks display? I have to believe you enjoyed yourself as well!"

After finishing his float, he exclaimed, "If I replaced all half-hearted, generic romance with something more personal, more interconnected, something like fun week, then I'd be like Wesley from The Princess Bride."

"Then you'd be Wesley-like," she countered. "I don't want someone else, I want you—and a long string of wonderful, shared experiences—great and small—with you!"

"If you're hormonally challenged, I'm romantically challenged. I guess I'm just not very good at it," he said.

She looked up at him and sighed, "Now, I didn't just hear the makings of an excuse, did I? Please tell me I'm wrong. Sure, there are plenty of excuses for not being romantic: you can't afford it, or you shouldn't need to prove your love, or you're too tired, or you don't have the time, or you're not very good at it. All those sound like great reasons for not working to improve our sex life too. Don't you think?"

"Okay, I get the point," Matt stated. "You're brutal!"

"A girl's gotta do what a girl's gotta do," she said. "You just gave me too good an opening. Actually, you've done lots of sweet, romantic things, and I wonder if you know how much I have appreciated them.

"The 'welcome-back' office party you threw for me a few years back comes to mind. You picked up on the difficulty I was undergoing, feeling like I didn't fit in very well as a part-timer, and you organized everything from the singing telegram, the flowers, and my co-workers' speeches, to the signs, the balloons, and the cake. Don't think I missed any detail. I felt a little embarrassed, but so affirmed by you, and, through you, by the office folks as well. You created that 'wow factor.'

"I loved it too when you organized the kids and made me a special Mother's Day video. You all obviously enjoyed yourselves, and you can bet I enjoyed watching it. All the effort spent made it special. Another big 'wow.'

"Then there was the surprise trip you set up to this very spot on our tenth anniversary. You got your mom to baby sit, organized the food, and picked me up at the mall, of all places. That was a nice touch. The whole trip felt like a second honeymoon, which is probably why we have such fond memories of this place."

He paused and replied, "That was a great trip."

Valentine Day's Three Most Popular
Gifts Celebrate the Three
Ingredients of Love

- Flowers: the beautiful connection of *intimacy*.
- Chocolate: the decadent sweetness of *passion*.
- Wine: the time-tested vintage of *commitment*.

Romance 101

Study your lover to find out what she or he likes.
Adventurous & Daring vs. Easygoing & Stress-Free
"Let's do something" vs. "Let's just relax"
Spontaneous vs. Scheduled

Romance 201

Take a romantic idea and give it a unique twist

Romantic Idea... Expanded... Expanded More

Picnic... in the backyard... at midnight... at work
Recite a love poem... write it yourself... put it to song
Birthday card... given each hour... with clues to find gifts
Sleep over at a hotel... honeymoon suite... a bed & breakfast
Give a flower... under a windshield wiper... daily for a month
Dinner... with wine... candlelight... dancing... a carriage ride
Go to the movies... leave work for a matinee... then a hotel
Dinner at home (no kids)... catered... with pianist/guitarist
Gift giving... on a "half-year" birthday... for no occasion
Massage... daily for a week... show up at his/her work

Romance 301

For Her

Occasionally weave a romantic experience (a week–long "fun week") into the web of her connections: the people, places, and interests dearest to her.

For Him

Go for something on his "fantasy wish list." (If sex and mischief are involved, it's hard to miss!)

"Then there have been the little one-day outings you've organized for the family. The kids really enjoy them, and I love the fact that you take over all the planning and off we go. They've been some of the best times.

"I do so much planning around the home that it's a real godsend when you step in and take over so I can relax without having to make a single phone call or arrangement. It's like those weekly dates you used to schedule. Whatever happened to them?" she wondered.

"Life, I guess. Going out together on a date does feel special because it's about just you and me," he replied.

"I like that," she replied. "Just you and me."

Matt touched Sarah. "Let me ask you, what is the most romantic thing I could do for you on a regular basis?"

"That's easy!" Sarah replied. "You romance me best by spending time with me—working and playing—doing whatever together. Our lives are so caught up in stuff that we don't have a lot left for each other. I love getting away like we're doing now, because when we travel it's like we're on a private yacht. We go from port to port together. There are people around, but we don't know them. We just have each other to explore things with—it's fun!

"You've often said that if we don't schedule it, it won't happen and that describes much of our problem. When we don't plan time together we settle into a bland, repetitive routine. The routine doesn't require much energy to keep it going, but it doesn't provide much new adventure in life either. I'm not looking for excitement as much as new op-

---

Vacations are not about "getting away"—
but about getting "in touch."

---

portunities to connect with you. Going places makes our togetherness that much more special because we're able to step out of our normal roles."

"Like when we talk for an entire weekend," he said.

"Yeah, or like when we took that car trip to visit used bookstores and read to each other along the way. Or, how about when we flew to our alma mater's bowl game? That was a bit expensive, but it was a lot of fun."

"In the past," he replied, "we've talked about a basic schedule that included a weekly date, plus a weekend once a quarter, and then a week together once a year to get out of the routine. Whatever happened to that plan?"

"Kids, my job responsibilities, your job responsibilities—you name it," she said, setting her glass down. "We could resurrect that schedule and make it happen."

"I'm ready to sign on. What do you say we use a date night to do some brainstorming for a longer trip?"

Com•mit•ment

The promise to give yourself;
to do or give something; to be loyal,
to work very hard.

A passionate lifelong love affair takes willingness and
work—a willingness to find out what it takes,
and work to get there.
Love is both the price and the prize

The Need:

Time for the two of you to regularly reconnect.

Meeting the Need: Bring Back Dating
(Being a date is a lot more romantic than being a spouse!)

Time Together Each Week

• Antique shops • Craft fair • Picnic
• Parking • Hot-tubbing • No-Tell Motel
• Comedy club • Karaoke bar • Dance club
• Mall • Zoo • Museum • Garden • Planetarium
• Window shop • Bike trip • Walk in the park
• Home with catered dinner, then dessert in bed
• Movie matinee • Brunch • Sleep under the stars
• Bookstore • Outdoor concert • Horseback riding
• Fashion show • Play • Tour of homes • Wine tasting
• Amusement parks • County fairs • Art festivals
• Home for the evening to look at photo albums
• Bowling • Miniature golfing • Roller skating
• Tape a program and watch it with popcorn
• Home with formal dinner and slow dance
• Kite-flying • Track meet • Ice skating
• Scrabble • Chinese Checkers • Uno
• Bicycle for two • Star gazing

Take turns being the creative date planner.

What could you do this week?_____

_____

And how about the next week?_____

_____

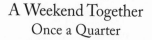

A Weekend Together
Once a Quarter

• Quaint bed & breakfast • Rafting • Ski weekend
• Have things ready for a weekend camping trip
at a moment's notice • Bicycle-built-for-two trip
• Cover up all the clocks/watches and spend a timeless
weekend together • Luxury, or less-than-luxury, hotel
• Horseback trip • Golf weekend • Hot air balloon
festival • Sign up for a couples' conference
• Go on a spiritual retreat for meditation and prayer
• Camp out in your own backyard • Just start
driving in the country and explore

Your favorite idea: _____

When could you do it?_____

A Week Together
Once a Year

• Instead of a trip to see the folks, go to Venice or San
Francisco or Paris or New York or Athens or Acapulco
• Five-day bicycle tour of wineries in Napa Valley, CA
• Take a cruise to Alaska or the Caribbean • Go to
Maui or Miami or any beach • Mountain retreat to
read and relax • Road trip of your state • Switch
homes with someone in another city/state
• Backpacking trip • Go on an intimate
conversation retreat and talk!

Your favorite idea: _____

When could you do it? _____

The Heart of Commitment

S arah stood up, and gathered the glasses. "That was rather good."

"Sure was," Matt agreed, finding the loveseat.

Reappearing from the kitchen, Sarah touched his shoulder and sat down beside him. "You know, I shouldn't play up 'the biggies' too much."

He paused briefly and asked, "The biggies?"

"The all-out, heart-stopping romantic things you've done. I certainly treasure the memories those experiences have given us, but I don't want you to focus on them to the exclusion of simple everyday acts of love."

"You mean 'the little-ies,'" he replied.

"No offense, but I've noticed men tend to think in all-or-nothing terms. So, when it comes to relationships, guys focus on the big, life-altering commitments like starting an exclusive relationship or getting married. After a guy makes that commitment, he thinks, 'Okay, now what's the next big challenge to conquer? I'm ready to move on.' It's like the process is finished rather than just beginning. I know there are also women who are out just to 'capture' a man, but I'd say they're the exception.

"The guys who have a big-commitment mind-set seem shocked that their mates question how their commitment plays itself out on a daily basis. Their attitude seems to be, 'I pledged my love to you when we got married. Unless I tell you differently, figure it still applies.'"

"Hey, that's unfair," he protested.

"Didn't we agree that it's okay for women to use extreme language when making a point?" she said, smiling.

"Either way, the point remains valid, even if it's one man in two, or five, or ten. A woman goes into an emotional meltdown relating to a man with a big-commitment mindset. She ends up suffering from love starvation. Instead of regular deposits of loving acts to build up relational reserves, constant withdrawals have drained her relational bank account. And a woman who is starved for love becomes everything men don't like in women. Right?!"

"I plead the fifth," he said.

"To fill the emptiness a woman may very well turn to eating or shopping or substance abuse or work or motherhood but ultimately those things prove to be short-term fixes. What she needs is love. Any woman can get that nourishment from herself, her friends, and her family, but if she is relating to a man in a committed relationship and not getting it from him, well, what's the point of the relationship? It creates a hollowness inside.

"Such a woman ends up like a starving person who loses the capacity to think of anything but food, and then can easily become irritable, cranky, self-focused, and just plain hard to live with. That negativity adds to her insecurity and it spirals down into—take your choice—clingy neediness or self-protective coldness. In the process the man gets self-protective himself, which makes the woman even more clingy or self-protective. Sound familiar?"

"We've taken that spiral down on a few occasions!"

"Of course, women want the big commitment, but I've looked at our marriage certificate maybe two or three times since our wedding. What I've looked for since is a re-commitment mind-set—the attitude that 'we've only just begun' to live out our commitment. That attitude produces a series of daily deposits. Not just a past 'I do,' but a present 'I still do'; 'I still want nothing else but to give you my heart and soul, now and for the rest of our lives.' Those renewed acts of love nourish my—"

"Craving-for-affection drive," he said, cutting in.

"That's right. That's the estrogen-charged drive."

"How do you define re-commitments?" he asked.

"Re-commitments are acts of daily thoughtfulness. They might reach the level of romantic zeal we just talked about, or be simple acts of service and appreciation within our partnership. We express those acts of thoughtfulness by what we say and write, what we give to and do for each other, and, of course, what we do with each other.

Making the Vow

I take you • a freely chosen commitment,
To be my husband/wife • in an exclusive relationship,
To have and to hold • as a friend and a lover,
To love, honor, and cherish • tender and affirming,
For richer/poorer, in sickness/health • unconditional,
Till death do us part • and secure over the years.

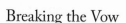

Breaking the Vow

In 1880: 1 divorce in every 20 marriages.

In 1900: 1 in 10. In 1920: 1 in 7. In 1940: 1 in 6.

In 1960: 1 in 4. In 1970: 1 in 3. In 1980: 1 in 2.

Half the children born in the last 30 years are children of divorce. Since 2003, the official divorce rate has dipped below 40% at times, but this doesn't reflect break-ups of cohabiting couples—and cohabitation has doubled since 1990. Of the 50% who stay together, only 50% rate their union as a happy one.

A *big-commitment mind-set* fails past intentions: "I do becomes "I did, at one time." It starves love through neglect or disrespect.

Renewing the Vow

A *re-commitment mind-set* honors past intentions: "I do" becomes "I still do, right now!" It feeds love through acts of thoughtfulness. Re-commitments renew the magnetism of attraction through what we:

•say to •write to •give to •do for

•do with... each other on a day-by-day basis.

The number-one reason for unhappy marriages and divorce is not irreconcilable differences, but the loss of attraction. Attraction takes the "ir" out of irreconcilable.

"Do you want specifics here?" Sarah asked.

"Definitely," Matt said, sitting up a little straighter.

"First of all, I feel important when you spend time talking to me. I really don't care that much about the subject. I'll talk to you about football or mechanics if necessary. I'll even talk all weekend about sex, but what I really enjoy talking about is people—our kids, our friends, our relatives, us. Maybe you've noticed, women love to gossip. It gets us in trouble if we use it as a means of putting others down. Often, though, we just want an outlet to talk about what we value most—our relationships.

"Given the fact that people rarely live in extended family groups anymore, our phones and our social meetings have become the primary relationship networking tool. That's why you see me on the phone so much and why I appreciate it when you call or text to check in with me. Communicating with me during the day, particularly if plans change, helps me relax. It reminds me that you really are the kind, wonderful, considerate guy I fell in love with."

"You've indicated that you love talking to me, oh, about a thousand times since we met," he grinned.

"Has it only been a thousand?" she said, matching his smile. "Well, I also love it when you write things: a note, a card, a poem, a drawing—you get the message. One time you left a note on the bathroom mirror in lipstick and the glass cleaner to take it off! But maybe you noticed, it didn't come off very quickly. Writing me a card or note for any occasion, or no occasion, is great because it reaffirms our connection. A couple of times I've even received a card from you in the mail. That's so sweet.

"You might not realize it, but I read and reread those notes. They're like a treasure chest of memories of your love for me. You've given me some beautiful handmade cards in the past, but I should tell you, I'm into quantity here as much as quality. How about a regular stream of notes with just X's and O's, or a heart with my name in the middle, or an 'I love you' on a sticky note. I treasure those concrete, black-and-white reminders that you think I'm the best thing that ever walked into your life."

"You are, Sarah," he said, taking her hand in his.

She squeezed his hand and replied, "Right up there with things you write for me are things you give to me."

"You're talking about gifts."

"Exactly. When I think of a gift, it's something special to the receiver, versus a present, which is more what the occasion would call for, or the giver wants to give."

"I'm not sure I see the distinction, but I wouldn't argue with it either," he stated.

"Maybe there is no difference. I just know what I'm looking for is the personal touch that reaffirms us. That's why women are forever giving gifts to each other. A gift represents the special value of a friendship; it's a symbol of love. As such, it doesn't have to be expensive. Although, what the heck, once in a while expensive is nice! Surprise is better, and timeliness and thoughtfulness are best. It's like when you got me a fancy umbrella the day after I lost mine, or when you got me a pair of earmuffs after I mentioned my ears were always getting cold. I don't think those times I even dropped you any hints, as I often do!"

"Those were pretty practical gifts," he replied.

"Yes, but they were thoughtful. They showed you knew me and were concerned for me. What I really loved about the earmuffs is that you wrapped them up in a blanket and attached a note, 'A little something to keep you warm.' You know, or maybe you don't, that women love the packaging almost as much as—or more than—the gift. It's that thoughtfulness thing again."

"I guess I'd better learn how to tie a bow," he said.

"The greatest gift of all is one you can't wrap—the time you spend doing things for and with me and the kids. I'd trade everything else for it. A woman dislikes laziness in a man. 'Couch potatoism' is a big turn-off, but industriousness is a big turn-on—it makes me proud of you.

"That's also why women love plans. Plans help us feel secure. So, a man with a plan is a real big turn-on. You don't necessarily need to take control, just be willing to put forethought into what we're doing. I love it, for instance, when you set up a family bike ride. I love it too when you bring home take-out to relieve dinner stress or when you take the kids out to relieve mother stress."

"Those things sound like they're right out of your love frame and your affection plan," he noted.

"There's one more thing I haven't mentioned. Anytime you compliment me—to my friends, to my folks, or in front of the kids—it warms my heart. A public compliment is worth five or ten of them in private. Think of them as verbal foreplay, because nothing gets me hotter."

"Is that right?" he asked.

"That's right," she repeated. "It all goes back to that relational bank account to which we either make deposits or withdrawals. Withdrawals are easy; anything we do that starves love, like being harsh or hurtful or emotionally distant, depletes the fund fast. Even if we're nice to each other, but just let things happen, sooner or later relational entropy sets in. Then, as the trust level drops, there's not much left for a rainy day.

Our Relational Bank Account

Withdrawals	Deposits
Things that starve love	Things that feed love
Withholding feelings	Communication
Criticism	Compliments
Flirting	Fidelity
Taking for granted	Expressing gratitude
Acting as a loner	Acting as a team
Building up resentments	Clearing up issues
Withdrawing	Reaching out
Working too hard	Spending time together
Blaming your partner	Taking responsibility for your part

Adapted from *What Women Want Men to Know*,
by Barbara De Angelis

"When I affirm you, say through a word of admiration, I put a deposit in your account. Likewise, each loving word, note, gift, and action becomes a deposit from you. Your reliability, consideration, sensitivity, and partnership feed a security and connectedness that keep me from becoming anxious, irritable, clingy, demanding and you name it—all the things that make you want to run and hide. I become more nag mate than soul mate."

"This is helpful, but if you don't mind, go back to a hero, like Wesley from *The Princess Bride*. Could you explain this soul mate idea a little more? Remember, I'm a left-brained guy. What would the ideal soul mate be like?"

"Sounds like two questions: What's a soul mate, and what's an ideal mate? Which answer do you want?" she asked.

"How about both," he requested, catching her eye.

"Okay, a little review. A soul mate would be a close friend—anyone—who loves you for who you are. You share a mental, emotional, and spiritual bond allowing you to freely express the most personal issues of your life.

"I'd say the ideal mate includes all that, but adds the physical connection as your lover and the long-term commitment of lifetime partnership. An ideal mate often brings you a strength of completion in the form of a very different personality type, like we talked about earlier."

"How about, more specifically, the ideal husband?" he asked.

"That's you, honey," she said with a grin.

"Right. Maybe then you could use me as an example of everything a woman wants in a man!"

"Sure!" She paused and asked, "What does a woman want in a man? Are you ready for a monologue?"

"Go for it," he replied, settling in. "I'll take notes."

"An ideal man listens," she began slowly, "looks into your eyes with genuine interest. He asks questions that reveal his understanding. He delights to know new things about you. He loves to hear you dream and cheers you on as you pursue your ambitions. He challenges mediocrity and selfishness, but you can relax because he accepts you completely and relishes your uniqueness.

"An ideal man shares his feelings. He's not afraid to open up about his struggles and fears, his hopes and joys. He is emotionally strong—not a wimp—but also available and vulnerable. He is quick to say 'I love you' at just the right time, which is any time he's not in trouble with you!

"An ideal man finds great satisfaction in partnering with his wife and kids—working around the house, doing projects together, going places. He surprises you with small acts of thoughtfulness and kindness. He anticipates your needs and jumps right in to help. He keeps refining his sexual and romantic skills to become a great lover.

"An ideal man gets discouraged and depressed, but he doesn't stay down. He rises again and takes on life's challenges with a positive attitude. He enjoys his life, his work, and the people around him. He is a joy to be with.

"An ideal man commits himself to personal growth. He is not a couch potato or TV-holic. He may love football, but not more than he loves you! He protects his health and treats his body with respect. He lives life with self-discipline and passion. 'Work hard, play hard' is his motto.

"Shall I continue?" she asked, receiving a nod. "An ideal man loves his kids and makes fatherhood a top priority. He finds time to be with them and is sensitive to their needs. He is always safe to be with and is their mentor and hero. He provides an umbrella of protection around his family. Likewise, he gives of himself to others and is caring toward the less fortunate. He is tough and he is tender.

"An ideal man pursues the important things of life, especially a relationship with God. He doesn't just leave the area of spirituality to others. He knows he's not the last word in the universe, and he puts his faith in the One who is. He values stillness, reflection, and prayer.

"An ideal man lives by a standard of honesty. He keeps his word. He can be trusted and relied on to come through for his wife, kids, extended family, and others.

"An ideal man does not carry resentment or anger for long. He doesn't avoid confrontation, but when it comes he is careful to fight fairly and without harshness. Forgiveness and grace extend through his life to those around him. He seeks to live by the golden rule, 'Do unto others as you would have them do unto you.'

"An ideal man doesn't manipulate to get his way. He asks for what he wants, but he doesn't succumb to self-pity when he doesn't get it. At the end of the day he carries no regrets or chips on his shoulder.

"An ideal man lives with an inner confidence and strength. He doesn't need to check himself in the mirror or showboat his abilities, money, or position. He enjoys reminiscing about great times together, but he lives in the present and looks to the future. He is known as a giver rather than a taker. Life is an act of service to him.

"Finally, good humor and humility follow him everywhere he goes. He lives lightly, spends little energy in worry, smiles broadly, laughs often, and knows how to have fun. He is taken seriously by everyone but himself."

"Wow. Are you describing an ideal man or a saint?"

"Maybe both," she said. "But those qualities are what women look for in a man. What do you think?"

"I think I have a long way to go," he replied, looking over the notes he had taken. "A very long way!"

"Now, there's the humility I mentioned," she said.

"I'm serious. I've really got a lot of work to do!"

"What's important to me is not where you are now or how far you have to go, but that you're willing to work on getting there. Obviously no one is perfect or ideal or even

---

In case you wondered what the companion
description is to the ideal husband:
An ideal wife is any woman who has an ideal husband.
—Booth Tarkington

---

close. It's that spark of willingness that gives me great hope for our future and keeps attracting me to you.

"It's why I married you. Notice I didn't include best-looking or most upwardly mobile or even most romantic on my list. I liked a lot of things about you, but first and foremost was your openness to learn and to grow. I thought we'd face challenges—and that's certainly been true—but I also knew you'd be willing to take on the obstacles that lay in our path including yourself, when necessary. Just the fact that you've taken the time to come here and get into all this means so much to me."

"Thanks," he said, reaching for her hand. "I love you, and I appreciate those words so much. They're as affirming as a night of wild lovemaking. Well, almost."

"I love you too. You're such a wonderful guy."

"You look tired," he said, touching her cheek.

"This has been a long day."

"Agreed," Matt replied. "Let's head for bed."

Arranged Marriages

Over 50 percent of the world's marriages (and 90 percent in India) are arranged. In such cases parents, family members or a matchmaker are given a varying degree of power, "forcing" a commitment on a couple who may know nothing or little about each other. Such a union will lead to empty love (see pages 342-344) if intimacy and passion do not grow and become important parts of the equation, along with their commitment. (Interestingly, it is estimated that only about 5 percent of arranged marriages end in divorce.)

Living Together

Whereas an arranged marriage forces commitment, living together avoids or delays commitment. The idea is to make a small wager (live together) and see if things work out instead of going all in (get married) with the risk of total loss.

Women often see cohabiting as a step toward marriage, whereas men tend to like the idea of shared living expenses and greater accessibility to sex. Maybe women should consider their mother's advice, "Why buy the cow if you can have the milk for free?"

Today 50-60 percent of marriages begin with cohabitation. Of those couples who do not break up, about 65 percent who eventually marry will divorce, compared to 45 percent of all first marriages of non-cohabiting couples. Also a higher percentage of couples living together cheat on each other, or experience abuse and depression. Finally, the saddest result of all: the likelihood of even more children left to grow up in broken homes, perpetuating the same destabilizing experiences in their own relationships.

It is understandable that many fear marriage because, being children of divorce, they fear divorce. But you can't practice permanence. Like love, marriage is not a conditional, semi-commitment to your beloved. By their very nature love and marriage are unconditional. It's not about "trying" but "doing." "Do you take this man/this woman…?" "I Do!"

The fact that you can't "unwind" marriage so easily makes its dynamics much stronger when the unsettling winds of difficulty come. A marriage commitment can provide an invisible hand of strength to help work through such difficulties to become a more united couple as a result. When the right time comes, don't try out marriage, get married.

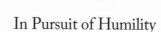

In Pursuit of Humility

A Sad Reality

Humility is not a popular human trait in the modern world. It's not touted in the talk shows or celebrated in valedictory speeches or commended in diversity seminars or listed with corporate core values. And if you go to the massive self-help section of your sprawling mall bookstore, you won't find many titles celebrating humility.

—John Piper, *Future Grace*, p. 85

One key to developing humility is to understand its opposite. Humility's opposite is arrogance—pride deprived of humility. We all dislike arrogance in others. Could they like it any better in us?

Humility Test

When problems arise between you and your partner, on a scale of 1 (never), to 10 (always), how often do you:

- listen carefully? ____
- stay non-defensive? ____
- not justify your position? ____
- realize your own contribution? ____
- appreciate your partner's position? ____
- advocate for his/her distinct viewpoint? ____
- change your attitude/behavior as a result? ____

Now for the ultimate humility test:
Ask your partner how accurate you are!

Interlude on Humility

Humility is a God-given conviction regarding our humanity. It allows us to see our part, how we fell short or made a mistake, or what we did to cause a problem or pain. It enables us to willingly admit and to work on this failing. Embracing humility liberates us from arrogance by reminding us that we are just as susceptible as anyone to moral failure. None of us has our act fully together, or even close. We're all a work in progress.

While the couple enjoys a peaceful night's sleep, let's pause to highlight a critical means they have—and we have—of turning a relationship into a passionate lifelong love affair.

At the core of such a relationship you find humility. Humility lowers defenses, sees another's point of view, deals with conflict constructively, and reminds us to listen and learn. It's the soil in which intimacy and love grow.

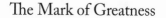

The Mark of Greatness

We look to the ideal,
strive for excellence,
and pursue life's greatest goal
of continual openness
to listen,
to discern wisdom,
and to implement change.

Humility,
resulting in a
willingness to learn
and to better ourself,
is the mark of a great person.
Faith, hope, and love stand on it,
and test its genuineness
over a lifetime.

Humility
is our greatest
character quality, our
greatest gift to those around us.

You haven't arrived but you know you're getting closer
when you're taken seriously by everyone—except yourself!

*Clothe yourselves with humility toward one
another, because, "God opposes the proud
but gives grace to the humble."*

—Peter, 1 Peter 5:5

Do you see humility as a great character quality? What
would it mean for you to pursue it more?

Sunday Morning

WAS IT GOOD FOR YOU?

S tretching the sleep away, Sarah wasn't yet sure if she was asleep or awake. The voice she heard, however, sounded quite familiar.

"Qui-ck-ie. Qui-ck-ie. Qui-ck-ie," Matt whispered.

"What?" she exclaimed, stretching her legs.

"I hope this doesn't seem too out-of-the-blue. I'm getting you up with subliminal messages," he whispered, snuggling up behind her tightly.

"They're not subliminal if you verbalize them. Remember: Subtle. Subtle. Subtle. "

"Then I'll stay on a nonverbal level," Matt stated, as he slid his leg between hers.

"You're incorrigible! We're still on vacation, remember? I'm not ready to wake up yet."

"That's just the point; we don't have to get up!"

"I thought we had an understanding last night," Sarah reminded him, hoping to quiet him down. "It didn't expire at dawn, did it? Let's cuddle for now."

"Okay, but given that it is a new day can we talk about—you know?" he whispered.

"I'll make you a deal. We can dialogue about it this morning, or we can do it, but not both. You choose." She reached back with one hand to pull him closer.

"Now who's being incorrigible?! That's a tough choice. But we did say this weekend is about talking."

"Good then, you talk. I'll listen," she replied, using her other hand to rub some of the sleep out of her eyes.

He began, "You know, I really appreciate quickies."

"I think we've established the fact that you like sex—anytime, anywhere, any way. You don't have to be in the mood or 'feel right about it,' you just like it!"

"Right," he agreed. "But I didn't say I like quickies. I said I appreciate them. It's a personal message to you. I'm saying thanks for being open to my desires for increased frequency in the form of quickie sex."

"Is this your way of being subtle with me? You remember what we talked about regarding subtle, right?"

"There's no ulterior motive here. I'm just expressing my thanks. During the last few years you've been increasingly generous about having quick sex and not making me feel guilty about it. I've really appreciated that," he said.

"I think I've turned a corner regarding my feelings about quickies. In the past I could easily feel used, but your efforts to take our relationship more seriously, and make sex less of an entitlement, have softened me to your need for frequency. I want to meet it whenever possible."

"So," he said, smiling, "my plea that frequent sex helps keep my prostate healthy was not the motivation..."

"Okay," he continued, after her deadpan silence, "here's another word of appreciation. During the last year or so you have touched, stroked, and held me down south a lot more than ever before. It's a small gesture that means a tremendous amount to me," he said, hugging her more firmly.

"I know I've already mentioned it, but you seem to be a lot more aware that your attention down there brings me such feelings of acceptance and affirmation. For me there is just no better way you can say 'I love you,' even if your touch is for only a brief moment and doesn't lead to anything else. Although a hand job may not be quite as blissful as the oral version, blissful is blissful!

"Sometimes I wonder if I ever left my teenage years behind. The level of hormones charging through my body seems as strong as ever, particularly after I've slept all night next to a beautiful woman."

"How about a cold shower? I suppose you could get the job done yourself," she suggested, still hoping for a few more moments of rest. "Do you masturbate when you're alone? If so, you don't leave any evidence of it."

"Whoa, aren't you the daring one posing such questions!" he said, stretching out more himself.

"Hey, who's bringing up the embarrassing issues?"

"Have you heard the joke that 98 percent of men masturbate and the other two percent lie? Actually, I've heard the number is more like 80 percent, but whatever it is, I've always been with the majority on this. Your turn."

Realizing her morning rest was definitely over, she turned over and said, "I've told you before that I've done it—mainly out of curiosity. I've heard the percentage for women is lower; only 40 percent have ever masturbated."

"You told me before that as a younger woman you 'discovered' yourself. I took that to mean masturbation."

"You know that I'm not that comfortable naming body parts. But the first time I realized that my clitoris wasn't simply another one of those parts came when swinging sideways on the playground at twelve. I found that kind of rubbing enjoyable, but it took a while before occasional curiosity turned into self-pleasuring.

"So, I did it as a teenager but I've just not felt much need for it. I do know a couple of women who masturbate regularly, including an old friend who sometimes did it at work, and another who confided in me that she did it while she drove around town. If I could suggest anything along these lines, it would be for you to use a vibrator on me more often. I often like it. Now, how about you?"

"If you're asking about masturbation, I've actually stopped doing it," he said. "I realized it tends to drain off my sexual energy. If I hold off, my desire for satisfaction grows, and delayed gratification is not such a bad thing."

"It seldom is," she said with a sense of amusement.

"Maybe it's better to think of it as increasing my sexual dependency on you. I'll bet the more that happens, the nicer I'll be to have around the house!

"One urge I have had during lovemaking, though, is to take your fingers and join them with mine as I stimulate your breasts or clitoris or as you stroke me. Joining together—whether it's stroking you or me—could make sex more partner-like, if we could get comfortable with it."

"You know," she said, pausing, "another thing that I'd like to see us get comfortable with is keeping our eyes open during lovemaking—from start to finish. It's easy to get submerged into your own pleasure during sex, particularly when you close your eyes. Keeping our eyes open is like inviting each other to come inside our souls to participate together. I think it would be very intimate."

"Whatever we do, please approach me in a confident, but not pushy manner. That allows me to gain security from your strength and to lower my guard. Trying new things can bring up the issue of trust for both of us."

"Like," he replied, "when you've let me blindfold you

or tie your hands together. I remember the issue of trust even came up the first few times I came into you from behind, doggie style."

"I don't like that term. It's more guy-talk than girl-talk. It's so easy for a woman to feel used, and that kind of description doesn't help. I enjoy you entering me from behind; just be sensitive. Don't forget, your sexual interests can be very different from mine. You do our relationship a big disservice if you pressure me to go further than I want to go. I don't mind exploring your fantasy world, as long as I know I can come out of it at any time."

He paused and said, "Trust can be a fragile thing. There is a fine line between pursuing you with the confidence you like and crossing the line to the pushiness you don't like. When I initiate something new it often feels like it's all up to me instead of a shared event. I may be clumsy or embarrassed as I try it. Your openness to me and my advances is so helpful—it's in my love frame!

"You mentioned that you like a confident, sensitive approach. What I desire from you is a little different. I like it when you approach me with confident vulnerability. When you let me know how much you are looking forward to sex, in any and every way it might come, you communicate that kind of open confidence with me.

"That's why I really enjoy it when we make love in the middle of the day or in the backyard or whatever. I'm not into the thrill of potentially being caught in an office or an elevator, but I can see why some people would be. Being a little daring can add a lot of spice and excitement."

"Remember," she replied, "feeling safe is a much bigger priority for most women than being daring. If it's anything more than garden-variety stuff—in our bedroom, in

Touching Yourself Is like
Tickling Yourself

A wife would do well to touch her husband, especially in the southern region regularly, or better yet every day before getting out of bed, after going to bed, or anytime in between, and to do so directly or through his clothing.

This elevates a couple's passion.

As you hold him there—every day—periodically go further, caressing him with powder or lotion. Sometimes use both hands and mouth. Don't feel pressured to bring him to a climax every time, but do it often!

For most men, being caressed conveys 'I love you' better than any words could express.

It reminds him of what an incredibly caring woman he has married and helps him face his world feeling affirmed and energized.

Figuring out a man is really quite simple. His genitals and his heart are directly connected. When you touch the one you can get to, you simultaneously touch the one you can't.

our bed, in the missionary position—then you should look for clues that I'm okay with what's going on."

Matt looked at her and smiled. "We wouldn't want our lovemaking to get boring, would we?"

"Again, it's not a matter of exciting or boring for me, it's a matter of feeling secure enough with you to do new, fun things. As I've told you before, security is important

...But Being Touched Is Very Different!

A husband would do well to hug and cuddle with his wife regularly, or better yet every day before getting out of bed, after going to bed, or anytime in between, and to do so in a non-sexual way.

This energizes a couple's intimacy.

As you hold her—every day—periodically go further and tell her what an absolute honor and privilege it is to be married to such a beautiful woman (and wonderful mother). Tell her often that she is the very best thing that has ever graced your life—maybe not each and every day, but very, very often!

For most women, hugging and cuddling convey 'I love you,' and words of appreciation cement the thought.

They remind her of what an incredibly sensitive man she has married and help her face her world with a quiet assurance.

Women may be more complex and mysterious and even confounding than men, but you can count on one thing: They love to be loved.

to me. Without it, sex becomes more fearful than fun. "I know men have anxieties about sex as well—whether it's the size issue or keeping an erection. You've said before that you sometimes worry about performance.

"We all bring anxieties and problems into the bedroom. Some of those problems come from the day's tensions. Other problems come from buried feelings from the past: relationships, our parents' attitudes, maybe even some traumatizing experiences—you name it. Whatever the issue may be, the solution is acceptance and patience. The greater the trust we build outside the bedroom, the more security will show up inside it.

"That's really why I started getting into quickies. It took me some time, but I figured out they are a way of meeting your need for more sex without overwhelming me. I could see how much they did for you and for us."

"Well, like I said, I appreciate your sensitivity. Periodic quickies are a real gift to me—especially in the morning when I often wake up aroused, my testosterone level is peaked, and I'm ready to go. They've gone a long way in providing me with a sense of peace and well-being. In just a few minutes I join with you and find the release my body

Premature Ejaculation

30 percent of men over all age groups express distress over climaxing too quickly, often less than a minute after intercourse. Men should be able to exercise more control over ejaculation (up to six minutes or more) and various treatments can help increase duration.

One is to strengthen the pelvic muscles with Kegel exercises. A second, the "stop-start" method, repeatedly ends motion before reaching the "point of no return." Another, the "squeeze technique," has the woman squeezing the base of the penis between the thumb and index finger to suppress ejaculatory reflex.

Coming too quickly can be a vexing problem. Through supportive communication, partners can approach it as a mutual issue and shared project. A doctor's input and counseling will likely help as well.

aches for. I feel so cared for and loved.

"You know," he continued, "I love long, drawn-out sex, too. But I must admit, when you say, 'Let's just have a quickie,' it's like getting a permission slip to not worry about the foreplay. I can just flat-out go for it."

"Quickies have grown on me, too," she stated. "They're often just what I want, like getting an extra big cuddle.

"They're also a relief for me in a different way. My body doesn't wake up craving release like yours does. But I enjoy sharing the moment with you and I appreciate the freedom of not having to get into an intense experience or have an orgasm my body doesn't want right then.

"Of course, this doesn't change what I've said about taking lots of time but that's five-course meal lovemaking. Quickies are more like a brief stop at the refrigerator."

"I'm glad you said that and not me," he replied.

"If quickies were all we ever did, I'd have a different opinion, but they're not. When we begin lovemaking with the intention of gourmet sex, I sometimes realize that my mind is into it, but my body just won't come along. Instead of forcing the issue, I want to back off and just relax. In those situations, forget about trying to directly stimulate me. That's why I stop you from kissing my breasts. It's just not an experience I need or want at that time."

"You want me to back off," he reiterated.

"Only from trying harder to get me aroused. You've said that you get pleasure from giving me pleasure—I can appreciate that, but please do not measure our success by whether I have an orgasm every time. I've heard it said that a man is like the sun—always shinning, but a woman is like the moon, sometimes hidden, sometimes a cresent, other times half out or full. We wax and we wane!

"If I don't want an orgasm, that's no failure on your part because for whatever reason I prefer comfort sex instead of passionate sex—no mind-blowing fireworks, just a warm glow. I know for you a non-orgasmic sexual experience is an oxymoron, but I get a great deal of fulfillment in the overall experience and count the closeness and togetherness as a great blessing in our marriage."

"Sometimes," he said with a disarming sigh, "I'm just not sure whether I should keep working on getting you aroused, or just relax. That's why any and all signals from you are helpful. You build my confidence by telling me how much you love to be touched here or rubbed there or when a rocking motion is just right. At the same time, tell me what's not working or redirect me—in a gentle way. I'm sure it could be possible for you to be too bossy, but I've rarely, if ever, experienced that."

"I don't always know how to read my own body. We might start elaborate foreplay, but my body does not want to prolong things. Other times, quickie sex turns into wanting longer, comfort sex or something of the explosive variety. I want one kind of lovemaking going into it, then something happens that changes my mind."

He looked over to her and said, "That's why men so often ask that famous question, 'Was it good for you?'"

"If you have to ask, you probably don't want to hear the answer. Either way, you do us no favors when you ask me to analyze the sex we just had."

"Guys can be so goal-oriented," he interjected, "and maybe, just maybe, a bit insecure. "

"It's fine to analyze later, with the motive of improvement," she said, reaching out to touch his arm. "But in the moment I'm not interested in improvement, I'm into mak-

> Don't ask that famous question right after sex, "Was it
> good for you?" unless you're prepared to
> hear that less famous response:
> "Oh...uh, yeah...sure."

ing the most out of the present experience, whatever it-
might have been. A play-by-play analysis makes sense on
the football field, but not in the bedroom.

"Any after-sex energy you have left goes into afterglow.
I realize making love tends to mellow you out, but don't
roll over and go to sleep right away! Remember, you've
opened me up, entered my body, and filled me up. Sex is
more external for you; an out-of-body experience. So, I'm
sure it's hard to understand the feelings of someone who
has their insides accessible to another. When you exit you
leave a vacuum, an emptiness.

"That's why I sometimes hold you tight as you start to
leave. You've got to go sooner or later, but don't leave me
without some sort of affirmation. Stay engaged. Fill in the
emptiness with your words of love and tender embrace.
The afterglow can be as important as the foreplay in giving
me a sense of well-being and fulfillment."

"I like the afterglow, too," he said, rubbing her arm.

"Then be as sensitive leaving as you were coming in.
I need to know that sex, especially quickies, is about us
rather than just about you. Sometimes I don't even mind
not getting into the act at all—I'm happy just providing a
warm place for you to climax in, just as long as I know I
mean more to you than that. I want to feel like my gift is
appreciated, especially through your after-sex cuddles.

"If I sense your interest only comes from your neediness, I end up feeling used. That's why I hate it when your pursuit turns to begging. It takes away my option of saying 'not now' in a relatively neutral environment and throws me into a dilemma: Should I do something I don't particularly want to do in order to please you? We'd be better off if you'd take that cold shower.

"It's okay to ask me, 'Can we have a quickie?' but don't overuse that question. If possible, communicate your desires non-verbally. Just don't come on to me in a timid way. The recipe is really quite simple: Mix in a little controlled passion with a dose of humble confidence. That and an extra portion of very sensitive lovin'. Got it?"

"Oh yeah, no problem. It's so easy being the guy!"

"Just remember," she continued, "whatever kind of sex it is, I might not want the foreplay, but I do want the affection. I assume this is all different for you. When I want to initiate sex, I don't need to worry about starting with affection. I have your permission from the get-go."

"More like enthusiastic glee," he replied. "Let's see, how many times have I turned you down since we've been married? I think I could count them on one hand."

She paused smiling and said, "As far as my permission goes, this may surprise you, but you've got my enthusiastic approval, too. Go for what you want. I love feeding off your passion. Just make sure I start to come along for the ride. It's good to know that as the hostess I make the final call on issuing the invitation."

"You mentioned," he said, sitting up straighter, "that you assume you have my permission to pursue me. Actually, I long for you to initiate lovemaking more often. It communicates that you want me—every part of me—just like my affection communicates that to you.

"Last month you texted me a rather cryptic message. It said if I could get away, you'd love to see me that afternoon. I couldn't call you back fast enough as I kept trying to interpret what seeing you included."

"You did seem a bit disappointed when I asked you to lunch," Sarah said, turning to look at him.

"I thought maybe, just maybe, you were interested in some afternoon delight. Even though it didn't happen, your message got my pulse rate up, and that's my point. Anytime you do the smallest thing to initiate sex, you've placed yourself in the situation I'm often in by opening yourself up to rejection, and I love it."

"Why's that important to you?" she asked.

"Because," he replied, "you're willing to become vulnerable. I could potentially tell you 'no thanks' or even make fun of the whole idea. You've put yourself at my mercy, in a sense. So you could get rejected, even though we both know that's not likely.

"It goes back to the fact that I'm affirmed by your vulnerability. Whoever initiates sex finds him or herself in the vulnerable position. Your initiative communicates trust in me—trust that I will take your desire seriously. Since I initiate sex more often, you probably don't think about this as much as I do. When a woman wants a man, a man can't help but feel special. When you go a step further and take on the role of an aggressive hostess rather than a passive one, the gift is sweeter still. And if the hostess actually ends up 'begging' for it, that is a huge dose of affirmation, not to mention a major turn-on."

"Maybe there's an inherent womanly shyness about taking initiative," she said. "Being too forward can feel awkward. My cues are more subtle. If you hear playfulness in my voice, I'm likely interested. If I'm forward with hugs or touches, I may well be communicating that I want more of a physical connection."

"You're not a shy person by nature—just the opposite. So, why do you feel shy about initiating lovemaking?"

"I don't know. Maybe it relates to my past, or my up-bringing, or gender roles. Who knows? I realize that early on I took more initiative with you, and I'd like to go back to that. Of course, we both know couples where the woman initiates sex more often than the man. All this is reversed and the woman ends up quite frustrated."

"I could see how that might become unnerving for a man," Matt said, stretching a little more.

Sarah paused and asked, "And why is it not okay for the woman to be the primary aggressor?"

"Well, for many men it would be a dream come true to have the woman in their life be so sexually assertive. If it gets too out of balance, though, a man may start feeling inadequate. Women can hide their lack of arousal and pretend all is well and good but there is no way men can. If we can't get up for the occasion, so to speak, it is embarrassingly obvious to all.

"I can guarantee guys aren't much for talking about such things, except to their doctor or maybe in counseling. As you said, we're very performance-oriented. Unhappiness expressed about our sexual performance can make matters difficult, and any hint of ridicule could bring on a total meltdown in a man's self-esteem."

"You haven't gotten that from me, have you?"

"No, you've been frustrated," he said, "but I've never felt anything approaching ridicule. As a matter of fact, as I look back now on our marriage, the opposite has been true. I wish you'd given me more, not less, negative feedback about my performance—nicely, of course.

"I know that my approach to sex has been similar to my approach to most everything in life. What I've lacked in experience I made up for in confidence, however misplaced it may have been. I am just cocky enough to think that anything I do is, if not great, at least good.

"Over the years—particularly the first few years—you allowed me to live with the delusion that my performance was fine. It felt great to me so I figured it felt great to you, even though that wasn't necessarily the case."

"You're a very strong personality type," she said. "Sometimes I didn't want to ruffle the waters so I didn't say anything and went along with it. Plus, I wasn't very tuned in to my own pleasure to start with."

He paused briefly and replied, "Looking back, I realize that my pushiness and your relative silence have not served us well. For too long I just figured you got as much fulfillment out of intercourse as I did. My hope all along was that we'd regularly have simultaneous orgasms. When we couldn't seem to make that happen, I just settled on having one myself. To this day I don't think you've ever had an orgasm from intercourse alone."

"I've heard 85 percent of women don't," she said. "Intercourse just doesn't connect us where I'm most sensitive. You have to really get the rocking rhythm just right and go on for a long period of time for that to happen."

"That long period of time thing has been tough," he said. "The first few years I couldn't control myself. Since then it's steadily gotten better, but I've never really been able to sustain that kind of penetration and motion for long enough to bring us to simultaneous orgasm."

"Since orgasm is a reflexive action rather than a choice, reaching that crescendo together can be like trying to sneeze at the same time—pretty tough. But I'd say simultaneous orgasm is more an invention of romance novels than a real-world experience. Like most women, I need direct manual or oral stimulation of my clitoris to come."

"I've said this before and I'll say it again: I would appreciate all the guidance you can give me on what you like, how you like it, and how I can provide it. I'm so affirmed knowing you enjoy my touch. It excites me to excite you. Your feedback is all I have to go on here."

"I know it's not healthy, but sometimes I've avoided the issue," she replied, "because it seems harder to deal with it than just to let it go. For a long time I settled into not expecting an orgasm. I don't think I realized I'd given up on something that brings so much pleasure. When you started 'camping down south,' as you call it, focusing on caressing my clitoris, all those feelings came alive."

"I finally dropped the idea of bringing you to orgasm through intercourse alone," he said, "and went for manual and oral stimulation. Now I wonder why it took me so many years to discover your clitoris. For so long I would give you a once-over there and move on."

"Or you'd keep checking me out to see if I was lubricated enough," she said, shifting herself. "Then you'd wait for a bit and check me again and again until you thought I was ready for you to come in. I'm really glad you stopped that, because it was quite the turn-off."

"You got on me for doing that," he replied. "Once you even said I was becoming 'sexually lazy.'"

"Well, after you finally discovered my clitoris, you needed to back up and remember that emotional foreplay still gets me wetter and faster than the best technique."

"But technique is important, right? If your clitoris could talk, wouldn't it say 'I might be small, but I'm important'?" he said, smiling at his own choice of words.

"If my clitoris could talk, yes, it would say that it is more than just a little bump. A woman's sweet spot consists of a whole system of nerve endings, muscles, and glands but it's all concentrated in a small, delicate space.

"A penis sticks out. It's a big target—okay in your case, it's a huge target—with lots of surface area."

"You're so affirming," he said, matching her grin.

"In any case, not as much skill is required with you; as long as I touch, lick, rub, and squeeze it a lot, you're happy. It's hard to get that wrong, but a clitoris is a tender little target that must be treated with gentleness and skill.

"First, you need to find it. When you do, let variety rule the day—slow, fast, up, down, sideways, in circles, diamonds, triangles, or even the alphabet, one letter at a time. But, while variety is important in the beginning, consistency is critical toward the end. That's why I often guide you and indicate how I want you to rub me. I sometimes rock back and forth because a steady rhythm acts as the key ingredient as I close in on an orgasm. And when I get close, that's the one time not to get creative. Keep doing that back-and-forth thing with your finger or tongue until my eyes roll back and I can't take it anymore."

"That is so much fun!" he exclaimed.

"Well, I should tell you that, overall, you've done well these last few years. I really like it when your hand finds my clitoris during intercourse. As for positions, my favorite one is whenever you press the weight of your pelvis against me. I press my clitoris up against your pubic bone at the base of your penis, and instead of thrusting in and out, we rock gently back and forth together in rhythm."

However they come, I'm having orgasms, and I like them. Sometimes they're light, like waves rolling in, one after another. Sometimes they're deep down and quite intense. I'm glad my orgasm is important to you, too—not that I need or even want one every time, but I definitely want it some of the time. Sex may be complex for a woman, but the simple fact is that there is nothing that fills my body with the kind of pleasure that having an orgasm does. So it's okay to focus on it as a goal, as long as you don't fixate on it as a goal."

"It's important," he replied, "to know that you like what I'm doing to you. If you don't like it, I want to know that, too. Of course, you don't have to say it, as long as you direct my movements with your hand—or your moans of delight. And maybe, just maybe, one of these days we'll find ourselves having simultaneous orgasms."

"I'll be sure to be there when it happens," she said with a grin. "Orgasm or not, multiple orgasms or not, simultaneous orgasms or not, it all doesn't amount to a lot of time in the life of our overall relationship—a few minutes a week, at best."

"Ah, yes," he said, "but those are the best moments of our life together—at least I hope that's true for you!"

"Oh, they're great all right, if our overall relationship

> *Secretly, a woman may feel...that if he really loves her, he will know what to do. These feelings are food for romantic fantasy but they don't create great sex.*
>
> —John Gray

is great. I'll bet if we looked back over the trust graph we made yesterday you'd find a correlation—our best sex has been during the times of our greatest trust.

"It just makes sense. For me, sex naturally flows like a spring from the pool of love between us. I treasure those sensual experiences in my locket. Those loving moments act as reassurance that you find me just as irresistible now as when we first met. The years have simply served to enhance and mature our attraction to each other.

"Ultimately, it brings me such joy to know that my love provides a harbor where you take refuge from life's storms; I know that, if it wasn't for me—my heart and soul, as well as my body—your life would suffer from a great void. With me, with all of me, you find a great measure of contentment and hope and purpose."

"Honey, you are all of that to me, and more," he said.

"Thanks," she said with a kiss that turned into an embrace. "I hate to change the subject but I need to take a shower. Could you make us some coffee?"

"How about my special omelet?" Matt asked.

"That would be great!" Sarah replied, "but shall we first take that shower together you suggested yesterday?"

"Now, that would be great!" he said with a smile. As he ran his fingers through her hair, he sighed, "It will have to be a 'quickie shower' though. I'm so busy this morning you know, with breakfast to make and all!"

Looking for the Perfect Gift?

Give your man a quickie, or your woman, a wonderful afterglow. Uninhibited sexuality is your gift to each other.

Anatomically, a man's genitals are revealed while a woman's are hidden. This is consistent with a man's tendency to project his life externally and a woman's natural inner dignity and mystery. Women tend to be turned on by sensitive confidence, and men by vulnerable confidence.

Very few women regularly come to an orgasm through intercourse alone. So, "camp down south" with lots of manual and oral stimulation of the clitoris and G-spot—*variety* at the beginning, and *consistency* toward the end.

No one is born an expert sexual partner. Even the most capable won't have all the moan zones mapped out. Don't be afraid to talk mechanics.

Ask yourself, "What is it like to make love to me?" Ask your partner which skills need the most work: before, during, after, or all of the above!

Avoid analysis right after sex, though, unless you both want to talk about it then.

Do your homework. Work hard at getting an A+ in Sexology by becoming your lover's dream lover!

Okay, the perfect gift. When and where?

Hey, you don't have to write it down, just do it!

An Entitlement or a Gift?

W alking into the kitchen, the first thing Sarah spied was her husband. The next was her omelet. "What a great breakfast, Matt. Glad I married a morning person."

"That's not what I heard a little earlier this morning," he replied, giving her a hug and a pat.

"There's nothing like a long, hot shower to change your perspective. It smells great."

"I put a little bacon in the creation," he said, joining her at the table. "I was wondering, would you mind if we finished our talk from yesterday—about oral sex?"

"We weren't finished?" she asked. "Can you give me a good reason why I shouldn't signal to move on now?"

"You're pretty uncomfortable with it," he stated.

"Like I've said, I'm not normally into analyzing our sex life as an activity or event. In a loving context, I enjoy sexual things with you that I don't feel altogether comfortable talking about. So if you proceed, do so cautiously."

"Thanks. I'll try. I'm puzzled about why you're sometimes hesitant about performing oral sex on me or enjoying mutual oral sex. Maybe I should explain my feelings about this. Oral sex feels wonderful. That area is the most sensitive square foot on my body. Having your mouth roaming around down there is so disarming, so captivating. Even the position you get in to do it helps me feel adored. I love intercourse, but your mouth creates a unique sensation. You do know how much I like it, right?"

"Oh, be assured, I know how much you like it," she replied. "Maybe it would help if you could convey to me a little more on why you like it so much."

"Sure. To me, oral sex communicates pure, unadulterated acceptance, absolute admiration. It's odd to talk about it in this way, but my penis represents my self-identity as a man. Hopefully it doesn't do my thinking for me! But in virtually every other way, it's me, only smaller. Well, not that much smaller!"

"Hey, you're not touchy about size, are you?"

"That was a joke," he said, grinning, "but almost every guy has some concern about it, unless maybe he's 'King Dong.' When it comes to size, you'd do well to say nothing at all unless you're commenting on how large it is. Like sometimes you've said, 'You feel so big inside me' or 'You're so deep inside me.' That's a great stroke to the male ego. I would say if you're ever looking for an occasion to use the word 'immense,' this would be it!"

"I'll remember that. But really, I don't think size makes the experience all that different for most women.

"There's more to it—like angles and technique! It's not the size of the ship that matters, but the motion of the ocean."

"I'm sure the ship matters more to men than it does to women, and that's why women need to be careful about what they say. I've heard that regardless of how big guys are normally, 90% of men are between five to six inches long during erection. It's more a matter of perspective than proportion, and most men don't realize average is not all that big. But believe me, nothing would crush a man more than being ridiculed about the size of his ship. It seems, though, we were talking about something else—like oral lovemaking."

"Can't we talk about ships?" she mused. "I promise to use big descriptive words. How about titanic?"

"Hey, save your 'sweet nothings' for bedtime talk, dear. I hate to be so graphic about it, but if possible, I'd like you to know what it's like for me."

She looked over to him. "I appreciate that."

"When you take me in hand and put me in your mouth you love me in my most sensitive and vulnerable essence. Think of my penis as a very special part of me. "

"I think I know what you mean, but women don't personalize body parts—especially our sex organs."

"I don't consciously think that way either—but on a subconscious level, well, a man's penis is important enough to him that it kind of takes on a life of its own!

"So, I don't know how you want to think about it, or if you want to think about it at all. But whenever you can, express your womanly delight with all the tenderness and affection you can muster for me down there. I also love it when you use your breasts to rub me there. It combines tenderness and a turn-on in the same act. It's a great combination of softness and hardness.

"Here's my perspective, and granted, it's rude, crude,

socially unacceptable, and everything else wrong about guys, but oral sex for a man could be as good as a counseling session for strengthening a marriage."

"That is so male," she said, meeting his gaze. "How is oral sex going to improve a marriage? Will it get you to listen more, or will you just come back for more and expect more? More than most things I do for you, oral sex only makes sense in the context of a loving relationship."

"Please hear me out," he said. "I'm not denigrating counseling. We've profited from it plenty. I just want to make the point of how 'going oral' helps a man feel loved in a very tangible way. Of course, it's not automatic that any given man will respond with thankfulness and love. Maybe it will just mean he'll expect more, but I guess that's the risk love takes. If a woman is willing, or even eager— whoa, that kind of attitude brings a guy to tears. I can't imagine anything that could communicate more love over the years, to a man who enjoys it, than oral sex.

"Maybe it would help to equate that small area of my body to your heart. My desire for attention there equals the sensitivity you want shown to your feelings. Only there isn't anything figurative about this. I just lie back, nothing to worry about or fix, no performance necessary, no work to be done. It's pure pleasure.

"If I feel any discomfort at all, it comes from guilt for the overwhelming sensation of receiving. I wonder how I can manage my strong desire to receive it without making you feel it's an expectation. I feel so admired, so affirmed, so adored. It's hard to believe I warrant so much attention and so much unconditional love."

She looked at him and said, "It would help to think that giving to you like that doesn't just end up creating more need, but actually creates great appreciation. Then it's not rude or crude—it's acceptable and respectable!"

"Talking about rude and crude, do you remember once, right after we were married, doing it to me while I was driving? I thought I had died and gone to heaven."

"Yeah, and I thought that just might happen—right there on the freeway. But we actually survived our youth!"

He squeezed her hand. "Since we did survive, those memories are reminders of our passion—part of that locket of sexual delights. So, driving may be out of the question, but it would really 'blow me away' for us to be watching TV some evening and all of a sudden..."

"That's blowing something all right—my mind!" she teased.

"Please don't think I'm expecting that. I'm not. When you do initiate the unexpected, though, it's like a beautiful sunrise of love and affirmation coming my way."

"I do want to surround you with affirmation. It's just that my role is so often that of the giver—with you, with our kids, with friends, with life in general. It goes back to the hostess–guest analogy. As the hostess I want to love you, and I enjoy meeting your needs, but your desires are so strong they can come across as demands, even if they're not meant to be. Just the fact that we're talking about this and you're expressing such strong opinions puts pressure on me to do what you want, rather than feeling free to do what I want to do for you."

"Looks like you may want to wave on the conversation to something else," Matt said.

"You're such a mind reader, but do you understand what I'm saying?" Sarah asked.

"I think so. You want to feel free to give rather than

pressured to give, which is not really giving at all."

"Yes. That's a form of taking. I don't believe this is a good way to think, but I'll be honest. I sometimes worry that if I give you oral sex on a more regular basis, your desire to get it will overwhelm my desire to give it. So, I hold back. But I appreciated your words, that you could never expect it from me as often as you'd like to get it.

"Also, just so you know, you have a tendency to push my head down on you while I'm there and that bothers me. All of a sudden I feel trapped. Instead of giving you a gift, it feels like you're taking what you want."

"Really? I didn't realize. Maybe it's a reflex action. I'll definitely try to avoid that," he said, pausing. "I'm surprised though. I have struggled knowing what to do with my feelings about liking oral sex more than I could expect you to give it. You're saying that your reluctance comes from the same worry of increasing my expectations. That's interesting. I've always thought you held back more because you were averse to the act itself."

"No, not really," she replied. "From what I've read, a clean mouth has more germs than a clean penis does, so it's actually a healthier choice for kissing. As long as you're clean and I'm in the right state of mind, I'm open to it. As a matter of fact, although the texture of semen isn't one of my favorites, I don't mind the taste so much."

"Do you know that swallowing is the ultimate act of admiration?" he asked.

"And do you know that what you eat makes a difference in the taste? So, if you want me to get into swallowing you'll need to think about a fruit salad diet with lots and lots of strawberries! Then you'd become like dessert!"

"I guess to sum it up," he stated, "you enjoy performing oral sex but worry that I'll take advantage of it."

"I don't have a burning desire to do it," she stated, "except that I find joy in your enjoyment, and I know how much you like it. For me, that's the motivation. I love you.

"As I've said, my larger struggle involves feeling pressured. I've been burned before by 'over-giving.' So, at times I approach sex, and especially oral sex, with caution, putting limits on how much I'm willing to give. With your strong drive you tend to be a 'boundary buster,' so that makes me even more cautious—sometimes too cautious. I think that if I just avoid it, it will all go away."

"That's sad," he replied, "because so often what you experience as pressure from me, I experience as a yearning—a deep-seated desire to feel loved. Ultimately it sounds like an issue of trust. You must feel I'll take advantage of you like a guest overstaying his welcome."

"Can you blame me?" she asked.

"Not at all," he replied. "I know in the past I've used everything from force of will to guilt to threats of leaving, I'm sorry to say, to get my sexual desires met. During those times I've acted out of fear. I've felt like I'd dry up and blow away—like I'd die inside, if I didn't get enough sex.

"It's not a good defense for my behavior, but like I mentioned yesterday, there have been times I've felt rejected. It seemed that no matter what I did, the answer was going to be another 'No.' The feeling of rejection would hit me like a lead weight in the stomach.

"If I were to guess, I'd say that after motherhood your desire for sex went down to maybe two to three times a month at most, while I'm still at two to three times a week. For me, the partner who wants to increase the frequency, the sobering reality is that outside of infidelity, the only love life I can have is the one you're willing to give me, and the one I'm willing to work for.

"The low point for me came after our last child was born. We went without sex during the last part of the pregnancy, the recovery, and then through some of the depression you experienced afterward. I hate to admit it, but the only thing sadder than your depression was my self-pity. I backed out emotionally just when you needed me most and fall turned into a frosty winter as far as our relationship was concerned!"

"That was a hard time for both of us," she said.

"One day I remember feeling overwhelmed with rejection and despair. I came face-to-face with the fact that I had limited options. Was having sex with you or having a relationship with you going to be more important to me? The decision seemed that black-and-white.

"I believe sex is a right of marriage, but giving up the mentality that you owed me sex as an entitlement was a big attitude adjustment for me, and it felt like death. I looked at it in the same terms as that book on the five stages of death and dying. You know what I'm referring to?"

"You mean the one by Elizabeth Kubler-Ross?"

"Right," he replied. "The first stage she identifies when a person faces death is denial. I remember very early in our marriage when I clung to the notion that we were on the same wave length sexually. Our problems were just a matter of communication and would work themselves out. If not, I could bring you around.

"When that didn't happen I went into the second stage, anger. For me anger has usually taken the form of a cutting comment or the silent treatment. I was too proud or embarrassed to tell you what was really going on—that

I wanted more sex and felt the pain of rejection.

"When I realized that bullying you and pushing the 'guilt button' wasn't getting me very far, I began the bargaining stage. You remember me proposing some stupid things like, 'I'll do all the laundry for a week or take out the trash for a month if you'll have sex.'"

She smiled at the thought and said, "The amazing thing is that I agreed to some of those proposals. I guess I was desperate for a little domestic help!"

"In the stages of death and dying, depression comes next. If a person can go through the hard work of depression, he or she finally comes to stage five—acceptance. Genuine acceptance, though, is rarely achieved. When it does come, people experience an inner peace and calm, almost as if they already had died and been resurrected.

"Acceptance is reached so rarely because stage four—depression—is so painful. Depression is so hard to work through that we often revert back to denial, anger, and bargaining in one form or another."

"Interesting," she sighed. "We go through the stages whenever we seek to rid ourself of a harmful habit or take a new step of personal growth. Then we must face the death of the old habit or way of thinking before we can

---

Anytime we seek to adopt a new attitude or behavior, we have to let the old one "die." When dealing with this "death," we cycle through the stages of:

Denial • Anger • Bargaining
Depression • Acceptance

To reach acceptance—adopt the new attitude or behavior—we must do the hard work of depression because we are leaving a familiar habit for a new one.

---

embrace something better. How did it work for you?"

"Depression is a natural response to loss. For me the loss amounted to a realization that I could not make you have sex or want sex. Before, I lived with the illusion that I was in control of our sex life, that it was mine for the taking. Slowly but surely I came to understand the reality of the situation: it was yours for the giving, as the hostess.

"Call me dumb, but when a man goes to sleep one day thinking he's in control of sex and wakes up the next realizing how foolish he has been, well, can you spell a big, fat, rhinoceros-sized, d-e-p-r-e-s-s-i-o-n?"

"You did say this was positive for you."

"It was," he replied, "but it doesn't mean I don't still struggle with the loss of control. From my male perspective, women have all the power. Your gender dictates when, where, how, and how often our gender gets sex."

"What? Hardly," she disagreed, looking over at him.

"Oh, yes you do, and I think I can prove it. Have you heard the joke about the little boy and little girl who were playing, and the little boy pulled his pants down and with pride said, 'I have one of these and you don't'?"

"No, but I think I'm about to."

"Well, the little girl went home crying to her mom. The next day, the same thing happened. 'I have one of these and you don't,' he said again, taunting her but the second time the girl just kept playing. He couldn't rattle her. 'Why aren't you crying?' the boy asked. 'Because,' she said, as she lifted up her skirt, 'my mommy says I have one of these, and with one of these I can get as many of those as I want.'

"Okay, so much for that story. How about a real-life example? Any woman could walk into a singles' bar to find a guy—some guy who would gladly go home with her for the night. Not so with a man, however."

"Yeah," she replied, waiting for more.

"Hey, I'm not advocating the behavior, I'm just using it to illustrate my point. The same situation exists in a marriage. Statistically speaking, what percentage of wives will be denied if they want to make love? Whatever it is, most husbands in most marriages will get denied much more often than their wives. That's just how it is."

"Look, your observation may be accurate," she said, reaching for his hand, "but your interpretation leaves a lot to be desired. Maybe women do have more power when it comes to sex—as you said, we're the gatekeepers, the hostesses. As I said, though, the power you're talking about is not the power to create a special, loving bond. It's simply the power to deny. It's the power of last resort, veto power.

"I can assure you that women in fulfilling relationships do not get their kicks out of turning their men away. Actually we'll use everything available, including sex—particularly sex—to nurture the relationship.

"Don't underestimate your 'indirect control.' I love you, and I love making love with you. I want to be swept off my feet—and into bed. Even though I am the hostess, I'm also your wife, and a woman who's a natural-born nurturer. I gain deep satisfaction from caring. The power to deny does not wear well on a nurturer.

"The more you help create an emotional bond between us, the more control you'll exercise over sex. Exercising power in this indirect way is your and my only guaranteed way of experiencing lifelong sexual passion."

"I agree," he stated. "It's just taken me a long time to see it so clearly. You'll never guess what acted as the turning point from depression to acceptance for me. One day the realization hit me that I went many years as a hormonally turbo-charged single guy without having sex—and I actually lived through it. Having sex or not did not have to define the quality of my life. I could live the rest of my life without having sex, and I'd be okay."

"That sounds like a healthy perspective," she said.

"Yes, or a recipe for self-pity! Mostly, though, I've found strength, even joy in it. I am free to love you for who you are and not for what you give me or what I may think I'm entitled to. I still struggle; it's like an attitude adjustment, or maybe a paradigm shift. It's certainly brought a measure of humility. I hope you've seen some results."

"Oh," she said, meeting his gaze, "I've definitely sensed the change you've described. It has helped me relax and let down my guard. I can't imagine this conversation happening otherwise. I hope you've seen some results, too—namely, me being more sexually open."

"I have," he replied. "For me it's all about exercising patience in a short-term loss for long-term gain. I've realized I have limited choices, the glass is either going to be half-full or half-empty. I'm either a grateful guest for the sex I get or a resentful one for the sex I don't get. I just keep telling myself, 'If I don't get as much sex as I want or in the way I want it, I will not die of sex starvation!'"

"So in dealing with your fear of death you've actually realized you won't die—of sex starvation, at least," she reiterated.

"Not any more than I'm likely to die of regular starvation," Matt said, looking over his half-eaten omelet.

Who Has the Power?

Whether the man or the woman, the one with the least desire for sex exercises the most control over it.

As hostesses, women have the final say—veto power, but as natural-born nurturers, the power to deny does not wear well on them.

If it is the man who has the greater desire for sex, he can dramatically increase his power (his "odds" or "luck") by creating a deeper emotional connection with his woman. Such indirect control is a man's only non-abusive way of gaining more sexual power. A lifelong emotional bond is a couple's only hope of experiencing lifelong sexual passion.

Willingness—freely given, freely received—is the key to sustaining that passion.

Willingness on the man's part is to be a grateful guest for the sex he gets rather than a resentful one for the sex he doesn't get.

Willingness on the woman's part is to be a gracious hostess, joyfully giving sex rather than begrudgingly "giving up" sex.

P.S. A woman's bottom line on giving oral sex is this: She will want to give it much more if she feels like she is, in fact, giving it rather than feeling it is being taken from her.

Sex is not an entitlement, but a gift: A gift from the One who created it—God—and from the one whose body we join—our lover.

How does this issue affect your relationship?

Playing Baseball on Opposing Teams
vs. Enjoying Pizza Together

Playing baseball is the dominant cultural metaphor we use to think and talk about sex. In a TED Talk, Al Vernacchio offers an alternative way to envision the place that sex has in our lives: enjoying pizza together (see Ted.com).

Playing Baseball	*Enjoying Pizza*
Two opposing team	Cooperative
One wins/other loses	Both fulfilled
Play by the rules	Our pleasure wins
Sexist	Reciprocal
Run the bases	Let it happen
Goal to Score	Invites exploration

No analogy is perfect, but the baseball metaphor is not just imperfect, it is one-sided and degrading. The pizza metaphor lends itself to a two-sided mutuality full of cooperation, exploration, and satisfaction for both partners.

At what point should we begin enjoying pizza together?...

When in sync, *intimacy* fosters deep friendship, *passion* fuels great sex, and *commitment* creates a magnificent marriage—producing love's exquisite elixir!

But sex before marriage fast-tracks a couple's experience of passion beyond their growth in commitment. This misbalances relationships, often with negative repercussions for growth in intimacy (see pages 342-344).

If you've consummated your relationship, it's not too late to back off, choose abstinence and wait to enjoy pizza together once your commitment rises to the commensurate level of your passion and intimacy—in marriage.

Expectations Are Premeditated Resentments

Ex•pec•ta•tion

The act or state of expecting, anticipation;
a strong belief that something should happen,
or someone should act in a particular way;
an expectant attitude.

Quiet settled over the room. Finally, Sarah asked, "Do you remember the bumper sticker I saw a few years back: 'Expectations are premeditated resentments'?"

Matt looked up and replied, "How could I forget? That statement has caused more discussion in our household than anything else, besides our present subject."

"I began thinking about it again after our little food experiment," she said.

"How so?"

"We have such a strong inclination," she continued, "to

change our partner's behavior, which results in all kinds of undignified, controlling behavior on our part."

"Yeah, undignified, like dumping salad on your husband's head!" he said, making a jab at her side.

"The emphasis here is on 'controlling.' We often communicate expectations of what we think we deserve from each other. I'd say that eliminating those demands has constituted the single greatest struggle between us. What do you think, Matt?"

"Well, isn't it safe to say that when we were dating, we exceeded each other's expectations? You were the most affirming, positive, and friendly woman on the planet, not to mention quite the flirt. As for me, I was the most sensitive, affectionate, and romantic guy in the world."

"Yeah," she agreed, "you'd open the car door for me. You'd listen and talk for hours. You'd call me all the time, write wonderful notes. My Prince Charming, destined to fill my life with romance and intrigue."

"You're swooning again!" he said, smiling. "Actually, our serious conflicts didn't start when we stopped going out of our way to do nice things for each other, but when we assumed that same free-flowing experience would continue after marriage."

"That's a bit simplistic," she said. "Dating and courtship has its own set of rules, with an escape clause that allows either partner to leave much more easily than in marriage. In marriage, you sacrifice the freedom of easy escape for the security of commitment. That security then allows more of the real you to emerge and blossom."

"Or creates a rude awakening for your spouse."

"True," she replied, pausing a moment, "but just think about how marriages were once set up by parents and still are in some traditional cultures today. Those arrangements forced newlyweds to either work it out or be miserable. Like the old adage says: 'Don't marry the person you love. Love the person you marry.'

"A couple in an arranged marriage would not date or court beforehand. So they would not know what to expect from each other, but they would still come into the relationship with expectations. Whether arranged or not, couples' expectations largely come from what they grew up seeing go on between their parents. Our parents' marriage—healthy or hostile or somewhere in between—goes a long way in forming what we think a marriage relationship should and shouldn't be like.

"We grew up in very different families," she continued, pausing briefly. "Your parents kept it together and you went through childhood in a secure environment. My dad left home when I was young, and I was raised mostly by my mom until my stepfather entered the picture. Male approval is so important to a girl, and I spent my teenage years trying to find in guys I dated what I didn't get early on.

"Add those unique family-of-origin experiences to our different personalities, toss in gender traits and some extra need for approval, and we both face lots of adjustments to make our relationship work."

He nodded. "What I'm trying to say is that those adjustments largely take place after marriage. During dating and engagement, couples frequently deal with differences by overlooking them in light of the positive qualities they see in each other. When someone appeals to us, we tend to see them in their most ideal state.

"Looking through rose-colored glasses blinds both partners in the beginning. We think we're relating to a human being who is a shining new car, when in reality we're dealing with a guy or girl who is a jumbled box of mis-fitted parts—of issues and problems."

"I agree," she replied. "Obviously more evaluation comes into play as dating moves toward engagement. I'd assume that the more varied and stressful the situations a couple faces, the better means of evaluating each other they have. But, you're right, we all still tend to believe the best about our loved one and gloss over imperfections—which then grow to their real size after the wedding.

"It's like comparing grandparents' love for their grand-kids and parents' love for their kids. Grandparents' love includes the appreciation of a little extra distance! When a couple gets married, they lose that extra distance and now must work out their differences 24/7. The wonderful, sen-sitive, caring person they dated and courted just vanished. Now Mr. and Mrs. Who-They-Really-Are shows up."

"It's all a little sobering," he said, getting up to pour some more orange juice. "People are in their impression stage before marriage and their comfortable stage after marriage. That's why I think it's unfair for a woman to use her sexual charm to capture a man's heart and then do a U-turn. You've heard that scientists discovered the food that reduces a woman's sexual desire by 90 percent? It's called wedding cake."

"That's a tired joke. Let's apply it to a guy's roman-tic gymnastics before marriage. Is it fair to court a woman with romance and then do a 180 after the ceremony?"

"You've got a point," he said, "I guess I'd just say that courtship sets us all up for a fall, with those unrealistic ex-pectations that stem from our ideal mating behavior."

"Sometimes the hardest thing to do is to identify those

expectations. I like that G.K. Chesterton quote the pastor used at our wedding. I didn't think it was very romantic then, but I think it has served us well since."

"You remember that? How did it go?" he asked.

"He said something like, 'If we can be divorced for incompatibility, I can't understand why we're not all divorced. I've known many happy marriages but never a compatible one.' So, he's saying the issue does not boil down to whether we're compatible, but how much we're willing to stay connected with each other despite our incompatibilities. We have all these expectations of a perfect relationship with a perfect spouse, and we miss the point."

"Here's a small example of an expectation I carried into our marriage," he stated. "I assumed you would fold my clothes—just because my mom did it during my youth—until you pointed out one day, in no uncertain terms, that you were not the 'designated clothes folder.'"

"Did your dad leave his laundry scattered around the bedroom, too?" she asked with a grin.

"Maybe it's genetic," he smiled back. "If we can identify our expectations and begin to set them aside, we give each other the precious gift of freedom. Instead of feeling obligated to make our life good, our partner is released to love us in the only way that love works, out of free choice—not compulsion.

"It's not that we stop telling each other what we need and want. We just stop doing it in a demanding way. Our main question should be, 'What must I do so that my happiness doesn't depend on your behavior or choices?'

"Learning to let go like that frees me from being a prisoner to your choices or trying to force you to meet my needs. So you're freed up to love me without the threat that I'm going to be unhappy if you don't do it the right way. The more we try to ensure someone's loyalty and love, the less we're going to get it.

"As force disappears, love fills up the space left behind. With our partner freed from the burden of making us happy, he or she will be more willing to freely give us what we want and need. It just works that way."

"Well, I'd agree," she said. "When we give a person their freedom, we become much more attractive to them. They become much more likely to make sacrifices for the further growth of our relationship—the very thing we wanted in the first place! Now we have the love we always wanted because we didn't try to force it."

"Or, we pursued it in the only way that will work—by giving our partner the freedom to not love us."

"Exactly," she replied. "My only issue here is that there are some legitimate and realistic expectations, such as those that come from wedding vows. Those vows include a very specific commitment—to remain sexually faithful to each other—and a very general one—to love, honor, and cherish each other. Can we not expect our partner to follow through on those commitments? In marriage, personal freedom takes a back seat to commitment.

"So, it seems that any expectation which proceeds from mutual agreement, such as the vows of faithfulness and love, gives us the right to expect that agreement will be carried out—albeit imperfectly and often not in the way we desire."

He paused in thought. "I think that's the key—mutual agreement with no assumptions. If you ask me to go to the store to get some milk and I say I will, then it is reasonable for you to expect me to carry through with your request.

If I promptly forget about your request, you certainly have the right to be perturbed. If you also expect, though, that I'll get non-fat milk when nothing has been said about it, then your expectation has come from an assumption instead of mutual agreement.

"And this is the problem with so many expectations— they are based in assumptions made outside of a couple's mutual commitment, like: 'that's how my parents did it' or 'my friends do it' or 'you should know what I like' or 'that's the way I dreamed it would be growing up.' These expectations are the toxic ones because they are essentially demands from voices outside of our mutual commitment."

"So, how do our love frame lists relate to all this?" she asked. "They could become our expectation frames!"

"That's true," he replied. "I'd say our love frames need to be considered love guidelines. If you want to love me— and I hope you do!—this is the best way to do it. I surrender my love frame list to you and receive your list with the hope that our love will grow more deeply through a better understanding of each other.

"Of course, we're going to miss the mark and fail a lot, but that's where a spirit of no expectations, which is another way of describing unconditional acceptance, also applies. In the final analysis I can't demand that you love me in a certain way because true love can never be coerced or forced. But when you do love me in a certain way—a way described in my love frame—you can be quite sure I'll be filled with lots of appreciation.

"So, we can't demand that our partner love us in a cer-

> Love frame lists are not love's demands,
> they're love's guidelines.

tain way, but we can expect them to consider our desires, given our vow to love, honor, and cherish. Our mutual commitment should embolden us to communicate our desires, just not in a demanding way."

"Yes," Sarah replied, "but even that falls short in an ideal relationship. The very best approach is to adopt our partner's position, as we talked about Friday night. If I am an advocate for your desires, and you for mine, then the trust built between us will be enormous. If, however, I'm always just talking about what I want, sooner or later it will start to sound like a demand.

"I could say, for example, 'Hey dear, it's been a long time since we've done something together and partnering is in my love frame, so I'd appreciate it if you'd take another long look at that list and get with it.' My dissatisfaction is real, and likely legitimate, but such an approach will tend to weaken the trust between us because I'm simply talking about what I'm unsatisfied with. Otherwise, we'd have to call them duty frames.

"However, it would make a huge difference if you were the one to take my side and plead my case for me, saying something like: 'I've felt pretty stressed lately and that's affecting our time together. I'll bet that's been really hard on you. Let's talk about how I could pace myself better and do some more things together as a couple.'

"Being each other's advocate dramatically deepens trust, but there is a real fear in it. The fear is, if I don't make sure I stand up for myself, will I then give a green light to being run over and used? There may possibly be weeks, months, even years between one spouse extending the kind of freedom from expectations we're talking about, and the other responding in kind. What about responsibility? How about when a spouse abuses the freedom given and uses it as a license to do anything he or she wants?"

"Surely you're not talking about me?" Matt asked.

"Of course not, dear—it's purely hypothetical!"

"Well," he said slowly, "abusing freedom is always a possibility—otherwise it wouldn't be freedom. But slavery to each other's expectations hardly provides an attractive alternative. In the end, expectations that are not clearly agreed upon are premeditated resentments, because they set us up for frustration and anger. The only thing I should expect from expectations is to be disappointed, and probably sooner rather than later."

"Dare I bring this up again?" she asked. "In our sex life you've often communicated expectations. Instead of just leaving it at 'I love sex,' you've told me, in so many words, that I should love it as much as you do, at the same time you do, and in the same way you do. It's as if your hormone level defines what I ought to feel. I very much appreciate what you said earlier about not seeing sex as an entitlement. Are you really willing, though, to give up all your expectations in this area?"

"You're right about the fear element in giving up expectations," he said. "I'm not fully aware of what it all includes, but honestly, it scares the heck out of me. We both realize though, that neither of us wants the alternative of you living by my expectations and me living by yours."

"So?..."

"So," he replied hesitantly, "I'd plead for your patience on this. If I could rid myself of all expectations in this area of our life together, I could do it in any area!"

"There's another area of our lives where I feel expectations from you," she said. "Are you ready for this?"

"Go ahead," he said, looking over to her.

"Decision-making."

He looked surprised. "How so?"

"For good or for ill, our family reflects traditional gender roles in the sense that the man still has the most say. What we do, by and large, revolves around you and your choices and the moves we've made, have all resulted from your promotions. I know you now make most of the money, but your career advances have come at the cost of stability for our family and supportive friendships for me. I don't think you're aware that you can operate with a sense of entitlement when it comes to such decisions."

"Well, I think I've been open to your input," he said.

"Yes," she stated, "but that's what it's been—input. You've always made the final decision, or tried to. Let's take another example: our family life. Since we became parents, I've been the primary care provider for our kids. Because of that you've deemed me the kid expert, which supposedly gives me the most say-so in their lives.

"That's great on paper, but my problem is this: I make most of the parental decisions regarding their day-to-day lives, but when a big decision comes along, like choosing a school, you feel quite free to voice your opinion like it's the final decision. Again, what gives you the right to expect to make the big decisions after I've put in the time and effort to make most of the little ones?"

"I haven't really thought about this," he said. "You do have a point. Why didn't you bring this up sooner?"

"I guess it's been brewing underneath the surface."

He looked at her and said, "You know, honey, when I approach our relationship with those kinds of expectations, you'd be wise to take me on. Otherwise, you end up doing what I want just because I want you to. Instead of being a partner, you become an employee. You might not believe me, but I'm really sorry. I know I have a strong personality, but I truly do want a partnership with you.

"So, once again, let me say this: I do not want an entitlement mentality running our relationship from either end. Happiness doesn't actually come into its own until it creates a mutual experience. I propose we make a big sign and hang it over our front door. It would say 'Expectation-Free Zone.' Here we live with the joy of no guarantees. We are entitled to nothing but respect. When the gift of sex or love or romance is given, it comes freely and joyfully, not coerced out of guilt or obligation."

"Why not," she said. "We need to paint the place anyway. How about a giant sign on the house itself?"

"Now that's a serious commitment."

"It would be our little contribution to neighborhood awareness. This couple believes there is no such thing as forced love. Love comes from desire, not duty."

"I return to courtship love as a model," he said. "While courting, most couples give each other a reprieve from the heavy cloud of expectation. Maybe love blinds us to each other's flaws during courtship, but it also frees us from demanding that those flaws be fixed. Why should we not provide the same acceptance for each other in marriage? The flaws become more obvious, but the means of growing out of them become more powerful. Marriage provides security for the risky effort to change and grow."

"Excuse me if I repeat myself," she said. "Learning to relate to each other without expectations comes in fits and starts. You mentioned your fear that if you gave up sex as an entitlement, you'd just never get what you needed or wanted. I've had similar fears, and sometimes they've produced a hardened attitude."

"How so?" he asked.

She began thoughtfully, "I'll give you an example. For years I wanted you to be more involved with our kids, such as in promoting musical aspirations. I hoped you'd support this effort. When I realized it didn't appeal to you, I put on the pressure, which just led to conflict. Finally I decided if it was that important to me, I had to be the one to encourage them to participate and practice. I do it, but I don't really feel very supported in it.

"Here's another desire. I've always wanted you to make a bigger deal out of my birthday. You know how important celebrations are to me. I don't even want to tell you this, because it spoils it if I have to ask. For a long time I've just expected the minimum and have been grateful for anything more. Maybe that's relieved me of some resentment. I'll tell you, though, it's never been the fairy tale experience little girls dream of.

"My problem really goes deeper, and I think it's based in fear as well. If I give up my expectations, it feels like I have to give up my desires, too. It's like I'm alone in the world on this, and no one really cares. So I tend to repress those feelings and buck up. I start working on whatever it is without someone to partner with, trying my best to encourage our kids in their endeavors or being content with minimal birthday celebrations. But I long for more—more of a sense that you really want to meet my desires."

"I've appreciated your struggle to let me be a father and husband in my own way," he said. "It's similar to me letting you be the kind of sexual partner you want to be.

"When it comes to what we want from each other,

we can hope, we can ask, we can negotiate—we can even leave copies of our love frame list around the house, since they're the best description of our needs and desires—but we just can't expect. Otherwise we set each other up for failure to meet those expectations, and resentment inevitably follows. As we give each other freedom from our expectations, we respect each other as marriage partners and open the door for change without coercion.

"It seems the natural tendency is to treat others as extensions of ourselves rather than separate individuals. It's no small thing to grant another person the same worth and dignity that we assume for ourselves. At its core, respect identifies another person as a real person—not us but just like us, with the same set of rights and desires."

"Yes," she said. "A marriage license is not a sculptor's license to try and mold our spouse into our own image. I'd agree that the greatest compliment and measure of respect we can give to our partner is to refrain from trying to change him or her. If change is going to come, acceptance, not pressure, will provide its context.

"When we live in such an environment we can make changes that weren't otherwise possible. That kind of respect allows two autonomous beings to become companions. The two of us create a couple—two individuals who use our freedom not as a license to do anything we want but as the motivating energy of acceptance from which we can change and grow."

"Well said," he replied. "You know, it's another picture-perfect day. Do you want to go for one last walk?"

"Why don't we hang out on the veranda," she said, meeting his gaze. "I wouldn't mind some time to just sit and enjoy the peace and quiet before we head home."

Eliminating Expectations Is the Counterintuitive Way to Love Each Other

Given our mutual vow to love, honor, and cherish we can expect our spouse to consider our desires, that's simply being respectful.

But we can't expect him or her to fulfill our desires, in the way we assume it should be done.

Make your home an Expectation-Free Zone—where you live with the joy of no guarantees.

If I give up my expectations and my demands, it feels like I have to give up my desires, too, but that's not the case. I can hope, I can ask, I can negotiate for fulfillment of those desires. I just can't expect.

Yet there's an even better way—I can be the advocate for my partner and his or her needs and desires.

My example will act as a support to his or her growth in becoming my advocate as well.

Why is eliminating expectations difficult for you?

_____

_____

How could doing so benefit your relationship?

_____

_____

Intimacy and Interdependence

*A*s Matt stepped onto the porch, he met Sarah's gaze. The morning's light provided a warm glow to the serenity around them. "With all our talking, I've forgotten just how peaceful this place is," he said.

Sarah sat down. "You know, we've had more of a working vacation than a vacation vacation."

He nodded. "I hate the thought of going back to the real world today. What do you think, shall we stay here? People were meant to live in paradise, right?"

"Duty calls," she sighed, "but I'm open to that once-a-quarter weekend getaway, just you and me. Let's put it on our list of quarterly events we'll be sure to keep!"

"Speaking of events, I've been thinking about what you said about making a big deal out your birthday. It's just been the last few years that I've really noticed how important birthday celebrations are to you. You know how that began?"

"How's that?" she asked.

"For years I've seen you go overboard for our kids' birthday celebrations—maybe even more than the average mom. You'd think that would have given me a clue, but I'm slow. Then, a couple of years ago, it dawned on me that you are also more sexually open and responsive to me on certain days—like my birthday."

"That's because you always say you only want one thing for your birthday. Right?"

"For whatever reason," he continued, "I realized that on one day of the year you would often push the envelope with something from my fantasy wish list."

"You're not telling me anything I don't know," she added. "What you're missing in this equation is how much your attention to celebrations means to me. If you'd make a bigger deal out of events like my birthday, I'm sure to make even bigger efforts to celebrate your special events throughout the year, and in the way you like it."

"Well, that's my question," he said. "Where did the 'freely given, freely received' attitude go? Are we opening ourselves up to an I'll-scratch-your-back-if-you-scratch-mine kind of relationship? Surely we don't want that."

"No. I'd use another saying: 'What goes around, comes around,' or 'you reap what you sow.' This is where you have to be careful with a no-expectations attitude. At times it seems to me that guys take the 'No Expectations' sign from over the front door, where it applies to both partners, and hang it around their necks. Then it turns into a 'Don't you dare try to control me' sign, which carries with it a whole different set of assumptions."

"You said, guys, so I guess that may apply to me."

"Well, you can get touchy when you think I'm infringing on your rights or trying to control you. I don't want to bring up old stuff, but you remember our battles over you getting home late for dinner. You knew how frustrated I was about not having a set dinner time, especially with the kids. I tried to pout and nag you into changing. That led to a lot of defensiveness and fights. You felt when it came to your job, I didn't have the right to interfere. For you it became a hill to die on, while I thought you were making a mountain out of a molehill.

"Our impasse led me to give up on having you home at a certain time, and I let you deal with the consequences of eating a cold dinner, or no dinner, and missing out on the family time."

"I didn't much like those consequences," he stated. "It wasn't that long before I started getting home earlier."

"You weren't happy with me not making it work better for you, though," she continued, stretching her legs. "Not acquiescing to your wishes meant putting up with plenty of pouting and whining from you. You really wanted your cake, and for us to wait and eat it with you!

"I know there are times we need to set boundaries with each other, and even flash our 'no expectations' signs to let each other know one of those boundaries is about to be crossed. It seemed to me, though, that you were simply unwilling to compromise. You accused me of trying to run your life, when in fact your career was running your life. You needed freedom all right— freedom from the insanity that was taking over your schedule."

"I've told you this before," he replied, "but your determination to not bend over backward for me helped us avoid some of those weird, co-dependent behaviors that can happen in a marriage."

"Weird, co-dependent behaviors?" she asked.

"Yes," he continued, "Like when one spouse covers for the other and doesn't allow that spouse to experience the real consequences of his or her actions."

"It was just too difficult. I didn't want our family's schedule always revolving around your work habits."

"Exactly," he said. "If you would have repeatedly waited for me to get home late before you served supper because you didn't want to upset me, I would have avoided any negative consequences for my choices, but it was those very consequences that kept reminding me that life consists of more than just getting ahead in my job. My regret for missing family time made me even more open to hearing you out on these issues as time went on.

"I think your acceptance of letting me be irresponsible made the difference. You didn't like my choice, and you set appropriate boundaries. But you didn't force me to do it your way, and as things went along, I was able to lower my guard and entertain the idea that your perspective made a lot of sense. Wouldn't you say this has been true in curbing my workaholic tendencies in general?"

"Again," she said, "there's a fine line between giving someone the freedom to chart their own course and giving them a green light to act irresponsibly and carry on with living selfishly. I still wrestle with this. How can we have both intimacy with each other and independence from each other? Exactly how does this work?"

"That is the question, isn't it," Matt stated.

"Okay, so what's the answer?" Sarah asked.

"Each couple has to chart their own course," he said. "It seems that we can't have 100 percent intimacy and 100 percent independence. One gets limited from the other. Obviously, our wedding vows limit our independence, like that little phrase about remaining faithful!"

"Yes," she agreed, "but wedding vows are only meant to express the 100 percent commitment we make to intimacy. The question that remains is: What will that comitment produce? Think of our kids. We are responsible for providing them with a 100 percent loving and supportive environment. Why?"

"I see where you're going with this," he replied. "There's a purpose behind our love and support."

"That's right—we don't want our kids to remain dependent on us any more than we want to be co-dependent on each other, as you mentioned earlier. That kind of relationship stunts personal growth because it's based on fear and control rather than love and freedom.

"Instead, we want our kids to become secure, independent people in the sense that they know how to take care of themselves and, eventually, others. So ultimately intimacy's purpose is to produce independence."

"Which you're defining as growth and maturity," he said, reaching out to touch her arm.

"Yes. Independence can be pretty ugly if it's just another word for unfettered freedom to fulfill our own selfish whims. But if you think of it in terms of what we hope for our kids, it amounts to taking on the qualities of wisdom and perseverance and gratitude and patience. It's growing out of self-centered adolescence into other-centered adulthood. Maybe maturity is the better word.

"The more intimate our relationship, the more we will find in each other a source of affirmation that will help us become our best, most mature, selves. Then what unfolds between us is the give-and-take of interdependence. Sometimes I'm weak and you're strong; other times you're

> Women, generally speaking, seek intimacy and men seek independence. What is often not understood is that you can't have one without the other. Intimacy fosters mature independence, which in turn breathes the life of free association back into intimacy. It's the intriguing dance of interdependence.

anxious and I'm confident. We trade back and forth, which leads to both of us coming out stronger. Love feeds back into our relationship and to those around us. It's a non-vicious cycle. We spiral upward!"

"So, if we limit some of our independence for the sake of intimacy in our relationship," he said, "we actually gain more real independence. When we let someone come inside our lives through self-disclosure, we're inviting a companion whose understanding and acceptance help us shed our slavery to personal weaknesses and character flaws. Our partner's love strengthens us to take on the hard issues and find a way to grow through them."

"You know," she replied, "compromising is itself a strong sign of maturity because it requires recognition that another person's perspective and rights are just as valid as your own. That recognition is what growing into adulthood is all about—acknowledging the needs of others and looking for ways to meet them.

"So, allow me to raise one more issue we've talked about before—meal preparation. Let's say I'd like you to do more cooking, but you'd rather not. Hypothetically."

"Why doesn't this feel hypothetical?" he said.

"I realize life is filled with limited options. If you will not help cook, then I must do it or our family starves. At this point I can negotiate with other chores that you'd be more willing to do, but let's just say you're unwilling to do, anything but the barest of minimums.

"Just as life has limited choices, each choice has some kind of consequence. Do you want to live with the consequences of not taking my request to share such a household chore seriously?"

"Those consequences sound ominous," he replied.

"I don't know what they'll end up being," she said. "I just know if you refuse to compromise, my heart starts closing up. I'm sure the same is true for you as well.

"Here's a one-plus-one equation that makes sense. You plus me equals a couple. As a couple we bring two perspectives, two sets of needs and desires into the mix. If one of us refuses to enter into the spirit of compromise, that partner says, in effect, 'I am more important than us.' If one of us seeks to control or manipulate the outcome, we abuse the process and forfeit a lot of trust. If one wins and the other loses, we will both end up losing.

"By compromising, we both win because we say to our partner that their goodwill and trust are worth as much as the issue itself. We may be 180 degrees away from agreement, but if we can see why the other person feels the way they do, we honor them with our understanding and empathy. Often, all it takes is feeling like we're being heard, and the issue takes care of itself.

"I've heard it said that divorced people make the best marriage partners—that is, people who have divorced themselves from as much selfishness as possible."

"Yes," he said, "and I'd make a distinction between selfishness and self-interest. Selfishness seeks to get as much as possible, as fast as possible, in any way possible. In contrast, acting in our true self-interest recognizes that

> Short-term self-interest succumbs to selfishness.
> Long-term self-interest pursues maturity through love.
> Soul-centered people appreciate the benefits of
> interdependent relationships for personal growth.

character growth is our most valuable asset. So our best interest gets redefined to maturing as a person. A truly self-interested person will reject selfishness and embrace the maturing process of learning how to be more fully other-centered. You could call that soul-centeredness.

"As much as anything," he continued, "a soul-centered person values compromise. Compromising validates both people and both people's perspectives. Nobody goes away feeling unheard or belittled. The trust level deepens significantly."

"I agree," she said. "Failing to take your viewpoint into consideration is a sign of disrespect, while continually reminding you of mine is a form of nagging, and nagging may quite possibly be the most unbecoming thing we women do. Besides that, nagging does little to guarantee you'll do what I want anyway. What if I make my desire crystal clear, and you still don't do it? Won't that just lead to more disappointment and resentment?"

"Not if you tell me what you want from me but still don't expect me to do it—in the way you want, at the time you want, etc. We've got to be able to hear each other say, 'No, I can't do this part of it, but I can do that part.'"

"That's a delicate matter," she replied.

"Delicate, yes, but crucial if we're going to do away with an entitlement mentality and develop real intimacy."

"It's still delicate," she replied, "because we can be so quick to react defensively to each other's requests."

"I'd say that's the key," he agreed. "If I know that what you want from me comes in a request, then I don't hear it as a demand or obligation requiring fulfillment but as an opportunity to serve you and enhance our relationship. Isn't that what marriage vows are all about?"

She nodded, "When we got married we made promises that exist independent of our background, gender, personality, and feelings. You promised to be my loving and faithful husband for richer or poorer, in good times and in bad—all that good stuff."

"But did I mention I'd do 50 percent of the cooking or get immersed in our future kids' musical aspirations?"

"I knew," she said, "that I should have gotten more specifics nailed down when I had you up there at that altar! By the way, do you remember me mentioning that I'd be open to your wild fantasy life and to performing oral sex on you? I pledged 'to have and to hold from that day forward' not, 'to hold and, you know what!'"

"You've made your point! It's amazing how poorly we understood what we were getting into when we made those polite little promises to each other. That simple 60-second custom could well end up being a 60-year effort of working it out between us on a daily basis."

"I don't know," she said with a smile. "I'll bet it's going to take me at least that long to beat out your unenlightened self-interest and replace it with..."

"Soul-centeredness," he interjected. "It's comforting knowing I have a lot more time to hit on you too," Matt said with a smile and a little jab to her side.

Sarah squirmed and reached out to hold his hands away from her. As she looked up and met his eyes, she matched his smile. "I'll take that as an 'I love you.'"

Love Provides the Means to Mature

To *compromise* means to give up something, but don't forget what you get. Besides getting your way, partly, you gain your partner's trust that you're a considerate person. When two contenders seek middle ground they find themselves standing in the victor's circle together. People often call this a win-win and it leads to *intimacy*.

Intimacy fills the space between who we are and who another is, with a supportive connection of understanding. That *connection* helps bring hope to our darkest fears and energy to our brightest dreams.

But anything this valuable does not come easily.

The price intimacy exacts includes a willingness to share ourselves and ultimately *to grow up* pursuing mutual happiness and greater *maturity*.

Maturity discards comfortable behaviors and attitudes for better, soul-centered, life-affirming, other-serving alternatives.

An intimate friendship helps strengthen us to *be* ourselves, *see* ourselves, and *rise above* ourselves, with the courage of our convictions balanced by a consideration for others. And that is the definition of maturity.

> *Love creates an "us" without destroying a "me."*
>
> —Leo Buscaglia

> And intimacy creates a "better me"
> from the tribulation and joy of forming an "us."

Going Back—Home

Finally, the time came to to leave. So, the couple packed up, took one last look around the cabin and headed home. A long silence prevailed, giving them time to catch their breath after the weekend's intensity. After a pit stop at a roadside service station and some small talk, Sarah asked, "Well, what did we learn from all that?"

"Where do we start?" Matt questioned, looking in the rear view mirror. "You go first."

"I learned a lot," she replied, turning toward him.

"Yes, but what did you learn?" he asked.

"That you have a far greater capacity for talk than I ever thought possible!" she said, smiling.

"You think you're surprised," he replied. "Whoa. I'll have to go into some kind of silence hibernation for a year to recuperate. Just kidding, it shouldn't last longer than a couple of months!"

"Women and men are so different!" she exclaimed.

"This weekend has reminded me that love for a man starts with the exterior, the skin, and moves to his heart, while love for a woman starts with her heart, and moves to the skin. In the middle of it all, intimacy and passion act like flint and steel, igniting the fire of love. It's fascinating."

"And frustrating," he added. "Particularly if you're not tuned in to those differences, which we weren't when we got married, even though we thought we were."

"So, besides the value of humility, maybe that's the real lesson of the weekend," she said, touching his knee.

"What's that?" he asked.

"Getting 'tuned in.' It might look like we live in the same house, but it's more like we live on the same street in two houses next door to each other. Dating, courtship, and then marriage gets us involved in one giant remodel project to join our houses together under a new roof. We no longer need two kitchens, two living rooms, or two master bedrooms, but like any big remodel project, getting rid of the old to make way for the new can get messy."

"You create such good word pictures," he replied. "To continue the analogy, that new, haphazard house will become a home when heated by the warmth of attraction between its residents. A home forms wherever love exists. I've been reminded that as we experience love, acceptance, and forgiveness, it increases our own capacity to love, accept, and forgive. It's that wonderful non-vicious cycle."

"You're not bad at word pictures yourself. A house is a rendezvous point, but a home is a place of sharing, loving, learning, and growing. It's an environment where two of us, and then three, four, or more can find a safe haven to fashion lifelong character qualities and values. I really appreciate your efforts to make our house a home. Getting into it with me this weekend speaks volumes about your interest and investment. Thanks."

"My pleasure," he replied.

Long periods of silence continued to break up the couple's occasional dialogue. Eventually they neared their city and Matt spoke up. "I'm curious. When we do get home and settled in, what's the first thing you plan to do with what we've experienced this weekend?"

"Go get coffee, with my journal. How about you?"

He paused and said, "For me, writing out our love frames proved very helpful. I was struck by how we think we're loving our spouses—just because, but unless we know what's in their love frame they likely won't feel loved. We tend to love each other through our own love frames rather than through the other person's love frame."

"Last night you summarized our love frames in a rather concise way," she replied. "You said that my goal was to be your sex goddess and yours, to be my soul mate.

"That's a new but helpful perspective. Over the long-haul a 'sex goddess wife' will make her man feel admired and a 'soul mate husband' will make his woman feel cherished. Isn't that what it's about—a woman loving her man so he feels more like a man and a man loving his woman so she feels more like a woman. As that happens, we step out of the confines of parental love into the arms of a stranger—a stranger who not only takes a liking to us but who makes a lifelong commitment to us."

The car soon turned onto a thoroughfare with familiar neighborhood sights; home waited just down the street. At that moment Sarah caught a reassuring glance from Matt. Their weekend's conversation would not be quickly forgotten, and they both knew it.

Use "the Triangle" to Deepen Your Love Life

In his Triangular Theory of Love (yes, google it), Robert Sternberg puts the ingredients of love—intimacy, passion, and commitment—on the points of a triangle.

If a couple has just one element between them, such as intimacy, they have a "liking" relationship. If they have two, such as intimacy and passion, they have "romantic love" (the variations are shown on pages 343-344). When all three qualities are strong they have "consummate love."

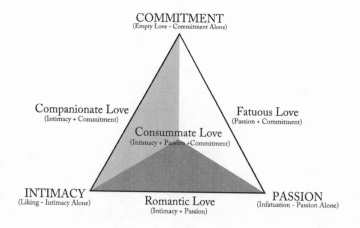

How do you enrich the love between you and your partner? Determine where you are—what side(s) of the triangle are weaker and what side(s) are stronger. The seven variations on pages 343-344 can help you identify which "love ingredients" need attention in your relationship. Use these graphs to talk through weaknesses and celebrate strengths.

Six Variations of Love

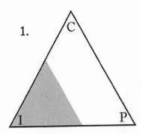 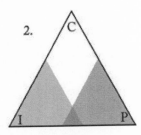

1. Liking: I like you. For both: We're good friends.

2. Romantic Love: We're in love and can talk for hours.

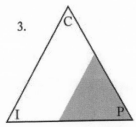 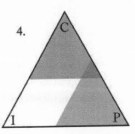

3. Infatuation: Crazy for you. Both: Crazy for each other.

4. Fatuous Love: We're committed alright, to pleasure.

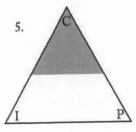 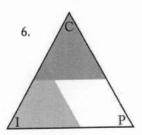

5. Empty Love: We're staying together. End of story.

6. Companionate Love: We're good frieinds... for always.

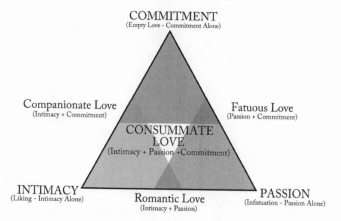

COMMITMENT
(Empty Love - Commitment Alone)

Companionate Love
(Intimacy + Commitment)

Fatuous Love
(Passion + Commitment)

CONSUMMATE
LOVE
(Intimacy + Passion +Commitment)

INTIMACY
(Liking - Intimacy Alone)

Romantic Love
(Intimacy + Passion)

PASSION
(Infatuation - Passion Alone)

7. Consummate Love: We enjoy a lifelong love affair. The triangle within the triangle is the "sweet spot" where intimacy, passion and commitment steadily deepen over time. The relationship becomes a safe harbor for not only the couple, but it's a blessing to all around them!

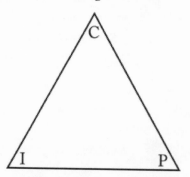

Our relationship ebbs and flows over time. Shade in your perceived level of intimacy, passion, and commitment right now. Start at the points and shade in to the interior.

Draw similar blank triangles with your partner and shade them in individually. Then Talk.

Interlude on Love

> Love is patient, love is kind. It does not envy, it does not boast, it is not proud. It does not dishonor others, it is not self-seeking, it is not easily angered, it keeps no record of wrongs. Love does not delight in evil but rejoices with the truth. It always protects, always trusts, always hopes, always perseveres. Love never fails.
>
> —Paul, 1 Cor. 13:4-8

As the couple unpack their car and settle back into their normal routine, let's review the big picture. We humans are complicated creatures who bring a multitude of desires, needs and perspectives into our relationships.

The intricacies of making them work offers life's finest challenge, and they keep us coming back to ask the bottom-line question: What makes for a lifelong love affair?

The short answer is love. A longer answer includes the key ingredients of intimacy, passion and commitment as described by the triangle and in the following pages.

Intimacy + Passion + Commitment

When we're in the midst of seemingly irreconcilable relationship difficulties, loneliness and pain can easily cloud our perspective. But whatever your circumstances, know that you are not facing a unique relationship problem.

Many of our problems begin with the simple fact that men and women are very different. While there are exceptions, women generally bring the gift of intimacy to the relationship and men, the gift of passion. Seeking to understand and respect that basic difference constitutes the first step in fueling ongoing love for each other.

The third ingredient, commitment, provides the underlying security to love. Committed couples work hard at acquiring the relational skills necessary to feel and express passion and intimacy. And while there are no guarantees, opening our hearts to intimacy, passion, and commitment goes a long way in providing us with the love we seek.

So whatever the misunderstanding and hurt up to now, it's time to call a stop to blame or guilt. Unless you're in an intimacy-busting relationship (see p. 23), the questions shouldn't be, "What's wrong with him/her?" or "What's wrong with me?" but, "What do I need to learn?" and "How can I apply what I know to loving him/her right now?"

Of course, the above questions are best asked by both partners, not just one. Partnerships are, after all, about two individuals becoming a couple. Each half plays a vital part in the growth of the whole. It's not about each giving 50 percent; it's a 100 percent proposition for both.

= a Lifelong Love Affair

We must also recognize that moving ahead happens at different rates. If one individual can't grow or refuses to grow, the couple's relationship will become unbalanced. So what do we do if we're the only team player on our team?

Because we cannot force our partner to change or grow, one thing we may have to accept about our mate is the very fact that he or she is not ready, willing, or able to make the relationship better, at least not right now.

In the meantime, one thing our partner must accept about us is our decision to do everything within our power to make the relationship better. To do that we will be loving him or her in increasingly radical ways—which means loving on the basis of his or her love frame. This isn't playing the doormat role or being a victim, it's simply exercising the sometimes difficult choice to love.

Unconditional love makes it hard for even the most resistant partner to not get sucked in. One might resist being loved for a while, but for how long? Such love tends to be contagious. Either way, we work on ourselves to be the best 100 percent of the equation we can be, and see what happens. Likely we will be pleasantly surprised.

When both partners find their joy in the joy of the other, a relationship turns into a passionate lifelong love affair.

The best thing in life to hold on to is each other.

—Audrey Hepburn

The Heart of Love

Start with a universal—everyone seeks happiness through selfishness or love:

Selfishness	Or	Love seeks
seeks happiness		happiness in the
at another's expense.		happiness of another.

Consider the implications: Selfishness actually betrays our happiness because it perpetuates immaturity and alienates the very people who can help us mature. Love secures our happiness. It increases our soul's capacity for caring, respect, kindness, and affection, and that is how we mature.

Ultimately, love is quite paradoxical. As Jesus said, "It is more blessed to give than to receive (Acts 20:35). The one giving love ends up benefiting more than the one receiving that love. They are more blessed.

To love someone often involves acting against our short-term self-interest—selfishness, because it requires us to sacrifice something of ourselves—take loving an enemy, for example! But such sacrifice actually promotes our long-term self-interest—true self-interest, since it helps us to mature as people.

Loving others—friends and foes alike, and a partner can be both at times—becomes the ultimate self-affirming act.

Finally we come to the meaning of love:

Love is finding our joy in the joy of another.
Their personal growth and fulfillment
becomes our greatest delight.

The Journey Continues

> We peel it all back to see what makes
> life worthwhile and find the core: *Relationships.*
> Then we identify what brings happiness and fulfillment
> to relationships and find the nucleus: *Love.*
> Finally, when we look to the source we find that:
> *God is Love.*

The man who loved making love and the woman who loved feeling loved found more common ground than they expected. Matt realized that he didn't love sex so much as he felt loved through sex. Likewise, Sarah realized she didn't love being cherished, exactly. She felt loved when being cherished. They actually loved each other.

That love included a locket full of wonderful sexual and romantic memories that acted as an underground spring, replenishing their lives with hope and harmony: "Someone out there, or better yet, someone right here, really cares for me." Learning each other's love frames—how the other feels loved—began to replace the self-focus of "getting what I need." Less concern for "my needs" and "your needs" meant more time for "our needs."

The couple also gained clarity on why the risks of intimacy meant replacing comfortable self-protective strategies with humility. It would be their greatest challenge and most rewarding joy. Real intimacy promised to nourish each partner with a growing interdependence, giving them strength to blossom and flourish in surprising ways.

In each other they found a source of passion to take on life's challenges and pursue its opportunities. Setbacks would come, but their combined couple-strength clearly outweighed the sum of the parts. Over a lifetime they were sure to see deepening trust, settling for nothing less than the intimate allies they once dreamed of being.

Sarah and Matt's weekend proved so encouraging and fun that they decided to plan other conversations—with each other, their kids, and a few friends. The simple confines of such dialogue gave them a chance to check the compass and regain their bearings—challenged by each other's perspective and fortified by each other's love.

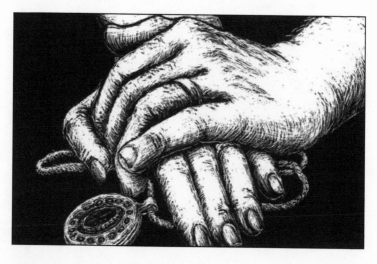

Matt's Goal: Cultivate Intimacy

Become Sarah's Soul Mate—and cherish her with whole-hearted affection. A woman feels loved through emotional intimacy.

Sarah's Goal: Cultivate Passion

Become Matt's Sex Goddess—and admire him with wholehearted devotion. A man feels loved through physical intimacy.

Their Goal Together:
Cultivate Commitment by
Becoming Intimate Allies in a
Passionate Lifelong Love Affair

Love each other in the way the other feels loved—within his or her love frame. Such love provides a dynamic environment for personal growth, and a safe haven of hope for family, friends, not to mention, society as a whole.

Your Goal in Your Relationship:

_____

_____

Love for a man starts with the exterior, the skin, and moves to his heart, while love for a woman starts with her heart, and moves out to the skin. In the fusion of it all, intimacy and passion act like flint and steel, igniting the fire of commitment, giving life's journey a rare but wonderful measure of warmth and light.

What insights have you gained from Sarah's perspective (or how do you disagree/differ with her)?

_____

_____

_____

_____

_____

_____

_____

_____

_____

_____

What insights have you gained from Matt's perspective (or how do you disagree/differ with him)?

_____

_____

_____

_____

_____

_____

_____

_____

_____

What are new things you learned or new ways to grow with the one you love?

In Intimacy: _____

_____

_____

_____

_____

_____

_____

In Passion: _____

_____

_____

_____

_____

_____

_____

In Commitment: _____

_____

_____

_____

_____

_____

_____

How can you love your mate better—so that she feels cherished or he feels admired?

_____

_____

_____

_____

_____

_____

_____

_____

_____

What can you do that will make an immediate difference?

_____

_____

_____

_____

_____

_____

_____

_____

_____

_____

_____

Acknowledgments

Through the companionship of their books, authors are the best friends I've never met. The following writers helped inspire this work and the book pages where they are found are cited below.

- Shmuley Boteach, *Kosher Sex: A Recipe for Passion and Intimacy* (New York, NY, Doubleday, 1999). On page 68.

- Henry Cloud and John Townsend, *Boundaries* (Grand Rapids, MI, Zondervan Publishing House, 1992). On page 196.

- Barbara DeAngelis, *What Women Want Men to Know* (New York, NY, Hyperion, 2001). On page 272.

- Gregory J.P. Godek, *1001 Ways to Be Romantic* (Naperville, IL, Casablanca Press Division of Sourcebooks, 2000). On page 245.

- John Gray, *Men, Women and Relationships: Making Peace with the Opposite Sex* (Hillsboro, OR, Beyond Words Publishing, 1993). On page 180.

- M. Scott Peck, *Further Along the Road Less Traveled* (New York, NY, Simon and Schuster, 1993). On pages 137-138.

- Dennis Rainey, *Lonely Husbands, Lonely Wives* (Dallas, TX, Word, 1989). On page 54.

- Robert Sternberg, *The Triangle of Love* (New York, NY, Basic Books, 1988). On pages 342-344

- Stan Tatkin, *Wired for Love* (Oakland, CA, New Harbinger Publications, 2011). On page 252.

- Michael Webb, *The RoMANtic's Guide* (New York, NY, Hyperion, the preface, 2000). On page 250.

Beside the authors above, much thanks to Sándor Lau for his creative support in getting this book off the computer and into the world, to Patti Sobel for 22 beautiful scratch art drawings (and her not so subluminal message on page 7), to Patricia Marshall for her artistic book design, to Matthew and Emily Flood for lending their attractive images with Samantha Davis and Sean Reber's help, and to David Sanford, Kent and Thomas Goodman for their wise marketing guidance.

Also thanks to many who have given astute critique, including my wife, Teresa; my brother, Jeff Syrios; my sister, Melinda Eckeberger, and a host of friends, especially Carolyn Rexius, and copy editors, Cyrena Respini-Irwin and Monique Kirby.

At a 1980 family reunion my grandmother, Nira Hamilton, said something I didn't appreciate until later. She stated that what she took greatest pride in was that there were no divorces in our family tree as far back as she, the family historian, could go. Granted, not all of those relationships were blissful ones, but it's been my great privilege to be heir to people determined to "work love out," including my parents, Bill and Barbara Syrios.

Finally, thanks to all who are not willing to settle for an ordinary relationship and even more so if you are transitioning from a generation who couldn't find a way to keep it together or, now after experiencing divorce yourself, are determined to set a different path.

It is to those of you, willing to take on humility by listening, learning and growing with the one you love, that inspires us all to make love count. This book is by you and for you.

Visit us on the Web

IntimateConversations.com

Enriching Our Lives—One Conversation At A Time

Intimate Conversations
affectionately shares wisdom
through fictional dialogue. We listen in as
people talk about issues near and dear to them—
and to us. Here we'll find allies who seek to
live by life's highest ideals, who learn to
achieve its greatest potential and who
partner with those desiring
to share the journey.

Our mission is to encourage
personal character growth and to strengthen primary
relationships by cultivating intimate conversation
among couples • family member • friends.

Continue the Conversation

E-book Resources

So Let's Talk: Questions to help you cultivate intimacy and passion.

Love Frame Guide: Identify the unique way you/your partner feels loved.

Audio Book

Intimate Conversations for Couples

Listen in as Matt and Sarah verbalize the conversations in the book.

Video and Podcasts
Keeping Love Alive

A series of entertaining and heart-felt teachings on how to achieve and sustain intimacy.

About the Author

Bill Syrios has honed his understanding of intimate relationships as a pastor, father and husband for over 35 years. He wrote *Intimate Conversations for Couples* for those longing to experience a deeper level of intimacy, passion and life-long commitment with the one they love.

Bill holds a Masters of Divinity from Fuller Theological Seminary and has authored three other books on spirituality and relationships. He and his wife, Teresa, live in Eugene, Oregon and have four grown sons: Luke, Andrew, Phillip and Mark. Bill is also the founding partner of Stewardship Properties, a real estate investment company with offices in Eugene, Kansas City and Dallas.